REFORM RESPONSA
FOR OUR TIME

REFORM RESPONSA
FOR OUR TIME

by

SOLOMON B. FREEHOF, D.D.
Rabbi Emeritus, Rodef Shalom Temple, Pittsburgh

THE HEBREW UNION COLLEGE PRESS

1977

Library of Congress Cataloging in Publication Data
Freehof, Solomon Bennett, 1892-
    Reform responsa for our time.

    Includes index.
        1. Responsa—1800-   2. Reform Judaism.
I. Title.
BM522.36.R385   296.1'79   77-24078
ISBN 0-87820-111-4

MANUFACTURED IN THE UNITED STATES OF AMERICA

To the dear and unforgettable memory

of my beloved sister

FAYE EVELYN FREEHOF

CONTENTS

SOLOMON B. FREEHOF
and the
HALACHAH

AN APPRECIATION
by WALTER JACOB

The Rabbinic Alumni Association of Hebrew Union College has previously published five volumes of selected responsa representing Solomon B. Freehof's work in the field over a period of almost two decades. Through this volume, *Reform Responsa for Our Time,* we pay special tribute to the author's eighty-fifth birthday; it is published by the Association with the generous help of the Rodef Shalom Congregation, which wishes to honor its Rabbi Emeritus through its assistance.

The responsa of Solomon B. Freehof, and his thoughtful introductions to each volume, show us something of the development of the Reform Jewish approach to *Halachah* in the last two decades. It is appropriate at the outset of this volume to summarize the Halachic activity within the Reform movement so that Solomon Freehof's labors can be seen in perspective.

The Reform movement was revolutionary when it

Rabbi Walter Jacob is Chairman of the Publication Committee, Rabbinic Alumni Association, Hebrew Union College–Jewish Institute of Religion.

began in Europe early in the nineteenth century. Although its initial concerns were liturgical reform and theological change, it soon sought to justify itself by using classic Halachic tools. In 1818 a small responsa pamphlet entitled *Nogah Ha-tzedek* was published; it was followed in 1842 by the publication of a series of responsa by the Hamburg congregation which supported changes in its liturgy (*Theologische Gutachten über das Gebetbuch nach dem Gebrauche des neuen israelitischen Tempelvereins in Hamburg,* 1842). Slightly later, a much more extensive review of the Reform position and its rabbinic roots was published in a series of responsa (*Rabbinische Gutachten über die Verträglichkeit der freien Forschung mit dem Rabbineramte,* 1843). Both of these volumes contained the work of outstanding individuals. They represented a vigorous attack upon the Orthodox establishment and some keen insights into possible new paths of religious development. Naturally, these volumes and others called forth strong Orthodox opposition, which was expressed in *Eleh Divre Habrit* and in the works of Moses Sofer, Akiba Eger, Jacob Lissa, Mordecai Benet, and others. Thus, even in its infancy, the Reform movement found itself engaged in an intellectual debate conducted within the historical framework of the responsa literature. This was, however, soon discontinued, and few liberal responsa were written during the next half-century. The Reform leaders could certainly have proceeded along these lines; for example, Samuel Holdheim (1806–1860), who began his rabbinic career as an Orthodox rabbi, and had written some Orthodox opinions early in life, was capable of reasoning in the traditional manner, but he, as well as Abraham Geiger, Zacharias Frankel, and others, felt that such a procedure was useless. It was not necessary for their own followers and did not influence the Orthodox. Furthermore, they probably felt no need to justify each detail of the changes undertaken.

Although no responsa were written during the next period of Reform development, vigorous Halachic debate continued at each of the synods and rabbinic meetings; they sought to establish a consensus of Reform Jewish theory and practice. The need for such conferences was felt early, and Abraham Geiger advocated the gathering of a broad general assembly through an open letter in 1837. Such a meeting took place at Wiesbaden in August of 1837, but few practical results were achieved except the impetus to publish articles on a wide variety of matters in Geiger's theological magazine. Subsequent conferences were held in Brunswick (1844), Frankfurt (1845), and Breslau (1846), as well as the synods in Leipzig (1869) and Augsburg (1871). Long and sometimes acrimonious debates on every aspect of the Reform movement's relationship with the *Halachah* were held. These debates were rarely entirely theoretical, but dealt with the practical matters of synagogue services, the Sabbath, holidays, marriage, divorce, burial, conversion, non-Jews, and much else. A wide spectrum of opinion was represented, at most gatherings, with the extreme left represented by Holdheim, who stated in Brunswick

(1884): "All the talk about a Talmudic Judaism is an illusion. Science has decided that the Talmud has no authority dogmatically or practically." The majority at that second German rabbinic conference, however, were more conservative. Individuals like Samuel Hirsch were concerned that resolutions passed by the majority of the conference would clarify changes of practice as codified in the *Shulchan Aruch*. Clearly, for most of the rabbis present, the *Shulchan Aruch* remained basic, and Reform made only limited changes. Although Philippson claimed that the majority of those present at the Brunswick rabbinic conference considered the Talmud and *Shulchan Aruch* no longer authoritative, the decisions there and at subsequent meetings constantly weighed changes against the tradition. This was especially clear throughout the debates on the Sabbath question and marriage laws.

Reform in Europe sought a balanced stance by continuing strong ties with traditional observances; no widely accepted theoretical basis was created by these meetings. In matters of Halachic theory, the Reform movement in Europe remained as vague as the Reform movement in the United States.

Developments in America began with the rabbinic conferences held in Cleveland (1855), Philadelphia (1869), Cincinnati (1871), and Pittsburgh (1885). The debates in the United States were concerned with practical matters, but each of these conferences also developed a theoretical stance toward the *Halachah*. In Cleveland in 1855 the discussion was based on the following criteria: "The Bible, as delivered to us by our fathers, and as now in our possession, is of immediate divine origin, and the standard of our religion. The Talmud contains the traditional legal and logical exposition of the Biblical laws, which must be expounded and practiced according to the comments of the Talmud." However, when it came to the adoption of a set of principles, the entire sentence on the Talmud was omitted, while other issues, such as Messianism, priesthood, the mission of Israel, resurrection, and the Hebrew language, were addressed.

It was different in 1885, for the third point in the Pittsburgh Platform stated: "We recognize in the Mosaic legislation a system of training the Jewish people for its mission during its national life in Palestine, and today we accept as binding only its moral laws, and maintain only such ceremonies as elevate and sanctify our lives, but reject all such as are not adapted to the views and habits of modern civilization."

The statement adopted a half-century later in Columbus (1937) changed this: "Revelation is a continuous process, confined to no one group and to no one age. Yet the people of Israel, through its prophets and sages, achieved unique insight in the realm of religious truth. The Torah, both written and oral, enshrines Israel's ever-growing consciousness of God and of the moral law. It preserves the historical precedents, sanctions and norms of Jewish life, and seeks to mold it in the patterns of goodness and holiness. Being products of historical processes, certain of its laws have lost their binding force with the passing of the conditions that called them forth. But as a depository of permanent spiritual ideals, the *Torah* remains the dynamic source of the life of Israel. Each age has the obligation to adapt the teachings of the *Torah* to its basic needs in consonance with the genius of Judaism." The Columbus Platform also dealt with specific religious practices by demanding "the preservation of the Sabbath festivals and Holy Days, the retention and development of such customs, symbols and ceremonies as possess inspirational value, the cultivation of distinctive forms of religious art and music, and the use of Hebrew, together with the vernacular, in our worship and instruction."

The latest statement, adopted in San Francisco in 1976, dealt with the tradition by stating that "Torah results from the relationship between God and the Jewish people. . . . Rabbis and teachers, philosophers and mystics, gifted Jews in every age, amplified the Torah tradition. For millennia, the creation of Torah has not ceased and Jewish creativity in our time is adding to the chain of tradition. . . . Reform Jews respond to change in various ways according to the Reform principle of autonomy of the individual." This Centenary Perspective contains no specific statement on the relationship of Reform Judaism to the *Halachah*. This has, however, been accomplished in a practical manner through a variety of publications of the Central Conference of American Rabbis, such as the *Shabbat Manual* and the *Tadrich*. There has also been more Halachic discussion in the *CCAR Journal* during the last years. The movement itself remains distant from a thoroughly thought-out approach to the *Halachah*.

We might say that the Reform movement has followed the pattern suggested by Solomon B. Freehof, who advocated that individuals rather than the Conference write codes, responsa, as well as theoretical articles on Jewish law. In this way an ongoing debate would create a consensus, and thus a link with the *Halachah* would be created. Polish and Doppelt's *Guide for Reform Jews* and theoretical articles by Petuchowski, Borowitz, Plaut, and others have partially accomplished this. Freehof has also stated that any theoretical basis must remain loose until we have decided upon a theology of revelation. The American Reform movement has thus decided to find its way to homogeneity of practice; it has refused to recommend observances which bear no relationship to the realities of modern life, whereas much Orthodox debate took place in an atmosphere of unreality, with the leadership discussing details while the vast majority of their followers do not even observe the broadest rubrics of the law.

The Central Conference of American Rabbis established its Responsa Committee in 1906; however, no responsa were published until 1911. This committee has had many distinguished chairmen, among them Kaufmann Kohler, Jacob Z. Lauterbach, Jacob Mann, Israel Bettan, and Solomon B. Freehof. Its procedures varied; occasionally full-length responsa were given in the *CCAR Yearbook,* sometimes followed by dissenting opinions or discussions by members of the committee. In addition, the *Yearbook* recorded the fact that other questions had been addressed to the committee;

they were answered either privately or briefly in the report made to the Central Conference. The committee's existence showed that despite a lack of theoretical basis, the Conference felt a need for an ongoing Halachic process. Solomon B. Freehof became involved in the work of this committee in 1947, and became its chairman in 1955. His own deeper interest in responsa began in 1941 with a lecture given at the Central Conference entitled "A Code of Ceremonial and Ritual Practice." In this he expressed the feeling that the demand for a code was premature. He stated that the necessary neglect of entire areas of Jewish law in such a work would be an embarrassment. Furthermore, he felt that since further experimentation on the part of the Conference and its individual members was necessary, codes should be left to individual efforts. This might eventually move the entire Reform movement closer to a unified attitude.

During World War II Solomon B. Freehof's interest in *Halachah* continued to develop through his membership on the Responsa Committee of the Commission on Chaplaincy of the Jewish Welfare Board. This committee consisted of Reform, Conservative, and Orthodox rabbis, with Solomon Freehof as its chairman; it published two booklets, *Responsa in Wartime* (1947) and *Responsa to Chaplains* (1953). They were unusual for their combined Halachic effort, which emergency conditions had prompted, and for being published in English. Up to this time, with rare exceptions, only specifically Reform responsa had been published in languages other than Hebrew, Aramaic, or Arabic.

Alongside Solomon B. Freehof's work for the military chaplaincy came the preparation of two volumes entitled *Reform Jewish Practice* (1944 and 1952). The subtitle of these volumes (*Reform Jewish Practice and Its Rabbinic Background*) clearly indicated the author's intent of binding Reform Judaism to the tradition. The dedication of the initial volume to the memory of Jacob Z. Lauterbach showed that Solomon B. Freehof wished to continue in the path of his favorite teacher, whose thoroughly argued responsa were full of citations. In the introduction to *Reform Jewish Practice,* Freehof traced the changes in Jewish practice caused by the destruction of the Temple and the creation of a large diaspora outside of Israel. Adjustments were made by the scholars as well as the people through *minhagim* which were often very important. Through the centuries, Orthodoxy remained sufficiently flexible to meet the needs of changing conditions, but this stopped in the middle of the eighteenth century. Reform then stepped in to adjust Judaism to modern life. Solomon B. Freehof felt that a fairly harmonious system of practice had developed after five generations of Reform Judaism, and he considered his book a summary rather than a guide for the future. In the second volume, which supplemented the first, he speculated that our neglect of the Sabbath and dietary laws might be due to the overdevelopment of Orthodox law in these fields. Little room for creativity remained. Furthermore, these areas had become marked by general nonobservance among most Jews; it was hopeless to deal with matters which would be ignored by the people.

Solomon B. Freehof's interest in the development of Jewish law was also shown through his report on mixed marriage and intermarriage to the Central Conference in 1947 and his analysis of "Jacob Z. Lauterbach and the Halacha," published in *Judaism* in 1952. The latter showed that Freehof wished to follow Lauterbach's pattern of sifting the entire tradition in order to find a modern, liberal approach to each problem.

Solomon B. Freehof then pioneered by introducing the responsa literature to the English-reading American Jewish public. *The Responsa Literature,* published in 1955, was followed by *A Treasury of Responsa* in 1963. Both volumes provided a nontechnical introduction to this large segment of rabbinic literature which had been totally neglected in English. Previously, responsa had only been used for an occasional doctoral dissertation. Both of Freehof's books spanned the vast literature from its beginning to modern times. In them, Solomon Freehof discussed the development as well as the problems of the *Halachah*. He dealt with a number of outstanding controversies which had led to major divisions in rabbinic Judaism. The books indicated the vast extent of Solomon B. Freehof's personal responsa library, which is among the best in the world, and has been largely given to the Hebrew Union College.

Solomon B. Freehof, the bibliophile of responsa literature, wrote an addendum to Boaz Cohen's *Kontras Hateshuvos,* which was published in *Studies in Bibliog-*

raphy and Booklore (1961). This study is an important tool as it brought Cohen's reference work up to date.

During subsequent years Solomon Freehof has devoted himself to a further development of the responsa through the practical answering of questions sent to him both as chairman of the Responsa Committee of the Central Conference of American Rabbis and in his individual capacity. Each volume has included a lengthy introduction which seeks to analyze the relationship of Reform Judaism to the tradition as well as the current mood of Reform Judaism. As chairman of the Responsa Committee, Freehof has published responsa for the Central Conference of American Rabbis with only a minimum of involvement by the rest of the committee.

In the first of these volumes (*Reform Responsa,* 1960), he expressed the feeling that because confidence in the prophetic approach of Reform Judaism had faded, a new path was needed. A strong impulse toward legal discipline had to be created. He pointed to the enormous changes which had taken place in Jewish law. Without the benefit of the Reform movement or any other attempts at modernization, Orthodoxy had quietly yielded to the wishes of the people and allowed vast areas of Jewish law to slip away. Yet the pace of that change was not sufficient for us and others. Nor has Conservative Judaism been able to adapt itself fast enough for modern needs, and its attempt to develop within the framework of Jewish law has led to violent Orthodox opposition.

In this introduction written in 1960, Solomon Freehof stated that he would approach the *Halachah* selec-
tively, for the law was human—it was advisory. The
volume largely reflected this permissive approach,
buttressed by traditional references whenever possible.
He was also willing to reject the tradition entirely when
it did not conform to modern times. In this introduction the author again mentioned Lauterbach and indicated his indebtedness to his teacher and friend.

The responsa themselves, in all the volumes, clearly
showed the relationship of Reform to tradition which
Freehof sought. We should note that each volume
was organized according to the sequence of the *Shulchan Aruch*. Even in lenient rulings the author tried
to pattern himself after tradition. All the questions
dealt with living issues and reveal a broad interest in
Jewish law. The chief problem of these decisions lies
in their constant permissiveness, though his *Halachic*
correspondence tends to be more restrictive.

The introduction to *Recent Reform Responsa,* which
followed in 1963, analyzed the needs of the Jewish
people in our time, especially the majority, who are
irreligious and antinomian. Orthodoxy has sought to
protect the law from the people rather than have it
serve the people. This brought the host of negative
answers in Orthodox responsa, which did not help the
people.

Although the law is logical, the lack of logic in daily
life necessitates its continuous development. Freehof
felt that our revived Reform interest in Jewish law was
partly sociologically determined and that it stemmed

from the background of the present-day congregant, which he found somewhat akin to that of the first generation of German Reform Jews in the middle of the last century. According to Freehof, this background was the reason for the nineteenth-century synods and books of responsa dealing with specifics of Jewish law. The recent changes in American Jewish life have led in a similar direction and simultaneously to greater diversity within the movement. The development of responsa would bring a renewed sense of unity. Three further volumes followed in 1969, 1971, and 1974. The dates themselves indicate that a progressively larger number of questions has been directed to the author; furthermore, he felt it necessary to answer them in detail. Some were answered more briefly in *Halachic* correspondence which has been deposited at the Hebrew Union College. In each of these volumes Solomon B. Freehof analyzed the mood of Reform Judaism and attempted to find his own way back to *Halachah*.

In *Current Reform Responsa* (1969), Solomon B. Freehof reviewed some tendencies which have brought the Reform movement closer to tradition. Among them was the general acceptance of Biblical criticism, which meant that it now was as logical to establish a religious position on the rabbinic tradition, which had been subjected to historical criticism a generation or two earlier. Furthermore, the movement had matured and so could abandon its earlier stance of rebellion without feeling any loss of freedom. The movement, as he saw it, need not hurry to reaffirm a relationship with the tradition, though it obviously felt the need for inner discipline. Realistically it was, of course, neither possible nor desirable to reestablish the old mood; changes would be selective and evolutionary. The responsa, as seen by Solomon B. Freehof, constituted a repository of human and divine wisdom through the generations.

By 1971 Solomon B. Freehof had added other facets to his justification of responsa. As the Reform movement became stronger in new lands, as witnessed by its rapid growth in England and its slow struggle in Israel during the last decade, it must once again defend itself as at its beginning. The pattern established a hundred years ago by Aaron Chorin and others through responsa or Halachic citations, and a generation later by the efforts of Geiger, Frankel, and Graetz to defend the movement historically, was now repeated. Orthodoxy in these lands and elsewhere continues to struggle vigorously against Conservative and Reform *Halachah*. The development of legal themes by Reform Jews was not welcomed by Orthodoxy either a century ago or today. The Orthodox attitude may be best summarized by a quotation from Moses Sofer, who wrote: "Everything new is forbidden by the Torah."

Freehof also pointed to the emergence of a new type of Orthodoxy, which has realistically appraised modern conditions and adopted many techniques and thoughts of the Reform movement; it may well use our methodology of responsa in the future. We could cite the modern Orthodox magazine *Tradition,* which publishes Halachic material in English, and is willing to print liberal opinions. This clearly shows a develop-

ment in a new direction which, of course, has been
vigorously opposed by the old-style Orthodoxy.

In his last volume, published in 1974, Freehof again
stressed the need for Halachic creativity and a harmony
between discipline and freedom. Although the Reform
movement has returned to many practices of traditional
Judaism, this has not been done in the spirit and the
manner of Orthodoxy. Our acceptance is based more
on *minhag* and follows psychology rather than logic
or the interpretation of the *Halachah*. In the current
volume, Solomon B. Freehof demonstrates that the
realities of modern Jewish life are mirrored through
the questions asked of the respondents. This has always
been true and shows that vast areas of the law are no
longer observed by anyone in modern Orthodoxy. The
Orthodox process of abandonment is, so to speak,
balanced by our slowly encompassing fields which
Reform had formerly neglected if not entirely abandoned.

Perhaps the best summary of Solomon B. Freehof's
approach to Jewish law was provided in his lecture
"Reform Judaism and the Law," given at the Hebrew
Union College a decade ago. In it he emphasized the
revolt of our movement against the strictures of the
law. While all legal systems depend on new inter-
pretations of old laws as much as on new legislation,
the latter path has been closed to the Jewish tradition
for a long time. The intense development of interpretation has often trivialized the law, and this needed
correction. In a sense, the Reform movement has accomplished this for our time.

The strength of the traditional system throughout the Jewish past lay in its emphasis on the universal study of the traditional literature. Reform in the past lacked the discipline of the tradition, but strengthened Judaism in the area of liturgy and equality for women, thus providing new paths and emphases. Reform is close to the Bible, which has become part of our conscience, but we have lost the Talmud and its intellectuality, which can now be regained. As Reform Jews, we can approach *Halachah* openly because we are not controlled by it; having declared our independence from *Halachah,* we are free to base ourselves solidly on it. As earlier, Solomon B. Freehof emphasized the reality of Reform Judaism, which has stressed Biblical ideas, while all our practices are rooted in rabbinic Judaism. Despite our emphasis on *Halachah* during the last years, it remains "guidance not governance."

During the last three and a half decades, Solomon B. Freehof has not worked in isolation. Others have sought different ways of dealing with the problems of the *Halachah.* Rabbis Doppelt and Polish published a *Guide for Reform Jews* in 1957; both had previously urged the Conference to edit such a volume, but it was reluctant to do so. The guide has been fairly widely used and appeared in a second edition. In the introduction the authors provided a rationale for their work. They clearly indicated that their work was a guide, not a code. The *mitzvos* were significant because many of them served as strong bonds to our history and made it meaningful in our lives; Jewish life fulfills itself through history. The *mitzvah* "has its source in an historic encounter of the Jewish people with God; hence, Jewish history is its basic authority. The *halachah,* on the other hand, has its origin in the perennial deliberations of rabbinical authorities; hence, its sanction rests precisely with its makers." The development of Reform Judaism was traced through various stages; following an initial emphasis on theology and ethics, it is now stressing practice and ritual. Doppelt and Polish also stressed the development of the *minhag,* enforced by popular usage and abandoned when its meaning was lost.

Halachic issues appeared more frequently in the *Journal of the Central Conference of American Rabbis* and in papers presented at the annual rabbinic conference. Some essays only indicated an isolated point of view, while others led further. Yet even the *CCAR Journal* eschewed *Halachah* after a few opening issues and turned to sociological and psychological questions of the rabbinate. Halachic matters were only treated incidentally.

We do not come to any substantive discussion of *Halachah* until April of 1960 in a series entitled "In Quest of Reform Jewish Theology." Later, greater concern with Halachic matters was shown.

In 1972 the Conference published a *Shabbat Manual* edited by W. Gunther Plaut. The book was published after a committee process of seven years. The introduction showed Gunther Plaut's approach to the *Halachah* as similar to Solomon B. Freehof's. He stated: "For us, mitzvah means that God offers an opportunity to introduce 'ought' into our existence. To accept this opportunity and act on it is not easy; it demands self-discipline." Later in the book, the same theme was continued in a chapter entitled "Catalogue of Shabbat Opportunities." The book concluded with a series of questions and answers about the Shabbat, often taken from the responsa of Freehof and Lauterbach. These were not responsa in the usual sense, with full citations from older authorities, but sought to provide straightforward answers and a brief historical background. The book has been widely used and will remain influential. Aside from these efforts, Stephen Passamaneck dealt with *Halachah* in his Founder's Day address of 1967, entitled "Reform and Halakha: The State of the Art." This essay analyzed the movement and what can be done to create a relationship with the *Halachah*. "Reform Judaism has always functioned within the juristic frame of reference which has characterized much of Jewish thought." This thought, akin to Freehof's, was placed in the theoretical framework by Passamaneck, who showed that the Reform movement differed from Orthodoxy in its theory of law, which was based on progressive revelation. He emphasized the persuasive effect of the law, which enables the free individual to make an ethical, liberal, and knowledgable decision. Passamaneck's view may be summarized in the statement: "Although *Halakhah* may no longer rule, yet it remains a central and vital role. The enterprise of *Halakhah* means turning the raw material of life into purposeful religious living. It is the ever unfinished task of generations begun at Mount Sinai, which has now become our own." This final emphasis on the tra-

dition borne continually since Sinai is especially significant.

Clearly, Solomon B. Freehof has been a leader in
this area of Reform Jewish development. He has continued and broadened a tradition rooted in the begin-
nings of our movement. Even as we express gratitude
for his guidance in the past, so we hope that God will
bless him with the vigor to continue his studies and
writing in the future.

INTRODUCTION

In every modern country the decisions of the law courts are accumulated and indexed and thus are instantly available to every lawyer. But the Jewish responsa literature, comprising hundreds of thousands of legal decisions, remains virtually unindexed, and so most of it is inaccessible except to the specialist scholar. The various attempts at indexing the responsa literature were developed mostly as appendages to the *Shulchan Aruch*. This reveals, of course, the sole purpose of the indexing, namely, to aid the rabbi in making his decisions when a religio-legal question comes before him.

While these Halachic indices (such as the *Pische Teshuva* or the *Ozar Ha-Poskim*) are of great value in making Halachic decisions, they all overlook other vital material in the responsa which is not directly relevant to Halachic needs, and which, generally, the respondent himself would consider only incidental to his main purpose. Actually, the responsa literature contains treasures for the historian, the sociologist, and the linguist. Except for a few special studies of certain individual

1

respondents, these treasures have remained unsought
for and untouched.

Now at last there is some prospect that a non-Halachic approach to the entire responsa literature may be
made. Menachem Alon of the law faculty of the Hebrew
University has made an index of the responsa of Asher
ben Yehiel, and in it he has included much more than
the Halachic decisions. His department at the university
is now planning the indexing and computerizing of the
entire responsa literature. This task will take many
years. As each individual book of responsa so indexed
appears, it will be valuable in itself, but the real value
of the projected work will become evident only as the
task approaches completion; for while the material in
these new indices to each responsa volume may serve
limited historical, sociological, and linguistic purposes,
a broader view of Judaism as a living experience can
come only from an overall view and a broader classification of the total literature taken as a unity.

Nowadays a broad view of Judaism must be based
upon a realistic knowledge of the actual state of religious observance of the Jews of the modern world. Such
knowledge is especially important today because even
in the religiously disciplined Orthodox Jewry, a drastic
(if unacknowledged) change is taking place. The very
variety of present-day Orthodoxy makes this fact clear:
Chassidic Orthodoxy, so-called traditional congregations, "modern" Orthodoxy, etc. The question then
suggests itself: Which of the basic commandments of
the Jewish legal tradition are still strong enough today
to discipline the life of the bulk of Orthodox Jewry?

How can one find the answer to such a broad question? Only through a total view of most of the responsa literature: a comparative statistical survey which would indicate which questions were frequently asked in a past century and which questions are no longer asked today. If a review of the modern responsa literature shows that a certain class of questions is no longer asked, that is more than a statistical fact. It may well indicate the falling away of an entire section of the legal literature.

For example, in the classic responsa literature up to modern times, at least a quarter of the total responses dealt with business matters, *Choshen Mishpot*. Now a quick comparison of the classic volumes with modern responsa finds a complete absence of questions concerning contracts, partnerships, etc., etc. What has happened? Obviously, in spite of the duty incumbent upon Jews to bring their business disputes to a *Bes Din* and not to a Gentile court, clearly the majority of Orthodox Jews generally do not make use of the *Bes Din* in settling business disputes but resort to the civil courts. This, surely, is an unacknowledged revolution in Orthodox Jewish life. Or further, the responsa literature up to about a century ago was full of questions of feminine hygiene. Such questions hardly appear in the modern responsa literature. Evidently another unacknowledged revolution has occurred. There are indeed *mikvehs* in every great Jewish community, but what proportion of the women make use of them?

On the positive side, the sudden multiplication of *agunah* questions a century ago revealed a new mobility

in Jewish communities, people moving westward, and a
resultant breakdown of family life. There is an increase
in modern responsa of a related question: What to do
when a husband divorced in the courts refuses or is
not available to give his wife a *get*. Once the Jewish
courts had authority to compel the husband to do so.
Now that authority is gone. In general, therefore,
besides the Halachic value of individual books of
responsa, an all-over picture of the total literature will
give a broad view of the actual realities of modern
Jewish religious observance.

Just as it becomes manifest (through an overview
of the responsa) that Orthodox Jewish life is undergoing basic change, so it is evident from direct observa-
tion that Reform Judaism is undergoing considerable
and even drastic change. Fifty years ago, Reform Judaism in America had a "classic" consistency. Every
congregation worshiped virtually in the same way as
every other, and the religious observances of the congregants were virtually the same all over the United
States. Now, manifestly, changes have occurred in
worship, in the religious life of the people. It would
be very difficult to make a clear description today of
what Reform Judaism looks like. All we can say is that
it has become variegated and is subject to constant
change.

As has been mentioned, we can study the changes
in Orthodoxy through an overview of the responsa
literature, but, unfortunately, for such a purpose such
a literature has not been available in Reform. We have
indeed had responsa written by scholars from the very

beginning, but we have never developed a responsa *literature*. The scholars who wrote responsa for the Central Conference of American Rabbis would present an annual report containing one or two responsa. This is still the custom of our Responsa Committee. Undoubtedly the past chairmen of the Responsa Committee received and answered many more questions than the one or two published in the annual report, but these questions were never published and remained hidden in their private correspondence.

Now a change has occurred. Owing chiefly to the foresight and generosity of the Alumni Association, I have been privileged and encouraged to preserve and publish not only the two annual responsa that go into the annual Conference report, but a selection from all the questions received and answered. Thus every two or three years a whole volume of Reform responsa has been published. The present volume, again published through the generosity of the Alumni Association, is the sixth volume of Reform responsa. This book series constitutes, therefore, the first responsa *literature* (or at least the beginning of it) in the Reform movement, not only in America but anywhere.

These six volumes contain 350 responsa. In addition to them, there have been preserved four manuscript volumes of responsa correspondence dealing with questions that could be answered briefly and without too much research. The six published volumes and also the unpublished responsa correspondence (most copies of which have been turned over to the HUC-JIR archives) can well serve to provide a broad view of the changing landscape of modern Reform Judaism.

The following examples might be selected as illustrating this possible use of our responsa. A question was asked whether it is not wrong of us to light candles, as we do in the synagogue on Friday night, after it is dark and the Sabbath is well begun. This question can be taken together with similar ones: May a congregational meeting be held on Friday night when business will be transacted? May a caterer be permitted to prepare the Bar Mitzvah meal on Saturday morning on temple premises? These inquiries seem to indicate a growing sensitivity of Reform congregants to older Orthodox prohibitions. At all events, such questions may never have been asked before.

The status of women in our service seems to be a growing concern. Questions are asked, of course, about women being called to the Torah. Another question is: When a woman is participating in the service, may she wear a *talit?* A woman asked if her son's Hebrew name might be given on his tombstone, not with the father's name, but with her name.

The new instability in family life reveals itself in questions about Bar Mitzvah. May the stepfather come up to the Torah in place of the father and ex-husband? What if the stepfather is an unconverted Gentile? What may his part be in the Bar Mitzvah? The growing interrelationship between Jews and Gentiles, which reveals itself in mixed marriage and intermarriage, also has its reflection in these responsa: May a child be named after a Gentile grandparent? May a mixed-marriage family, in which one partner has not converted to Judaism, become members of the congregation as a family? May unmarried couples living together join the congregation as a family? New medical questions and their impact on family life are the subjects of many inquiries concerning hysterectomy, fertility pills, transplants, easing the pain of a dying patient, etc.

These volumes, constituting our first Reform responsa literature, may well be of use, when studied as a totality, in revealing the changes in modern Jewish life. Thus it will be important to note which new questions are being asked and, for that matter, which questions are now not being asked at all.

I am deeply grateful to my many colleagues for the hundreds of interesting questions they have sent to me, and again and always, my heartfelt thanks to the Alumni Association for making the publication of these volumes possible.

1

SYNAGOGUE SABBATH CANDLES
PREKINDLED

QUESTION:

> If there is some objection to lighting the candles on
> Friday night in the synagogue because it is already dark,
> would it be proper to have the candles lit earlier, possi-
> bly by a non-Jew (or by a Jew, well before the Sab-
> bath), and then during the service for a woman of the
> congregation to bless the candles which have already
> been lit? (Asked by Rabbi Jack Segal, Houston, Texas.)

ANSWER:

I HAVE NEVER written on this situation, and it is a very
interesting one because, in a way, there is an analogy to
it which might justify this practice.

As you know, all blessings must be given immediately
before the action which is blessed takes place. If you
make a blessing over bread, the bread must be eaten
without delay, etc. Now this creates a problem with
the Sabbath lights. By normal practice at the home
table, the mother should recite the blessing and then
light the lights. But the problem with Sabbath lights is
this: Which of the two actions, the reciting of the blessing or the actual kindling of the lights, converts the

9

evening from weekday to Sabbath? It is possible that
the reciting of the blessing makes it the Sabbath. In that
case, how can the woman light the lights if it is already
Sabbath? This would be a profaning of the Sabbath.
But should she light the lights first? If it is the lighting
of the lights that makes it Sabbath, there would be no
violation of the Sabbath in reciting the blessing. However, the rule is that the blessing must come before the
action (*over l'asioson*). How can she solve the dilemma? She lights the lights first, covers her eyes so as
not to see the light, recites the blessing, removes her
hands from her eyes, and sees the light immediately
after the blessing. This explains the custom of the
mother covering her eyes and solves the legal problem
of how to avoid violating the Sabbath.

If it is the custom now in your synagogue to have the
lights lit first, then what can be done is this: The lights
could be screened by some nicely embroidered screen,
and then, when the woman comes up to bless the lights,
the first thing she does is to recite the blessing, and then
she can remove the screen so that she and the congregation will see the lights. This would be a fair analogy
to what is done at home.

2

SPORTS ON SABBATH IN COMMUNITY
CENTERS

QUESTION:

A controversy has arisen in our community as to
whether the Jewish community center should or should
not open its swimming pool on Saturday. It serves Jews
and non-Jews who pay a fee and use its facilities. However, the board is entirely Jewish. At present the center
is closed on Saturday. What is the standpoint of the
Halacha on the question of sports and athletic recreation
being allowed on the Sabbath? (Question from Rabbi
Abner L. Bergman, Salt Lake City, Utah.)

ANSWER:

THE QUESTION asked here is a delicate one. It concerns
the Jewish community center, which involves the religious mood and sensibilities of the *entire* community.
The center constitutes an important unifying factor in
the community, and a decision either way on the question asked is likely to offend one segment of the
community or another and lead to divisiveness. If the
facilities are opened on the Sabbath, then more Ortho-
dox-minded members will be offended. If the facilities
remain completely closed on the Sabbath, there may
well be growing protests on the part of those who are

11

not strict in their Sabbath observance. They will claim to be deprived of the facilities they are entitled to use on the day when they are, perhaps, free from business occupations. And besides that, there are Christian members who pay their dues and help maintain the institution, and their rights are to be considered also. For all these reasons the situation is delicate, and if the community is to remain united, it must be handled with great care.

Furthermore, the situation is complicated by the fact that the question is a difficult one from the Halachic point of view. Inasmuch as there *is* considerable disagreement on the question of these recreations on the Sabbath in the legal literature, perhaps the best thing, therefore, would be to indicate the various opinions in the Halacha, and thereby, perhaps, the community may be guided to a proper decision.

The question is asked here specifically about the swimming pool, as to whether it should be made available for use on the Sabbath. However, there are other and equally important questions implied. What about the handball courts, and the gymnasium for basketball? Should or should not these be made available?

Let us discuss first the stricter question of playing ball on the Sabbath. Basically, playing with a ball on the Sabbath and holidays is clearly forbidden. Joseph Caro, in the *Shulchan Aruch, Orah Hayyim* 308:45, definitely says it is forbidden to play ball on Sabbath and Yom Tov. But Isserles comments that many authorities permit it and that it is the established custom to permit it. The permissibility is based upon the statement of the *Tosfos* in *Beza* 12a (near the bottom of the page), who speaks of the fact that it is an established custom to play ball on the holidays (by the way, he uses the word *pelota* for "ball," the word which is still used for the "ball" in Jai Alai). The discussion there indicates that the basic question is the prohibition of carrying an object (in this case, the ball) from private to public premises on the Sabbath. If, for example, they were playing in a backyard and the ball were carried over into the street, this would be forbidden. Another objection, of course, is that the ball is played on soft ground, and a furrow or a hole might be created in the earth, which is forbidden on the Sabbath. It is, therefore, evident that if it is played in an enclosed court indoors and on a hard floor, there is no longer any objection to ball playing on the Sabbath. That is why Isserles says that the permissibility is by now an established custom.

Now as to swimming on the Sabbath, this seems to have a weaker basis for prohibition. First of all, of all the possible recreational and athletic sports, only swimming is, in general, recommended in the Talmud. In fact, teaching his son to swim is counted as one of the obligations of a father (*b. Kiddushin* 29a).

Nevertheless, the Mishnah specifically forbids swimming, together with dancing and horseback riding, on the holidays (and therefore all the more on the Sabbath; Mishnah *Beza* 5:2). The prohibition against swimming is analogous to the prohibition against dancing. Dancing was prohibited primarily as a caution against the danger of needing to repair the musical instrument if it happens to break. Repairing it is an act which is forbidden on the Sabbath. In an analogous fashion, the prohibition against swimming was incidental to the possible danger that water wings to buoy up a learner might be constructed on Sabbath and holidays (*b. Beza* 36b). (The phrase we have translated as "water wings" is *chavis shel shayetin,* literally, "the bottle for swimmers.") However, just as dancing is now permitted by setting aside the possibility of needing to repair the musical instrument, so on that basis, too, the caution against the danger of making water wings may also be set aside. But with regard to swimming there are additional objections besides the above-mentioned cautionary one. If one swam in a river, he might splash water onto the land and also create a ridge of earth. That is why one of the Gaonim, in a responsum cited by Jacob Mann in *Texts and Studies,* Vol. I, p. 557, rebuked the people for swimming in the rivers of Babylon on Sabbath. However, if the swimming is done in a pool with a rim which allows the splashed water to fall back into the pool, there is no objection to it on the Sabbath. (*Orah Hayyim* 339:2).

It will be noticed that the general tendency of the law with regard to these recreational and athletic activities is to begin with strict prohibition, but then gradually to accept the lenient observances of the people. Perhaps the older strictness is a heritage that goes back to the Maccabean era, when athletic contests and gymnasia were characteristic of the pagan Greeks and were imitated by young Greek-loving Jewish aristocrats. It was against this Hellenism that the Maccabeans waged their battle. There is, therefore, to be found in the earlier lore a general dislike for all such sportive activities. Besides, they were deemed to be a distraction from the more serious duties of observing the Sabbath with spiritual benefits of study, etc. However, as has been stated, it is clear that the prohibitions gradually weakened, and by now it can no longer be said that it is prohibited to play ball on the Sabbath in an enclosed court, or to swim in an enclosed pool. These may still be objected to as frivolous on the Sabbath, but they cannot be prohibited as forbidden.

Because of all these variations in the mood of the law, the present problem must be approached cautiously. Finally, however, this must be said: if the community center does decide to open these facilities on the Sabbath, it cannot be justly accused of violating the traditional law.

3

BAR MITZVAH ON YIZKOR DAYS

QUESTION:

A question has arisen in our congregation as to whether it is proper to have a Bar Mitzvah on the eighth day of Succos (Shemini Atzeres) since in many of our congregations we have *Yizkor* services on that day. (Asked by Rabbi Harold Waintrup, Abington, Pennsylvania.)

ANSWER:

THE POSSIBLE objection to having a Bar Mitzvah on Shemini Atzeres if the congregation has its *Yizkor* service on that day is based, evidently, on the feeling that there is an incongruity between the moods of the two observances, the *Yizkor* being somber, and the Bar Mitzvah being a joyous observance. The possible contradiction in mood brings to mind a much more serious incongruity. Is there not a glaring incongruity in mood between the *Yizkor* memorial service and the holiday itself? How is it possible that a memorial service can properly belong on a joyous holiday which is called *Z'man simchasanu,* "the time of our rejoicing"? Does not *Yizkor* violate the mood of the holiday? The answer

16

to this question brings us back to the history of the *Yizkor* service.

Originally the *Yizkor* service arose in the Rhineland as a memorial for the martyrs during the Crusades. It was held always on Yom Kippur, as is clearly appropriate and consistent. The sources speak of "atonement for the living and the dead." However, since it was also deemed appropriate that the prayers for the dead should be accompanied by gifts in their memory, the *Yizkor* was extended from Yom Kippur to the last day of each of the three pilgrimage festivals because on the last day of the festivals, the reading ends with the verse from Deuteronomy 16:17, which says that when the pilgrims came up to Jerusalem on the festivals, each was to give a gift according to the generosity of his hand (*k'matnas yodo*). So it came about that it was no longer considered incongruous (if ever it was so considered) to have a memorial service, a *Yizkor,* on a festival when we were bidden "to rejoice." See Maharil, end of the section on Hoshana Rabba; also my article "Hazkaras Nashamos," *HUC Annual,* 1965.

As a matter of fact, in many congregations a sort of *Yizkor* was extended from the last days of the three festivals to the service of *every* Sabbath. This memorial service took place in connection with the reading of the Torah. It consisted of the recital of the prayer *Av Horachamim,* "Father of mercies," which memorializes the martyrs of Israel, and with that prayer, when the man is called up to the Torah, he could give his charity in behalf of a departed relative who was named in the *Mi Sheberach.* In the Rhineland this Sabbath memorial was recited on only two Sabbaths, the Sabbath before Shavuos and the Sabbath before the Ninth of Av. In Eastern Europe it was recited every Sabbath, but with certain exceptions, which are of relevance to the question asked here. This memorial prayer and the *Mi Sheberachs* for the departed were recited every Sabbath *except* the Sabbath when the New Moon is blessed, and *also* if there is a bridegroom in the congregation married within the week, or if a parent has a circumcision of a newborn child during the week.

It is to be noted that the joyous occasions in the personal life of any single worshiper which prevent the recital of the *Yizkor* prayers do *not* include a Bar Mitzvah. Clearly a Bar Mitzvah is not considered to be the same type of family occasion as a wedding or the circumcision of a newborn child. The blessing recited for Bar Mitzvah by the father is not a joyous blessing. It speaks of being "disencumbered of a duty" (*Boruch sh'p'torani*), and in earlier generations not much fuss and celebration was made of the Bar Mitzvah. It often occurred on a weekday, Monday or Thursday, when the Torah was read. The calling up of the boy to the Torah at his Bar Mitzvah is essentially only an announcement to the congregation that the lad is now religiously an adult and may now be counted in the *minyan*. Of course it was natural that the family and also some guests should gather for a meal after the services.

It is only in modern times, when the Bar Mitzvah celebrations have become so elaborate, that some might feel a contradiction between the Bar Mitzvah joy and the memorial *Yizkor*. But it was not so in the past, and the Bar Mitzvah is not counted among the personal occasions of happiness in deference to which the Sabbath memorial prayers are omitted.

Of course, if the particular family involved is planning, as is customary nowadays, an elaborate family celebration, it might feel that a *Yizkor* day is incongruous with the spirit of family joy. But that would be this family's own decision, and if it feels that way, it can postpone the Bar Mitzvah for a week or so. But as a matter of traditional custom and mood, there is no contradiction between *Yizkor* and the holiday joyousness itself, and even on the Sabbaths, when the memorial prayers are omitted in deference to a personal happy occasion of a congregant, Bar Mitzvah is not counted among these occasions.

The answer to the question, therefore, is: Since there is a Torah reading on the eighth day of Succos, a Bar Mitzvah may be held on that day. The recital of the *Yizkor* is, from the point of view of the mood of tradition, no ground for postponing the Bar Mitzvah.

4

BAS MITZVAH

QUESTION:

In a neighboring temple, the ceremony of Bas Mitzvah was conducted at the Friday night service. Is this proper? Are there any rules or regulations that need be followed with regard to this ceremony?

ANSWER:

THE CEREMONY OF Bas Mitzvah, which was created during this generation, has now spread into Jewish Orthodox life in America (and also, I am informed, even in Israel). Hence questions have now arisen in the American responsa literature with regard to this ceremony. Usually the question asked is a very direct one: May an Orthodox Jew attend the Bas Mitzvah party in the family of a relative or close friend? Of course the question is not asked as to whether the questioner may or may not attend the service itself. This would imply asking whether he may attend a Conservative or a Reform service, which certainly would be forbidden to him. The question that is actually asked is whether he may attend the family celebration that follows the Bas Mitzvah service, just as there is a family celebration nowadays that follows the Bar Mitzvah service.

To this secondary question (whether to attend the Bas Mitzvah luncheon) the answer in the two responsa which have appeared is a definite and even a stern negative. The man should not go even to the party.

Moses Feinstein, the leading Orthodox authority in America, answers (*Orah Hayyim* 104) with a stern negative, and his reason is bluntly stated. This ceremony, says he, was established by the Conservatives and the Reformers, and that is reason enough to avoid any such celebration. The second opinion is by Moses Stern, formerly rabbi of Debreczin, now of Brooklyn (see his responsa collection, *Be'er Moshe,* I, #10). He likewise forbids the questioner to attend the celebration and gives a milder reason, namely, because it is a new ceremony, not established by our learned predecessors. But while coming to this negative conclusion, he speculates on the question as to why such a ceremony was not established in the past. Is it not the duty of a father to train a daughter as well as a son in the observance of the *mitzvos?* It would seem that he has such a duty. But there is a distinction as to the respective responsibilities pertaining to a son and a daughter, as is evidenced by the fact that the blessing which the father says at the Bar Mitzvah (*Boruch sh'p'torani*) was not ordained to be said for a daughter.

Of course with regard to the Conservative and Reform movements, these negative arguments have little weight. The Reform movement, from the very beginning, has proclaimed the religious equality of men and women, and the Conservative movement is striving with great effort these days to establish this equality.

Which of these two movements created the Bas Mitzvah I do not know. It is my impression that it began with neither of them; at least in the city of Baltimore, I know that it was started in the modern Hebrew educational system. But at all events, it is accepted in both movements since it fits their respective philosophies.

As for the basic Halachic justification for it, to which Moses Stern referred in mere theory (as an idea to be raised and then rejected), it deserves consideration. The Mishnah, in *Yoma* 8:4, says that parents should not compel young children to fast, but should train them, step by step, to become accustomed to fasting. To which the *Tosfos* (*Yoma* 82a top) takes for granted that this means training both boys and girls to the *mitzvah,* and it gives the respective ages of adulthood for each.

However, in *Nazir* 28b, in the discussion on the Mishnah as to whether a man may make Nazirite vows for his children, Resh Lakish says that he has a duty to train his son, but not to train his daughter. This would indicate that a father has no responsibility to train his daughter to observe the *mitzvos,* and therefore he does not need to recite the blessing when the daughter comes of religious age, as he does when the son comes of religious age. However, this is not the actual law. The opinion of Resh Lakish is explained away in the *Tosfos Yeshenim* to *Yoma* 82 as follows: What Resh Lakish means is that the father has no duty to train the daughter to Nazirite vows, but as to all the other commandments, he does have the duty. Then why does he not at a certain occasion in the girl's life recite the Bar Mitzvah blessing of disavowal? The *Pri M'gadim* to *Eshel Avraham* (*Orah Hayyim* 225, end of par. 5) says that the reason the father does not recite the blessing for the daughter, even though he *is* in duty bound to train her to the *mitzvos,* is because the daughter, being a woman, has many less *mitzvos* to observe than the son.

All these arguments to and fro are not decisive for us, but at least they indicate a strong feeling in the Halachic literature that a father has the duty to train his daughter to the *mitzvos,* as he has to train his son. The modern religious movements in Judaism, which have no psychological basis for objecting to novelty, are carrying out a strong line in the tradition by the establishment of the Bas Mitzvah along with the Bar Mitzvah. As for whether it should be held on Friday night, that depends: If the congregation in which it is held has a public Torah reading on Friday night, as some Reform congregations do, then it is quite proper to have a Bar Mitzvah as well as a Bas Mitzvah at that service.

Perhaps a word of caution might be spoken with regard to Bas Mitzvah in Reform congregations. The beloved and influential ceremony in Reform Judaism for coming of age religiously is the Confirmation ceremony held on Shavuos. When, due to a traditional mood, Bar Mitzvah was increasingly introduced in Reform congregations, many parents kept their sons out of Confirmation, feeling that Bar Mitzvah was quite enough. So, too, it might be that an increase in Bas Mitzvah ceremonies will reduce the Confirmation still further. This would be a definite loss to our Reform religious life.

If this unfortunate aftermath can be avoided, then on the basis of the principles of Reform Judaism, and also on the basis of a strong line in the tradition as to the duties of a parent to daughters as well as to sons, Bas Mitzvah is a worthy complement to Bar Mitzvah in a modern synagogue.

There has recently been published Volume VI of the responsa of Obadiah Joseph, the Sephardic Chief Rabbi (*Yabia Omer*). In responsum #29, he takes an attitude toward Bas Mitzvah opposite to that of Moses Feinstein, mentioned above. He approves of the ceremony and suggests that the father recite the same blessing that the father does for a Bar Mitzvah, and even considers the meal celebrating the Bas Mitzvah as a religious meal (*seudas mitzvah*), providing, of course, that words of Torah are spoken on the occasion.

5

TALIT AND MEZUZAH TO GENTILES

QUESTION:

A Christian minister is to participate in a joint service with us in the synagogue. He is eager to wear a *talit* as the rabbi does. May we give him one to wear? Also, a Gentile friend asked for a *mezuzah* to be affixed to his door. Should that be granted? (Asked by Rabbi Jay B. Goldburg, Des Moines, Iowa.)

ANSWER:

THESE QUESTIONS come up frequently in the increasing ecumenical meetings between rabbis and the Christian clergy. While in Reform Judaism we do not ascribe especial sanctity to ritual objects, nevertheless we should be considerate of their use. It is therefore of importance to consider the attitude of traditional Halacha on these questions.

The four questions asked are really two. The first two questions involve the lending of a *talit* to a Christian minister to wear during a joint service. The answer depends on the classification of the *talit* in the order of sanctity ascribed to the various articles of worship. Some articles, such as the mantle of the Torah and the ark in which the Torah is kept, are called "appurtenances of sanctity" (*tashmishey kedushah*). Other objects, such as a Succah and a *lulav* after the holiday, and fringes, are of a lower degree of sanctity. They are considered "appurtenances of a *mitzvah*" (*tashmishey mitzvah*).

The law has, naturally, a different attitude to the "appurtenances of sanctity" (such as Torah mantles, etc.) than it has to the "appurtenances of a *mitzvah*." The general principle is stated quite clearly in the Talmud (*Megillah* 26b), namely, that when these objects are no longer to be used, they, respectively, must be treated differently. The principle is stated there tersely as follows: Appurtenances of a *mitzvah* can be thrown away. Appurtenances of sanctity must be hidden away (*nignozin*), i.e., kept in a special place or buried. The *Shulchan Aruch,* in *Orah Hayyim* 21, says that the threads of a *talit* no longer used or broken "may be thrown onto the ash heap because it is an appurtenance of a *mitzvah* and not inherently holy." Of course, as long as the fringes are in the *talit* they should be treated respectfully. However, it will be noticed in *Orah Hayyim* 21:3 that it is permitted to go to the toilet wearing the *talit,* and Isserles adds that it is permitted to sleep in it.

If, therefore, the *talit* may be worn in all sorts of places, and if its fringes (when separated) may even be tossed onto the ash heap, there is no question that one may lend it to a Gentile minister who will handle it reverently. In fact, thus we will fulfill the basic *mitzvah* of acting "to follow the paths of peace" (*mipney darche shalom*). As you will see, the same principle is involved in the second question.

The second question is whether it is permitted to give a *mezuzah* to a Gentile to affix on his doorpost. Or if a Jew moves from his house or rents it to a Gentile, whether he may allow the *mezuzah* to remain on the doorpost. Actually, only a house inhabited by a Jew *requires* a *mezuzah*. Thus, for example, if a Jew rents a house from a Gentile landlord, he must affix a *mezuzah*. If a Jew rents a house to a Gentile tenant, the *mezuzah,* if there was one there, must be removed (see the discussion in *Yore Deah* 291:2).

The note of Isserles is of considerable interest in this matter. He cites a responsum by Maharil of Mainz (14th cent.) that even if the Gentile asks for a *mezuzah* to be affixed on his doorpost, we may not give it to him. It is of interest to note that even in the fourteenth century in the Rhineland, Gentiles occasionally would ask for *mezuzahs* to put on their doors. However this prohibition by Maharil was evidently not firmly based because Isserles, in the sixteenth century, contravenes it. He says: "If the refusal to give the Gentile the *mezuzah* would create ill will, we may give it to him."

Thus we see that both the question of the *talit* and the question of the *mezuzah* are related in the question of ecumenical relationships. In Jewish law such relationships are stated in two ways: in a positive way "because of the paths of peace," and in a negative way "to avoid ill will" (*meshum evah*).

6

MUGGERS AND MONEY ON SABBATH

QUESTION:

An elderly Orthodox Jew, walking home from the synagogue on the Sabbath, was, of course, carrying no
money. A hold-up man accosted him and, because the
old man had no money to give him, shot and killed
him. It was suggested that elderly Orthodox Jews, living
in high-risk areas, should carry a token bill with them,
say a ten-dollar bill, to hand over to the hold-up man
and thus save their lives. Is there a liberal Jewish attitude applicable to this opinion? (Asked by Rabbi Reeve
Brenner, Hebrew Center of Westchester, Tuckahoe,
New York.)

ANSWER:

NON-ORTHODOX JEWS do not hesitate to carry money
on the Sabbath. Therefore there is no need for "a liberal
Jewish posture" in this matter. The only type of permission to carry money that would be convincing to an
Orthodox man would be that which is based firmly on
Orthodox law. Let us, therefore, consider the strict
Halacha on the question as to whether a man may
carry money on the Sabbath if that act is likely to save
his life in case he is held up.

First of all, there is no question that the carrying of money is forbidden on the Sabbath. (See Maimonides, *Yad, Sabbath* 25:6 and *Orah Hayyim* 301:33.) The reason for the prohibition is not directly Biblical but is based upon the rabbinical concept of *muktsa*. There are numerous types of *muktsa*. The one that applies here is the *muktsa* prohibition to handle such objects as are normally used to perform the type of work which is prohibited on the Sabbath. Since, therefore, it is prohibited to do business on the Sabbath, and money is considered to be specifically "set aside" (*muktsa*) as an instrument for doing business, money may not be handled or carried on the Sabbath.

However, it is to be noted that in this very matter of carrying money on the Sabbath, there are some grounds for leniency. Isserles, in his note to the law in the *Shulchan Aruch* (*Orah Hayyim* 301:33), says: "Many permit the carrying of money on the Sabbath if one is afraid that if he leaves the money in his lodging, his money will be stolen." There are some discussions in the commentators as to whether the money should be sewn in the garments or carried loose. But be that as it may, Isserles says: *Nohagin l'hokel* ("It is customary to be lenient in this matter").

Now, our problem here is primarily how to persuade the pious old man to carry the money for his safety's sake. Therefore one could well argue with him as follows: Since it is permitted to carry the money in order to save the money from being stolen, should it not be permitted to carry the money to save one's life from danger from injury or death? Of course, this is, in a

way, the reverse of what Isserles permits. He permits
the money to be carried on the Sabbath in order that
it *not* be stolen, and we here would permit it to be carried on the Sabbath in order that it could be stolen.
However, as we have said, danger to health or even life
is more important than safeguarding the money.

Further discussion of this problem should also consider the laws of healing the sick on the Sabbath. If a
person is dangerously sick, all Sabbath laws must be
set aside completely. This applies not only to the secondary Sabbath laws like *muktsa,* the carrying of
money, but also the strict Biblical laws, such as lighting
fires, etc. (*Yad, Sabbath* 2:1 and *Orah Hayyim* 328,
329). Furthermore, this violating of the Sabbath for the
sick must not be done surreptitiously but openly by
adults and men of standing (*Orah Hayyim* 328:12
based on *Yoma* 84b).

Yet actually there are provisions in the law much
more relevant to our question than the fact that money
may be carried to save it, or that a dangerously sick
person may be saved by means which are in violation
of Sabbath laws. The important and the direct law in
this case is the law of *pikuach nefesh,* direct danger to
life from accident, fire, violence. The law, as stated in
the Talmud (*Yoma* 84b), and as codified in the *Shulchan Aruch* 329:1, 2, is clear and forthright. It is as
follows: "All danger to life sets aside the Sabbath, and
whoever is most active [in violating the Sabbath to save
life], he is most praiseworthy." Mugging is clearly a
source of danger to life, and if a life can be saved by
carrying money, which is based only on the laws of

muktsa, then certainly one is to be praised who can save a life by this violation.

Of course, it can be argued that we do not know whether the man might be mugged at all, or if mugged, whether or not the mugger would kill him. However, the law is also clear that when there is such danger of violence to life, we do not stop to count the probabilities. Thus, for example, if a wall falls, and if we think that someone is buried under it, but we really do not *know* whether or not a person is there under the ruins, though we suspect that he may be, or we do not know whether he is already dead or perhaps still alive, we must simply take for granted that there is danger of accidental death, and we dig into the ruined heap on the Sabbath (*Orah Hayyim* 329:2). This mugging situation is so frequent, especially in certain neighborhoods, that we may not stop to count the probabilities. We *assume* that the danger is present; and just as we are in duty bound to violate the Sabbath to save an endangered life, so the endangered person is equally in duty bound to save his own.

Maimonides, in his discussion of saving life on the Sabbath, cites the verse in Leviticus 18:5: "My statutes and ordinances which a man should do and live by" (*Yad, Sabbath* 2:3). To this he adds the Talmudic amplification: "live by but not die by." This amplification of the Biblical verse is derived from the Talmud (*Yoma* 85b) where, in the discussion of saving a man from danger, one scholar says: "Violate one Sabbath in his behalf that he may live to observe many Sabbaths." Clearly, then, it is a man's duty to save the lives of others regardless of whether the action involves violating the Sabbath. In fact, the law is that if we see a man attacked on the Sabbath, we may even prepare or use weapons to defend him, even if such actions are forbidden on the Sabbath (*Yad, Hil. Sabbath* 2:24). Obviously, too, just as a man is in duty bound to violate the Sabbath in order to save others, so a man is clearly in duty bound to save himself if he can. If, for example, a wall fell upon a person, we must, as mentioned above, remove the debris on the Sabbath to save him; so too, certainly, if the man is only half-covered by the debris and has the strength to struggle, he is in duty bound to remove rocks and stones and dirt (on the Sabbath) in order to save himself.

The old man and those like him are actually in duty bound to violate the Sabbath (by carrying money) or even to carry some repellent, such as mace or the like, if this is likely to save him, as the Talmud says, "to observe many Sabbaths."

7

HAVDALA BAR MITZVAH

QUESTION:

Has the CCAR taken a position regarding the increasing use of *Havdala* Bar Mitzvah services? Our board passed a resolution limiting these services to one per month. However, members are telling me that they are seeing these services elsewhere and are more and more anxious to see them here. My concerns are several:

1. They will come to threaten the centrality of the Saturday morning service.
2. They are contrary to the tradition in that (a) next week's Torah portion is not read; (b) the time of the service is arbitrary, leading to a *Havdala* often earlier than the sunset.

There are probably Halachic issues to be raised as well. Is anybody working on this? (Transmitted through Rabbi Joseph B. Glaser, CCAR.)

ANSWER:

ABOUT A DECADE AGO, I was asked whether it was appropriate to have a Bar Mitzvah on a Sabbath afternoon. I answered at that time that it was quite appropriate, since a Bar Mitzvah must take place in connection with a Torah reading, and there is a regular Torah reading at the Sabbath afternoon service. Since that

time I have not received a single inquiry about Bar
Mitzvah services on Saturday afternoon, until this one;
and judging from the text of this inquiry, Bar Mitzvahs
in this community have been so frequently arranged
for late Saturday afternoon that the congregation has
felt compelled to take measures restricting them to one
a month.

These late Bar Mitzvahs are arranged as follows:
The boy is Bar Mitzvah at the Torah reading on Sabbath afternoon. Then, soon after, there follows a *Havdala* service to mark the close of the Sabbath, and then
there is the Bar Mitzvah dinner and dance, etc. The
congregational complaints against these Bar Mitzvahs
are indicated above in the question.

However, it is doubtful whether the congregation
will succeed in holding down these Bar Mitzvahs to a
small number (one a month or so) because evidently
this Bar Mitzvah arrangement must fit the present social
situation as well, if not better, than any other arrangement. First of all, the Bar Mitzvah party, dinner, dance,
etc., is very important to the family. Otherwise they
would not spend so much money on it, as has become
the American custom. When the Bar Mitzvah is in the
morning on Saturday, the luncheon that follows has to
be orderly and sedate. Rock and roll bands and dancing
are not appropriate on the Sabbath. That is why we
also get inquiries as to whether a Bar Mitzvah can be
held on Sunday. The real reason for these requests is
that a dance and a party on Sunday would be free from
Sabbath restrictions.

The best time for this sort of a party is always Satur-

day night. It can go on to a late hour because people
will not need to go to work the next day. Then why can
they not hold the Bar Mitzvah as is customary on Saturday morning and then hold the dinner and dance Saturday night? The objection is that people would have to
come twice, and it is much more convenient and acceptable and desirable, from their point of view, if they
can go to the Bar Mitzvah service and then, without
too much of an interval, have the dinner and the dance.
It is evident that this arrangement fits the social wishes
of the people, and if it is otherwise acceptable, will
undoubtedly increase, as can be seen from the fact that
in this community the board of the congregation had
to restrict their number. Since, then, we are dealing
with a situation which may well spread over the country, it is well to go into the matter in detail from the
point of view of the Halacha, congregational welfare,
and the mood of the community.

As to the Halachic side of the question, it is obvious
that since there is regular Torah reading at the Sabbath
Mincha service (the first section of next week's *Sedra*),
Bar Mitzvah can well take place then. Of course, if the
Mincha service is early, say at two-thirty or three on
a summer Sabbath, the people would have to wait about
five more hours before they could have their dinner and
dance. Therefore it is clear that they would want to
hold the *Mincha* service as late as possible, so that there
would be only a brief interval between the service and
the festivity. The question therefore is: How late may
Mincha services be held?

The time of the *Mincha* service in the synagogue

is connected with the *Mincha* service of the Temple in Jerusalem. The question is: What is the time limit before which the *Mincha* service could be held? The Mishnah gives two varying opinions. In *M. Berachos* 4:1, the general rule is that the *Mincha* service may be held up to evening; but Rabbi Judah disagrees and says that it must be no later than "half the *Mincha*" (*plag ha-Mincha*), which is reckoned, in general, to be about an hour and a quarter before sunset.

The reason for the lack of exactitude as to which time *Mincha* is still permissible is due to the fact that the "hours" referred to in the Mishnah are different from our hours. Our hours are of uniform length, sixty minutes; their hours varied in length from winter to summer, according to the length of the day. The Mishnah divides the daylight period into twelve hours. Therefore these hours are larger in summer (being one-twelfth of the daylight period, which is longer). So when Mishnah and Talmud speak of the ninth hour of the day, it is virtually impossible to say which hour of our time that is. The ninth hour would mean the time when nine-twelfths of the daylight has passed. At all events, Rabbi Judah's time limit of *plag ha-Mincha* is about an hour before sunset, at any season of the year.

As between these two opinions, the law is that either time is permissible. Since the general statement is that *Mincha* can be conducted "up to evening," the custom has developed, certainly during weekdays, for people (especially working people who might come into the synagogue *after* the day's work) to pray *Mincha* late, at dusk, and go immediately into the evening service, the *maariv*; in other words, to pray both services together.

Nevertheless, this practice varies for Sabbath and holidays because of the desire to "add from the profane to the holy," in other words, to lengthen the Sabbath and the holiday by beginning it early and ending it late. However, even in the case of the Sabbath, under special circumstances, it is permitted to pray the *Mincha* service quite late and to close the Sabbath with the *Havdala* service somewhat earlier.

The chief source of this permission is the Talmud in *Berachos* 27b and the *Tosfos* (ad loc.). The Talmud speaks of Rabbi Josiah, who would pray the weekday service (i.e., *Maariv*) while it was still Sabbath; to which the *Tosfos* comments that normally this should *not* be done; we should lengthen the sacred day, not shorten it. But in case of necessity, for the sake of a *mitzvah*, the Sabbath may be thus shortened. So it becomes the rule in the *Shulchan Aruch,* in the discussion of the Sabbath evening service (*Orah Hayyim* 293:2), that under special circumstances, he may pray the Sabbath closing prayer and make a *Havdala* at and after the *plag ha-Mincha* (i.e., before it is quite dusk), but that one should leave out the blessing over the kindling light (*M'orey ho-esh*) because it is still actually forbidden to light fire since the Sabbath is not really over.

This rather early *Havdala* is therefore permitted for the sake of a *mitzvah*. But is it really for the sake of a *mitzvah* that this early *Havdala* is being done by the families discussed in the question? Actually, it is done for the sake of a Bar Mitzvah dinner and dance. Can we actually say truthfully that this Bar Mitzvah party is a *mitzvah?*

The question of whether the party has any sacred nature at all is actually discussed by one of the greatest rabbinical authorities, Solomon Luria (*Maharshal,* 16th cent.). His discussion of the Bar Mitzvah party must have come at the time when the whole idea of such a party was new, because he refers to it as "the *seudah* which the Germans have." His discussion is in his *Yam Shel Shelomo* to *Babba Kama* (chap. 7, par. 37), in which he discusses various feasts as to which may be considered religious feasts (*seudas mitzvos*). He includes a feast at the completion of the study of a Talmudic tractate (a *siyyum*), at a circumcision, and other such occasions. He denies that the party given at the dedication of a new house is to be considered a religious party because he says, frankly, that the people use that occasion to fill their gullets and to be hilarious. Then he mentions "the feast which the Ashkenazim give at Bar Mitzvahs" and he declares that to be a *seudas mitzvah,* or sacred occasion.

If, then, some words are spoken at the dinner table referring to the religious nature of the ceremony, this may be considered a *seudas mitzvah,* as Solomon Luria says, and for that purpose a late *Mincha* service and a somewhat earlier *Havdala* service (say at dusk, before the three stars appear) is permissible. So, in general, one may say that *Mincha* may be conducted quite late and then *Havdala* before the stars appear, all of this in accordance with the Halacha.

But why did the board of the congregation object

so much to this arrangement that it passed a law restricting it to only one a month? Their objection is that it will weaken the Sabbath morning service. That is certainly true. The Sabbath morning services everywhere and in all types of synagogues are greatly strengthened by the Bar Mitzvah. If, therefore, the late afternoon Bar Mitzvahs increase, the Sabbath services will certainly lose attendance. Of course one may argue that to make up for it the Sabbath *Mincha* service, which had become even weaker than the Sabbath morning service, would now be strengthened and revived. However, in the Sabbath morning service the Bar Mitzvah relatives and friends join in worship with the general congregation, but the afternoon service would tend to become exclusively the Bar Mitzvah service. People not connected with the Bar Mitzvah family are not likely to attend.

However, it well may be that it is futile to attempt to prevent these late Saturday Bar Mitzvahs. They are increasing, and they very well may continue to increase because of the social convenience mentioned above. What must be done is to keep it within the decencies of tradition as much as possible. Let it be a late *Mincha* service, close to dusk. Then it will be followed by the *Maariv* and the *Havdala* service when it is definitely dark. Then the Bar Mitzvah party, in mood and in the words spoken, should certainly begin as a *seudas mitzvah*. In that case, the new custom may be deemed quite acceptable.

8

CANDLES AT THE SATURDAY NIGHT SEDER

QUESTION:

> At the Seder in the Jewish old folks' home, it is customary for the ladies to have a candle-procession as part of the candle-lighting for the holiday. This year, however, the Seder is on Saturday night, and since the Seder will begin rather early, the candle-lighting would take place while it is Sabbath, which is forbidden. The suggestion has been made to postpone the candle-lighting until later in the Seder, say, before the door is opened for Elijah. By that time it would be quite dark. Is this procedure permissible? (Asked by Louis J. Freehof, San Francisco, California.)

ANSWER:

THE FACT THAT this year Erev Pesach is on the Sabbath creates many ritual difficulties. This occurs rather frequently, since the first day of Passover may occur on Sunday, Tuesday, Thursday, or Saturday. In fact, there is a whole section in the *Shulchan Aruch* (*Orah Hayyim* 444) dealing with this situation, namely, when *Erev* Pesach comes on the Sabbath, as it does this year. However, this section deals only with the ritual matters in preparation for Passover, namely, the searching for the *chometz* on Thursday and the removal of the *chometz* the next day. But it gives us no guidance as to the problem of the Saturday night Seder ritual itself.

If the Seder this year is held when it is fully dark, there is no problem at all because, since it is the end of the Sabbath, *Havdala* is recited. The *Havdala* is combined with the *Kiddush* in the merged formula called *Yaknahaz,* which means the blessing over the wine, the *Kiddush,* the light (which may now be kindled), the *Havdala* (marking the end of the Sabbath), and *Zeman,* i.e., the blessing *Shehechionu* (cf. *Chaye Adam,* "Laws of Passover; the Seder"). Thus the light is lit at the very beginning of the ceremony, and no violation of the law has occurred since the Sabbath is over.

However, clearly it is the custom at the Home, and in many institutions, to begin the public Seder before it is dusk, and it is this custom which creates the difficulties this year.

There is a basic question involved in this enquiry. Is the kindling of the *Yom Tov* lights indispensable to the beginning of the Seder, or can the Seder begin without it? First, it is important to note that the Mishnah and Talmud and all the Codes lay heavy stress on the *Sabbath* lights on Friday night: the Mishnah, in *Sabbath,* chap. 2, toward the end; the Talmud (*b. Sabbath* 25b), which declares the lighting of the light on Friday evening a religious duty; and the *Shulchan Aruch,* which discusses the Sabbath lights in six full sections (*Orah Hayyim* 261 to 266). By contrast, the kindling of the lights on the holiday eve has only scant mention. (The statement in the Mishnah, 2:2, and the Talmud, 24b,

is that we do not kindle with oil of burning, i.e., oil
obtained from burning unfit heave-offering, on *Yom
Tov.*) This does not refer to the lights for the ushering
in of the holiday but to the light ushering in the Sabbath which comes at the close of the holiday. The
kindling of the light on a holiday receives only a passing reference in the *Shulchan Aruch* (*Orah Hayyim*
263:5) and is not even mentioned in the *Chayye Adam*
in the description of the Seder. Of course it is an established observance to kindle lights ushering in the holiday meal according to Jacob Emden in his *Siddur*
(Laws of Passover Eve 4:2). But the lack of adequate
reference to it in the Codes indicates that its status in
the law is not very firm.

Not only is the kindling of the light on a holiday of
much lesser importance than the kindling of the light
on the Sabbath; it is also of lesser importance than the
Kiddush which ushers in the holiday. The *Kiddush* on
Passover, for example, is the first of the obligatory four
cups of wine, and is discussed fully in the law (*Orah
Hayyim* 473:1). Yet even this important ceremony, the
Kiddush, may at times be postponed. For example, generally the Seder should take place when it is dark because it is analogous to the Passover lamb eaten in
Egypt, which, according to the Bible (Exodus 12:8)
took place at night. Nevertheless, according to the law
(*Orah Hayyim* 472:1), if for the sake of the children
(and we may well say if for the sake of older people
also) the Seder is to be held earlier than nightfall, then
the head of the house must postpone the *Kiddush* until
it is dark. If, then, the *Kiddush,* which is indispensable

to the Seder and to the announcing of the holiday, may be postponed until after the Seder has gone on for a while, it stands to reason that the holiday light, which is not so firmly founded in the law, may certainly be postponed.

Actually, we do not need to rely solely on the above inference. There is, in fact, a close analogy to this proposed postponement of the candle lighting. The Talmud (*Berachos* 27b) speaks of Rabbi Josiah, who would pray the weekday prayer (i.e., *Maariv* or *Havdala*) while it was still Sabbath. The *Tosfos* comments that normally this should not be done, for we should lengthen the sacred day (the Sabbath) and not shorten it. But in case of necessity, for the sake of a *mitzvah,* the Sabbath may be thus shortened. This becomes the rule in the *Shulchan Aruch* (*Orah Hayyim* 293:3) in the laws of Sabbath-closing, namely, that we may recite the *Havdala* at *plag ha-Mincha,* i.e., just before dusk. But if that is done, one must leave out the blessing over kindling the light (*M'orey ha-esh*) because the Sabbath is not really over, and it is still forbidden to light fire. Thus there is a real precedent in the law for delaying the candle-lighting at this Seder.

The above refers to any Saturday night, but the law is even more direct and refers precisely to the situation this year, when the Seder comes on Saturday night. On that occasion (see *Orah Hayyim* 473:1 and *Chayye Adam,* Laws of Seder), the first of the four cups, which is the *Kiddush* cup, must be part of the larger Saturday night *Yom Tov* prayer (*Yaknehaz*), which combines both *Kiddush* and *Havdala* (especially the blessing over light, *M'orey ha-esh*). The law states that if, when the Seder is on Saturday night, the man forgets to recite (with the first cup) the blessing for the light and the other *Havdala* prayer, then he should nevertheless continue with the Seder and wait to pronounce the light-and-*Havdala* blessing till after most of the Haggadah is over and before the meal begins. This is very close to the procedure that is suggested by the question (*Orah Hayyim* 473:1).

Therefore, the proposed idea to light the candles later in the Seder not only is unobjectionable, but may even be considered desirable, since it avoids the violation of the Sabbath and, further, has a firm basis in the law.

9

THE PERMANENT SUCCAH

QUESTION:

A congregation in the South plans to build on its grounds a permanent boothlike structure which is to be used as a Succah during the festival. Is it permissible to use a permanent structure for this ritual purpose? (Asked by Rabbi Kenneth Segel, New Orleans, Louisiana.)

ANSWER:

AT FIRST BLUSH it would seem to be forbidden to use a permanent structure as a Succah. The law governing the building and the use of the Succah is based on Leviticus 23:44–45, in which the commandment to "dwell in booths" is based upon the statement that God provided booths (Succahs) for the children of Israel in the desert. Upon this verse the Talmud, *Succah* 2a, comments as follows: On the festival of Succos a man must move from his fixed dwelling place to a temporary or makeshift hut (*diras aroy*). Therefore, all the laws as to the building of the Succah speak of its light or makeshift construction.

Furthermore, the first Mishnah of the tractate speaks of "an old succah," and that is defined as a Succah that is already as much as thirty days old. Such a thirty-day-old Succah is deemed invalid by the school of Shammai. On the positive side, it has become an established custom to start building the Succah as soon as Yom Kippur is over—in other words, no earlier than four days before the festival begins. This custom is based upon the chief source of our Ashkenazic customs, Maharil (in his laws on Succos), and is confirmed as a custom by Isserles in the *Shulchan Aruch, Orah Hayyim* 625:1. All the above regulations would indicate that the permanent structure suggested in the question would be deemed invalid by Jewish traditional law.

However, a deeper study of the matter would reveal that the above objections are not at all crucial. First of all, as to the requirement that it be a "temporary structure," it is quite permissible to build a Succah, for example, in a garret, provided that the roof or skylight is removed so that those who sit in the Succah can see the sky and the stars through the covering of fir branches (*s'chach*). There is, of course, a further requirement that the permanent roof of the garret shall not overlap onto the Succah as much as four cubits. If there is less than four cubits of permanent roof over the rims of the Succah, this Succah which is part of the permanent house is quite valid. This is discussed in the Mishnah 1:10 (cf. Bertinoro).

As to the objection to "an old Succah," i.e., one that is more than thirty days old, the objection is confined only to the school of Shammai; but the school of Hillel declares such a Succah quite valid. This is discussed in the first Mishnah of the tractate; and in the Talmud 9a, the following becomes clear, that it makes no difference how early a man builds it, provided he builds it for the purpose of a Succah. If he built it to be a Succah, not merely to be any sort of booth, then there is no such objection as "an old Succah." See especially Rashi's statement (ibid.).

As a matter of fact, it became an established custom in many places to have a permanent structure with a hinged roof—provided, of course, that the hinged roof be lifted out of the way and its place taken by the usual branches (*s'chach*). It would be invalid to put the *s'chach* on while the permanent hinged roof is still on the building. The roof must be raised, and when the roof is opened to the sky, the *s'chach* must be put on. See Isserles to *Orah Hayyim* 626:3 for a full statement of the use of such a structure. In fact the Talmud itself (in 8b) speaks of buildings built by Gentiles for cattle, or for people to live in, which may properly be used for a Succah if prepared as described above.

Of course, whether the permanent Succah described in the question is a valid Succah would depend, therefore, upon the following: First, that the congregation from the very beginning *intends* it to be used for the purpose of a Succah. This, indeed, is the fact. Second, that it is not at all sufficient merely to decorate the building with fruits, etc.; the roof must be removed and a temporary roof of branches made. If that is done, the all-around Succah is quite valid according to Jewish tradition.

10

PROCLAIMING A NEW FAST

QUESTION:

American Protestants and Catholics are planning to proclaim a fast day in order to intensify awareness of world hunger, and also to observe this fast day as a day of prayer for the relief of world hunger. Since this proposed fast day is thus a religious observance, is there any objection to the Jewish community joining in its observance? Also, does such a fast day need to be on any special day of the week or not? (Asked by Rabbi H. B. Waintrup, Abington, Pennsylvania.)

ANSWER:

As far as the Bible is concerned, there is only one regular Jewish fast day, namely, the Day of Atonement. But after the return from the Exile, other fast days were added marking national tragedies, such as the destruction of the Temple, the breaching of the walls of the city, etc. (i.e., the Ninth of Av, the Tenth of Teves, etc.) In addition, special fast days were frequently ordained for natural catastrophes, such as drought or the mildewing of crops or earthquakes. The whole tractate of Mishnah *Taanis* is devoted to a discussion of such fasts.

Then, of course, in addition to these fasts (because of the threat of drought and famine, etc.), there were fasts for special groups, such as the fast of the firstborn before the Passover. Also, the custom developed to fast on the anniversary of the death of a parent, and also to fast after a terrifying dream (*taanis cholom*). In addition, chiefly among the Cabbalists, there was an ascetic motivation in adding many fasts. Thus there were fasts for the eight weeks beginning with the weekly portion *Shemos* (*shov'vim tat*), etc.

Now, on which days of the week or year may a fast day not be held? This question, interestingly enough, is the basic theme of the earliest post-Exilic, post-Biblical book, namely, the *Megillas Taanis,* which lists about thirty days of the year on which fasts may *not* be held. In other words, in general, according to the *Megillas Taanis,* fasts may be held on *any* day other than those enumerated in the booklet. However, the *Megillas Taanis* long ago went out of vogue, and fasts could be on some of the days on which the booklet prohibits fasting.

In Mishnaic times the fasts were generally held (at

least those for drought-famine) on Monday and Thursday because these were the market days on which the country folk and the villagers came into the larger cities. As for days on which fasts are not permitted, there is only one fast which may take place on the Sabbath and that is the Day of Atonement. No other fast, public or private, may take place on the Sabbath, nor may a fast take place on a holiday or a half-holiday. There is some objection to fasting during the month of Nisan. Other than these restrictions, a fast can occur at any time. If a fast day happens, because of the calendar, to fall on the Sabbath, it is postponed until the next day.

Now as to the purpose of the fast described in the question: Certainly to fast because of world hunger is in conformity with the ancient Jewish custom described in the tractate *Taanis,* in which almost all the fasts were for drought and hunger. If, in addition, one of the purposes of this fast is to get material help to starving lands, then certainly the purpose conforms to the spirit of Jewish tradition. The Talmud says (*b. Berachos* 6b) that the reward earned by fasting is deserved because of the charity given in connection with the fast.

Of course if a Reform rabbi or a group of Reform rabbis proclaim such a fast, Orthodox rabbis will not agree to it, but that is not surprising. However, if the cause is worthy, as it is, then the Orthodox rabbinate may have their own fast, as they frequently do for certain calamities which are impending.

As for the fact that the Christian churches, Catholic

and Protestant, ask us to participate in such a fast, that there can be no objection to. We simply make our own declaration concurrent with theirs.

11

THE USE OF TOBACCO

QUESTION:

> Should not the use of tobacco be prohibited by Jewish law on the basis of the growing consensus of physicians that it is injurious to health? Also, what are the chief responsa which deal with the question of the use of tobacco? (Asked by Dr. S. Z. Hulman, Leeds, England.)

ANSWER:

TOBACCO WAS introduced into Europe in the sixteenth century (in England, in 1565). The use of it in various forms spread immediately all over Europe. Both Church and State expressed strong opposition to its use. At times the Church threatened excommunication, and the State imposed fines, imprisonment, and even capital punishment.

Naturally the Jewish legal authorities, likewise, reacted to the sudden spread of this new habit. But the attitude of Jewish law was not entirely prohibitive. It could more properly be described as deprecatory and, to some extent, restrictive. The first full discussion of the use of tobacco was by Chaim Benvenisti of Constantinople (1603–1673) in his long supercommentary to the *Tur, K'nesses Hagdola* (in the supplementary volume, *Shiurey K'nesses Hagdola,* #567, sec. 3). He gives a description of how smokers have become so deeply addicted that they cannot wait for the Sabbath to end. They watch eagerly for the stars to appear so that they can begin to smoke. He tells how smokers crowd the streetcorners, puffing clouds of smoke. Specifically, he deals with the legal question of whether tobacco may be smoked on fast days (on personal fast days, on semi-strict fast days, such as the Fast of Esther, etc., and on the strict fast day of the Ninth of Av). In general he is opposed to smoking on any of the fast days because, he says, it brings Judaism to shame in the eyes of the Moslems, who strictly refrain from smoking on *their* fast days. He also discusses the fact that smokers claim that tobacco calms their nerves, making them forget their poverty and their troubles. He responds to that claim by saying that is the very reason why it should be prohibited on the Ninth of Av, when it is our *duty* to mourn and weep over the destruction of Jerusalem.

The next early authority to discuss smoking was Abraham Gumbiner, in his classic commentary to the *Shulchan Aruch* (*Mogen Avraham* to *Orah Hayyim* 210, par. 9). The question is whether smoking requires a blessing before its use, as all foods do. His opinion is given in commenting on the law in the *Shulchan Aruch* which says that when a person is a mere taster, not an eater (as a woman at the stove who takes a small amount into her mouth and then spits it out), such tasting requires no blessing. Since tobacco is inhaled and then exhaled, is it not similar to mere tasting and, therefore, requires no blessing? But perhaps it is like incense, which does require a blessing. He leaves the matter undecided.

The next important discussion is by Isaac Lampronti of Ferrara (1679–1756). Isaac Lampronti was both the physician and the rabbi of Ferrara. His scientific alphabetical encyclopedia of Jewish law contains a number of articles on tobacco. First he has an article under the heading "Apalto," in which he discusses the question of a license granted to a Jew to have a monopoly in the tobacco trade. This article reveals the fact that the Jews were active, and perhaps leaders, in the tobacco business.

Under the heading "Tobacco," Lampronti has a whole series of articles on the matter. Perhaps the most significant of them is the one in which he describes the prevalence of the use of tobacco in the synagogue. He describes the conviviality this arouses and how it destroys the whole mood of sanctity of the synagogue, and he declares that if he had the authority, he would abolish its use in the synagogue.

Elijah of Lublin (d. 1735), in his responsa *Yad Eliahu,* #65, refers to the spread of the tobacco habit among women. He discusses a rather curious question. Since a husband must avoid any contact with his wife during her menstrual period (for example, he may not drink from the same cup), may they both take puffs from the same tobacco pipe?

There is an interesting statement about smoking by

Moses Hagiz (b. 1671). Hagiz was an emissary from
Jerusalem to collect funds, and so visited many Jewish
communities. He finally settled in Amsterdam, where
he compiled his work *Leket ha-Kemach,* which is
composed chiefly of an epitome of the responsa literature. At the end of the volume, he speaks of the fact
that many scholars have prohibited the use of tobacco
on Yom Kippur, but he says the prohibition is not
sound and that it is really permitted. Of course, he adds,
those who are strict with themselves should remain
strict. Naturally he refers not to pipes or cigarettes,
which would require lighting, or to chewing tobacco,
which might be swallowed; he refers to snuff. This
statement is found on the last page of the original edition. The new edition is not yet complete and therefore
does not contain this statement.

Another full discussion of the matter of smoking is
given by Chaim Mordecai Margolis (d. 1818), the
author of the index commentary to the *Shulchan Aruch,
Shaarey Teshuva.* He has two lengthy discussions of
the question, one to *Orah Hayyim* 210 and the other
to *Orah Hayyim* 511. To *Orah Hayim* 210, he mentions that no blessing is needed before the use of tobacco. He mentions the discussion of whether it is permitted to light a cigarette or pipe at the flame of a
tallow candle, since tallow is prohibited food. By the
way, Isaac Lampronti, in his discussion of this question, describes a scientific experiment he conducted
to prove that the smoke of the prohibited tallow actually enters into the tobacco, and so such a lighting
should not be permitted. To return to *Shaarey Teshuva,*

Margolis discusses the question frequently dealt with, whether tobacco may be smoked on the holidays. In 511, he discusses the relationship or a comparison of the use of tobacco with the use of incense. He tends to permit that use.

A more recent responsum is one by Abraham Sofer, the son of Moses Sofer of Pressburg and his father's successor. In his responsum (*K'sav Sofer,* #66) he discusses smoking on the holiday. He must have been a pipe smoker himself, because he describes precisely the question of extinguishing the fire in the pipe (which would be prohibited on the holidays if the pipe has a cover which is not perforated).

The above include most of the important responsa on the various questions involved in smoking, namely, whether a blessing is needed; whether it may be lighted from a candle made of prohibited tallow; whether it may be indulged in on holidays or on fast days; and whether it can be used in the synagogue at all. But as to the second question raised by the inquirer, whether it should be prohibited because of the increasing medical opinion that it is dangerous to health, the fact is that the healthfulness or harmfulness of the use of tobacco was not especially discussed in the past. The opposition of Church and State to its use was based upon a general conservatism and a superstition that it was "burning incense to the devil." But, understandably, the users of tobacco in the early days praised it as beneficial. In fact it was called *herba panacea,* an all-healing herb; thus the only references to its effect on the body seemed to be, rather, in favor of its use. We mentioned above that smokers would tell Chaim Benvenisti that tobacco calmed their nerves; moreover, Abraham Sofer, in his responsum, speaks of the fact that smokers would tell him that the smoking was good for their health, especially for their digestion after a heavy meal. But the idea that tobacco could be harmful to health is a modern one, and if it is proved to be fact, then certainly the Jewish traditional law would have a clear attitude toward its use.

It is distinctly a duty incumbent upon every person to protect his health. The Mishnah, in *Baba Kamma* 8:6 (and the Talmud in 91b), states that a person may not injure himself. The law continues that if one does what he is forbidden, he is not punished for it. The statement means that if a man injures someone else, the courts punish him, but the courts will not punish a man who injures himself, even though it is a sin. So, too, the law is that a man may not even live in a city that has no physician (*Sanhedrin* 17b). The Talmud is full of laws which speak of what to do to prevent sickness and protect health. Maimonides, the great legalist and physician, said (*Yad, Hil. Rotzeach* 11:5): "Our sages have prohibited many things because they involve bodily danger, and everyone who transgresses against and says, 'I am only harming myself and it is nobody else's affair,' or if he says, 'I do not pay attention to such things,' such a person deserves to be flogged." This statement of Maimonides is repeated at the very end of the *Shulchan Aruch,* which adds, after Maimonides' statement, that such a person deserves to be flogged: "He who is careful about such matters will receive the blessing of happiness." Isaac Rifkes, in his commentary *Be'er Hagola,* explains this statement as follows: "The Torah warns us to be careful of our health because God, blessed be He, created the world in kindness, to do good to His creatures." In other words, he says that to neglect one's health would be a denial of God's merciful intention to us.

Therefore, if, for example, a man has had a heart attack or has some lung infection or some other bodily ailment, because of which his physician orders him to stop smoking, it is not only ordinary caution for this man to obey his physician, but it may be considered a mandate of Jewish law that he should do so.

As for other people who smoke, whether Jewish law would have them give up the habit would depend upon the degree of conviction that the medical profession has come to with regard to it. If ever the medical profession definitely agrees that the use of tobacco is of danger to every human being, then, of course, it could well be argued that Jewish law, which commands self-preservation, would prohibit its use. Until such time, we can only say that those for whom it is surely harmful would be carrying out, not only the recommendation of their doctor, but the mandate of Jewish law if they give up their use of tobacco.

12

CEMETERY MEMORIAL SERVICE ON SECOND DAY ROSH HASHONAH

QUESTION:

Our congregation plans to have a congregational memorial service in our cemetery on the second day of Rosh Hashonah. Does this type of service on that date comport with the traditional spirit of Rosh Hashonah, or should the service be discouraged as contravening the mood of the holiday? (Asked by Rabbi Elbert Sapinsley, Bluefield, West Virginia.)

ANSWER:

IT IS NOT CLEAR from the question whether this cemetery memorial service on the second day of Rosh Hashonah is one that had been held by the congregation in past years, or whether this is the first time that such a service is being proposed. If it is a service which already has been observed for a number of years, then it already has some standing as an established local *minhag*. Such a local *minhag* always has some validity unless, of course, there are certain strong objections to it. However, if this is the first time that such a service is proposed, then it should be subjected to still closer scrutiny as to its possible disharmony with Jewish tradition. In either case, we are dealing here with a type of service which at present is not widely observed in Jewish life, nor is it spoken of in Jewish traditional literature. Therefore it must be judged on the basis of a careful analysis of the mood of the New Year.

Does the mood of Rosh Hashonah include any element of festivity and happiness which might be marred by such a memorial service? The *Shulchan Aruch* is quite clear on the matter. In *Orah Hayyim* 597:1 the law states definitely: "We eat and drink and rejoice on the New Year, and we may fast on it." This law is based upon Ezra's statement when he addressed the people on the New Year (Nehemiah 8:9–10). He said: "This day is holy to the Lord. Mourn not nor weep, neither be ye grieved, for the joy of the Lord is your strength." This festive mood is also expressed in our custom of eating apples dipped in honey and of asking for a "year that is good and sweet."

Since, then, Rosh Hashonah is a day on which "we are forbidden to grieve," does it not seem that a communal cemetery service would contravene the mood of the festival? This question is answered clearly in the synagogue's tradition. Fasting is indeed forbidden, but a communal memorial service would not at all mar the mood of the day. This is evident from the services on Passover, Shavuos, and Succos. These three festivals are *completely* joyous. Not only are we forbidden to grieve on them (as the *Shulchan Aruch* ordains for Rosh Hashonah), but we are ordered positively to rejoice on them and do nothing to spoil the happiness of the festivals. Yet in spite of this mandated rejoicing, the last day of each of these three festivals has a communal memorial service for the dead, namely, the *Yizkor*. This memorial service was originally held on Yom Kippur alone, a day on which it was completely appropriate. But from Yom Kippur it spread to these three festivals.

Surely this memorial service, *Yizkor,* would seem to be a violation of the mandate to rejoice on the three festivals. However, the contradiction in mood is explained away to some extent by the statement of Isserles in *Orah Hayyim* 288:2, where he speaks of the memorial mood in relation to the Sabbath (for example, the reciting of *Av Ho-Rachimim,* the prayer for the martyrs). He says that to weep for the departed is not entirely sorrowful. After all, tears often relieve the heart and bring consolation. Whether or not this explanation is adequate, the fact remains that for centuries now the *Yizkor,* a public and personal memorial service, has been a regular part of the synagogue ritual on the three joyous pilgrimage festivals.

Now the basic mood of Rosh Hashonah is quite different from that of the three festivals. We are indeed forbidden to grieve or fast on this day. Nevertheless, the main mood of it is not joyous at all. This is to be noted from the liturgical rule that for Rosh Hashonah we must change the happy phrase regularly used in each *Shemone Esra* of the three pilgrimage festivals. On these festivals we use a sentence thanking God for bestowing on us "festivals of joy and seasons of gladness." This sentence must be omitted from the *Shemone Esra* of the New Year. The liturgical rule is given in *Tur, Orah Hayyim* 582, and goes back to the authority of the Gaon Hai.

Rosh Hashonah is primarily the *Yom Ha-Din,* the day of solemn self-judgment. If, in the development of the liturgy, it had happened that the *Yizkor* service had expanded from its original place on Yom Kippur and moved to the Rosh Hashonah service, this would certainly have been more appropriate than its moving to the three pilgrimage festivals, which actually occurred. Perhaps the reason that *Yizkor* did not carry over to Rosh Hashonah is that Yom Kippur, which already had the service, was only a few days away and both days are a unit as "Days of Awe." At all events, it is clear that a memorial service as here proposed would not be at all discordant with the mood of the New Year.

Besides this question of the basic mood of the festival, a second question arises. The regular synagogue Rosh Hashonah services are solemn enough. Would it not be excessive, therefore, to add another solemn service in addition to the synagogue service and outside of it? Here again tradition gives us a clear precedent. In the Middle Ages there had indeed developed a service of penitential type on Rosh Hashonah outside of and in addition to the regular synagogue liturgy. This is the widely observed *Tashlich* service. On the afternoon of the first day of Rosh Hashonah, the people go to the river, shake crumbs from their garments, and speak prayers dealing with the forgiveness of sins. This custom is comparatively new. It is not mentioned in the Mishnah or the Talmud. Nevertheless, by the

Middle Ages it became firmly established. Some authorities say that the water to be visited for the *Tashlich* should be a lake or a river where fishes are seen to swim about, thus to convey the idea that like fishes in a net, we are caught in the toils of life and death and must repent. The penitential mood of *Tashlich* is certainly close to the mood of the proposed communal memorial service on Rosh Hashonah.

A third and final question needs to be mentioned. Is it appropriate that this communal memorial service should be held in the cemetery? For a communal service in the cemetery there is more of a precedent than for the *Tashlich*. The Talmud, in *Ta'anis* 16a, says that on every fast day that is proclaimed, people should go to the cemetery to pray. In fact, if there is no Jewish cemetery available, they may go to a non-Jewish cemetery, for there too they would achieve a penitential mood.

Of course Rosh Hashonah is not a fast day for which the Talmud speaks of holding cemetery services. Nevertheless, it is worth noting that among the days when it is customary and appropriate to visit the cemetery are the "Ten Days of Penitence." Since we in Reform Judaism observe only one day of Rosh Hashonah, the second day of Rosh Hashonah may well be deemed for us to be the first day of the Days of Penitence on which cemetery visitation is traditional.

To sum up then: The mood of a communal memorial service, such as *Yizkor,* has spread from its original observance on Yom Kippur to the last days of the three joyous pilgrimage festivals and is not considered as marring their mood of happiness. Rosh Hashonah has some touch of the joyous holiday spirit but is mainly penitential, and therefore a communal memorial service, such as *Yizkor,* would have been even more fitting had it developed on that day. As for our adding a new memorial service on Rosh Hashonah to be held outside the synagogue, this too has its precedent in the post-Talmudic ceremony of *Tashlich.* Finally, among the days deemed most appropriate to visit the cemetery are the Ten Days of Penitence; and for us, who observe one day of Rosh Hashonah, the second day of Rosh Hashonah counts as the beginning of our penitential days.

For all these reasons, one may well say that a congregational cemetery memorial service on the second day of Rosh Hashonah is not at all inappropriate and might well become an established custom among us. Possibly it might be preferable if this service is not held in the morning, when the regular Rosh Hashonah services are being held in Orthodox and Conservative synagogues, but, perhaps, on the afternoon of the second day of Rosh Hashonah, which is exactly when the *Tashlich* service is held when the first day of Rosh Hashonah happens to be on the Sabbath.

13

ORDER OF SUSTENANCE

QUESTION:

What is the Jewish attitude with respect to the order of
distribution of a diminishing world food supply? On
what basis should priorities be established? (Asked by
Rabbi Kenneth J. Weiss, Glendale, California.)

ANSWER:

THE JEWISH LEGAL literature gives a clear-cut order of
social importance in the Jewish community. This leads
to a series of laws as to who or which group, in time
of need, should be sustained first. The list is given
most clearly at the end of Mishnah *Horayos* 3:7 and 8.
It reads as follows: A man precedes a woman in being
saved alive and in having his lost objects restored to
him. A woman precedes a man in receiving clothing
and being ransomed from captivity. A priest precedes a
Levite, a Levite an Israelite, an Israelite a *mamzer,*
etc., provided all of them are of equal degree of learning, but if the *mamzer* is a scholar and the high priest is
an ignoramus, the scholarly *mamzer* precedes the ignorant high priest. With this remarkable statement the
tractate *Horayos* and the whole Mishnaic order of
Nezikin come to an end.

In *Ketubos* 67a ff., the Talmud analyzes these statements and develops the laws in more specific detail.
The basis of the discussion there is the Mishnah
Kesuvos 6:5, which ends with the statement on that
page that if a man marries off an orphan girl, he must
give her as much dowry as he can afford. This leads to
the statement that if an orphan boy and an orphan girl
both need food, we feed the girl first because men grow
accustomed to beg from door to door, but a woman is
too embarrassed to do so.

On this basis the law is established that a woman in
need should be given food before a man in need. This
seems to contradict the Mishnah in *Horayos,* namely,
that a man precedes a woman. But the contradiction is
explained as follows: The Mishnah in *Horayos* means
that a man must be saved from mortal danger first, but
clothing and food should be given to a woman first.
This is the form in which the question of sustenance as
between man and woman is recorded in the Codes (in
Maimonides, *Matnos Ani'im* 8:15, and in *Shulchan
Aruch, Yore Deah* 251:8).

The precedences mentioned next—namely, Kohen
before Levite, Levite before Israelite, etc.—are explained as follows: They apply only if a man has such
limited resources that he cannot give as much as he
would wish to give to all who apply. He then gives first
to the Kohen, and then to the Levite, etc. But even this
sequence is modified by a more basic thought, that the
recipients earn their sustenance to the degree of their
learning; hence the statement that a learned *mamzer*
has precedence over an ignorant high priest.

There is still another test leading to precedence given in the Talmud, in *Ketubos* 67b. What a recipient is given must depend as much as possible on what he has been accustomed to. The Talmud there gives cases in which poor people were rather lavishly maintained because that had once been their accustomed mode of living. In fact, the Talmud tells there that a man came for food to Rabbi Nechemya, and the rabbi sustained him on a diet of lentils, although the man had told him in answer to a question that he was accustomed to finer food. The man died, not having been accustomed to this harsh diet of lentils, and he was thereafter referred to as "the man whom Nechemya killed."

There is still another test of charity. A man's obligation first is to his own family, then to the poor of his own city, then of his own country, and so on. In other words, charity does indeed begin at home (*Yore Deah* 251:3). This is a dominant rule. Samson Morpugo, rabbi of Ancona (d. 1740), in his responsa *Shemesh Zedakah* (*Yore Deah* #19), states that even if the poor of another city are learned men and the poor of one's own city are ignoramuses, the poor of one's own city have precedence.

If we would analyze the rules given above, we might derive certain principles of the order of sustenance according to the spirit of Jewish law. First, consideration must be given to the temperament of the recipient. A woman must not be shamed to have to ask for food. She must be fed first. Also, consideration must be given to the previous standard of living of the applicant. Then, learning entitles a recipient to precedence because the learned man is of special value to society. Also, the needy at home must first be provided for. All this is based on the assumption that there is a limit to the resources available and choices must be made; but if resources are relatively unlimited, then all receive as they need.

14

CONVERTS AND THE RABBI'S RESPONSIBILITY

QUESTION:

> A number of candidates for conversion have been living together without marriage. Some of them state that they will not marry for a time, if at all, but will continue living together. What if there are children and some of the children remain Christian? What if a Christian comes for conversion but the spouse intends to remain a Christian? In general the question is asked: What is the rabbi's responsibility as to the mode of life of candidates for conversion and their mode of life after conversion? (Asked by Rabbi Irving Cohen, West Palm Beach, Florida.)

ANSWER:

ONE OF THE basic attitudes in the Jewish law of conversion is a careful investigation of the motivation of the candidate. The Talmud, in *Yevamos* 46b (and in the *Shulchan Aruch, Yore Deah* 268 ff.), states that we must actually discourage a would-be convert. We ask him why he should accept the status of Jewishness when Jews have to endure so much suffering in the world, and also (268:12) we tell him of the "burden" of the *mitzvos,* how if he becomes a Jew he will be punished for the violating of the many *mitzvos,* whereas if he remains a Gentile, he is free from the danger of such punishment. If, after all these discouragements, a candidate persists in wanting to be converted, we then proceed with the ritual of conversion.

Of course one cannot always be sure of motives. Hillel, after all, converted the Gentile who admitted he wanted to become a high priest, and Rabbi Hiyya converted a woman who confessed she wanted to marry a Jew (see the discussion in the *Tosfos* to *Yevamos* 24b). On the basis of this discussion, many Orthodox rabbis refuse to accept proselytes whose intention is to marry a Jew, while some do accept them. However, in all such matters in which motives and future conduct are involved, it is hard to be sure. Joseph Caro, in his comment to *Tur, Yore Deah* 268, says that it all depends on the judgment of the rabbinical court (*Hakol l'fi r'os bes din*). So in all these cases the rabbi's judgment must count. If his estimate of the couple is that after conversion they will establish a decent Jewish family, he may decide to convert them.

But the question now is: If he is uncertain in this matter as to what sort of life they will live, what then are his responsibilities? Since much depends, as we have said, on the judgment of the rabbi as to the character and the probable future of the candidates, we must understand that his judgment nowadays is inevitably affected by modern moods and standards. If this question had come up a generation ago, the judgment of the rabbi would likely have been different from that of a rabbi today. In those days sexual and family morality were generally strictly observed. If a couple lived together without marriage, it would be an exceptional couple, scorned by society, and themselves well aware that they were living in sin. But today the situation is quite different. Sexual morality and family unity have greatly loosened, and we can no longer declare that all people who live together without marriage are consciously libertine. The mood of the world is so different that some couples who for one reason or another are living together in this way are otherwise quite decent.

This changing mood cannot mean, of course, that the rabbi condones this mode of life, which violates both civil and Jewish laws. However, he can no longer make sweeping judgments, refusing to have anything to do with all such couples. Here, perhaps, a Talmudic dictum applies: "Always let your left hand push them aside while your right hand brings them near." In other words, as Joseph Caro would have said (above), it all depends upon the judgment of the modern rabbi.

However, while the rabbi can no longer summarily reject such people as candidates for conversion, but must judge the character and probable future of each candidate individually, there are certain definite situations in which the rabbi cannot possibly accept the candidate. Suppose, for example, one of the couple is a Jewish man and it is the woman who is coming to be converted. According to Jewish law (Mishnah *Yevamos* 2:8), if a Jewish man is even suspected of living sexually with a Gentile and she converts to Judaism, he may never marry her. This is codified as law in the *Shulchan Aruch* (*Even Hoezer* 11:5).

Sometimes in this situation the Jewish man does not intend to marry the girl. He may tell her that because she is a Gentile such a marriage would cause great grief for his parents. She then, on her own accord, asks to be converted, so as to deprive him of any excuse for refusing to marry her (or to divorce his present wife in order to marry her). We are certainly not justified in giving a weapon to this woman to force a Jewish man into a marriage which is forbidden by Jewish law.

Another situation in which the rabbi cannot justly convert would be if the man is a Gentile and the woman is Jewish and they are living together. If she is a married woman, she is an *eshes ish,* and her Jewish husband no longer has the right to live with her at all since she is an adulterous woman. If, then, we convert the Gentile man, we would be rewarding her for her adultery. If, however, the woman in this couple is an *unmarried* Jewish girl, then perhaps it would be right to convert the Gentile so that they may be able to marry in accordance with Jewish law and custom.

Now if it is a Gentile couple and only one of them requests conversion, in that case, again, I believe the rabbi should refuse to convert. Please see the answer that I gave to the *CCAR Journal,* published in *Current Reform Responsa,* pp. 216–17. The reason given there is the following: This was a case of a married Gentile couple in which one of the partners wanted to become Jewish. If we converted the husband (or the wife), then he becomes a Jewish man married to a Gentile woman. Becoming a Jew, he is now, as the *Shulchan Aruch* says in *Yore Deah* 268:12, under "the yoke of the law." He was a righteous Christian before we converted him. Now, if he is the head of a Gentile family, he becomes a sinful Jew. We have no right, therefore, to convert him.

Of course, these couples of which you are speaking are not actually married, and we are not thereby breaking up a Christian home. But we are again creating the situation of a Jewish man living with a Gentile woman or a Jewish woman living with a Gentile man, as discussed above.

The only situation that is beyond all question is when both members of the couple are Gentiles. If it is the judgment of the rabbi under modern circumstances that this couple, when it becomes Jewish, will marry and establish a Jewish home, he should convert them. If he believes that they will not establish a Jewish home, then if he converted them, they would become a Jewish couple living in concubinage, which is against present Jewish law.

Now as to the children: If it is a grown child who is to remain Christian, we may accept that. But young children who are of religious-school age should enter the religious school (or if very young, be recorded in the Cradle Roll) and when they have gone through the school, that, as the Conference had decided, shall be accepted as full conversion of the child.

To sum up: The situation is complicated, and each type of complication must be handled differently. In modern times, with moral standards relaxed, the rabbi cannot summarily reject a couple living together without marriage, but he must use his judgment, deciding on the basis outlined above and his feelings as to the future career of the couple.

15

CIRCUMCISION OF PROSELYTES

QUESTION:

Is there any Halachic justification for the practice of some Reform groups of accepting adult proselytes without requiring circumcision? (Asked by W. V. d. Z., London.)

ANSWER:

THE QUESTION OF whether to admit male proselytes without circumcision was one of the questions which greatly troubled the Reform movement in the United States in its early days. At the second and third sessions of the Central Conference of American Rabbis (1891–93), the subject was vehemently debated and finally decided by a vote of 25–5 (see *CCAR Yearbook,* Vol. III, p. 36), adopting the resolution to accept proselytes without any initiatory rite (i.e., bathing or circumcision).

The debate, which is found chiefly in Vol. II, drew in almost all the leaders of the Reform movement in America. Many of the arguments repeat each other and use the same rabbinical quotations over and over again; but finally the whole question is summed up in the formal report of the Committee signed by Isaac M. Wise himself. This summary is systematic and in many ways original. It is worth epitomizing here because it is as good a statement of the case as has been found anywhere.

The essence of the argument is that there is no actual requirement of an initiatory rite for a proselyte to be found in the Torah; nor is there any definite legal requirement for such a rite found in the Mishnah. Therefore the Talmud is still debating whether or which initiatory rites are required, and therefore, also, there are some medieval authorities who consider that the initiatory rites are not indispensable.

If this statement can be proved adequately, it is of considerable importance because the Torah has over fifty detailed references to the *ger,* as to his rights and his privileges and the treatment due him. If, then, in spite of the full Biblical discussion of the *ger,* there is no mention at all of initiatory rites, the silence is eloquent indeed and would certainly tend strongly to prove that actually there were no such rites required. Of course, it was necessary for the Conference Report to explain away the trick which Simeon and Levi played on Shechem and his son Hamor. This action was denounced by Jacob in his blessing. Besides, it was before the giving of the Torah, and, in addition, we do not derive laws from stories or incidents. Next, the statement in Exodus 12:45 must be explained, which says that the *ger* must circumcise all the males of his household before participating in the paschal lamb, "for no uncircumcised may eat of it." This verse does not prove that any initiatory rites were required for the *ger* himself. It means that when the *ger* becomes a Jew, he has the Jewish duty of having his household circumcised. This is proved by the fact that the close of the sentence, "no uncircumcised shall eat of it," means "no uncircumcised *Jew* shall eat of it." See the clear statement in *Targum Jonathan* and Rashi's commentary to the verse. We see, then, that the Torah, which speaks in such detail of the *ger*, never clearly mentions any requirement of initiatory rites when he becomes a Jew.

As for the statement in the report that there is no clear law in the Mishnah requiring initiatory rites for *gerim,* there are two passages in the Mishnah that need to be explained away. In *Eduyos* 5:2, Bes Hillel says, with regard to a *ger,* that to be rid of the foreskin is like escaping from the grave. This is not taken as law, but is just a moral opinion, one which is mentioned only incidentally with regard to other matters. (But, of course, in *Pesachim* 8:8 it is mentioned by Bes Hillel more clearly; and it is taken for granted that circumcision is required.) Rabbi himself, the author of the Mishnah, says definitely in a *boraita,* in *Kerisos* 9a, that with regard to circumcision *gerim* are like Jews and have this initiatory rite; but the report insists that this is only a *boraita,* and nowhere does Rabbi Judah mention it as a definite law in the Mishnah.

There is value, of course, in all this argumentation. It indicates, at least, that there was no legal requirement in Torah and Mishnah, only these chance, off-hand, and debatable references. Certainly this fact must explain the debate in the Talmud itself as to initiatory rites of a proselyte (in *Yevamos* 46a and b). There Rabbi Eliezar says that circumcision is the more important of the two rites, and therefore if a proselyte has been circumcised but has not bathed, he is a full-fledged *ger.* Rabbi Joshua, on the other hand, considers the bathing more important and says that if a *ger* has bathed and not been circumcised, he is a full-fledged *ger.*

Then, at the top of 46b, the statement is found that "all agree that if he has not been circumcised, he is a full-fledged *ger*"; but further on it says, in the name of Rabbi Yochanan, that he is not a *ger* unless he both bathes and circumcises. So clearly the initiatory rite was still, for a time at least, open to some debate and question.

This explains, perhaps, why in the Middle Ages there were occasional opinions which indicate that circumcision is not a *sine qua non* for the validity of conversion. There is the remarkable statement of the great Jewish polemical writer, Lippman of Mulhausen (14th–15th cen.), in his *Sefer Nizachon.* This book, developing as a commentary on the Bible, defending our interpretation of it against Christian charges, makes an unusual statement in the commentary to Genesis 17:10, where the circumcision of males is enjoined upon

Abraham as the sign of a covenant. Lippman of Mulhausen refers to the sneering statement of anti-Jews
that if it were a covenant, why was not a type of covenant chosen which would include women? To which
he makes the following answer: "Our faith does not
depend upon circumcision but upon the heart. One
[i.e., a candidate for proselytizing] who does not believe sincerely is not converted to Judaism by his circumcision. But one who believes sincerely, is a full Jew
even if he is not circumcised."

Some participants in the older Conference debate
quote a responsum of the famous rabbi of Constantinople in the fifteenth century, Elijah Mizrachi, in his
Mayim Amukim #27 (the correct reference in the
Berlin edition should be #34), in which there is discussion of a Gentile woman and her child who are to
be converted, in which he says, with regard to the
child, the law *m'd'oraisa* is that the acceptance of the
Torah is sufficient even without bathing or circumcision. (However, he proceeds to say that for adults
both rites are required. Still he *does* indicate that according to *Torah-law* [*m'd'oraisa*] the rites are not indispensable.) There is an analogous statement in the
Kol Sochol (*Bechinat Ha Kabbalah*) by Leon of Modena. On page 59, where he follows the order of the
Shulchan Aruch, he speaks about proselytes. He says
we ought to give the proselyte the usual explanatory
warning and ascertain his sincerity. Then he adds: "We
should tell him of the worth of circumcision and its
reward. If, then, he wishes to be circumcised, well and
good; if not, let him take the ritual bath, and that is

sufficient to make him a full Jew in every sense. But
when his children are born, he must circumcise them."
It is clear, Modena continues, that as for the proselyte
himself, the only Biblical drawback to his not being
circumcised is that he cannot participate in the paschal
offering, but otherwise the Torah makes no mention
of circumcision being necessary for a proselyte. (Evidently those who participated in the Conference debate
got their chief arguments here. But it is clear that
Modena does not give the law as it is, but as he believes
it *ought* to be.)

On page 226 of the book *Behinat Ha Kabbalah,* the
editor, Reggio, does not deny that Modena was correct in saying that one can be a full Jew even if uncircumcised (even a *born* Jew, if his lack of circumcision
is due to sickness), but he says that circumcision is a
vital commandment and should be obeyed (see also
p. 230).

All the above debate is significant and must have
some bearing on our attitude in the matter of requiring
circumcision of proselytes. Nevertheless, there is, I believe, a difference in attitude toward tradition between
us and our predecessors. The official report signed by
Isaac M. Wise begins with a statement of a basic principle, namely, that our religious life is based upon the
Pentateuch. Even though we may interpret it somewhat
differently from other Jews, it is the Pentateuch which
unites us with the rest of Jewry. In other words, it was
the tendency of the early Reformers to go back to
origins. Therefore, it was of weighty importance to
them that the Bible itself, and also the Mishnah, has no

clear requirement of initiatory rites for proselytes. I believe that our standpoint is different, though we may not have formulated it as clearly as they did their standpoint. The *total* tradition is vital to us as guidance, at least, if not as rigid governance. Therefore it is important to us that the Talmud and Maimonides and the *Shulchan Aruch* (*Yore Deah* 268) have circumcision as a firmly established law and that, therefore, it is the widespread practice of our people to circumcise proselytes. The fact that these laws are post-Biblical and post-Mishnaic has no strong importance for us, at least not as strong an importance as it did for our predecessors.

Therefore, the matter remains as one for our own decision, based upon our feelings in the matter. The American Reform movement, because of the early decision, has long ceased to insist upon circumcision for proselytes. What English Jewry should do depends upon its own conscience. If it seems contrary to the spiritual and ethical spirit of Judaism to insist upon this ritual, let them do as we did two generations ago. It might be noted that the *Shulchan Aruch, Yore Deah* 268:1, says that if the proselyte is mutilated and therefore cannot be circumcised, "the [lack of] circumcision does not prevent his conversion, and it is enough if he takes the ritual bath." It is also a fact nowadays that most male infants, whether Jew or Christian, are circumcised by the obstetrician; therefore there are very few actually uncircumcised, or at least less of them, among would-be converts. It might be a worthwhile decision on the part of the English Reformers not to insist upon taking "the drop of blood of the covenant" if a convert is already circumcised (cf. the discussion of Asher b. Jehiel to the passage in *Yevamos*). If the English Reform movement decides to give up the requirement of circumcision, the fact that the Bible and the Mishnah have no such clear requirement, and the fact that this has been the practice of American Reform almost from the beginning, might aid them to the decision. If they wish to insist upon the requirement, then perhaps they will waive the requirement of taking the drop of blood from one already circumcised.

Addendum

Since writing the above, I have come across an interesting discussion of the question in the responsa *Chazon La-moed* by Mordecai Dov Eidelberg, who was rabbi in Nickolayev, Russia. The book was printed in Bialystok in 1923. The problem that confronted him was this: A Russian officer was converted to Judaism by a well-known rabbi. The officer, however, was not circumcised at the conversion because he was not well at the time. He promised to be circumcised at a later date when he would be restored to health. The rabbi who converted him insisted that under these circumstances the officer was a full proselyte even though he was not yet circumcised.

The problem came before Rabbi Eidelberg because the convert was to marry a young woman in Rabbi Eidelberg's congregation. The rabbi, therefore, had to decide whether he agreed with the converting rabbi that a man can be a full proselyte without circumcision. He discusses the question of hemophiliacs and diabetics, for whom the operation might be a grave danger, and also the question of a mutilated person who cannot be circumcised. Can such individuals ever be considered full converts? He ends his responsum by saying that the matter of conversion without circumcision can be argued either way and needs final decision by the leading scholars of our time, and so he refuses at present to make a decision and act upon it. The responsum is #7. However, David Hoffman, in *Melamed L'ho-il, Yore Deah* 86, says forthrightly that he would not convert any man who is too sick to be circumcised.

16

PRESERVING A TORAH FRAGMENT

QUESTION:

Congregation Habonim of New York has a membership composed chiefly of refugees from Germany. The congregation had built a memorial to the Six Million composed of stones from the debris of wrecked synagogues in Germany. Now the congregation is in possession of a fragment of a *Sefer Torah* which consists of one roller (*etz chayim*) surrounded by about an inch of parchment. Can this fragment be preserved in a receptacle built into the vestry wall near the memorial of the Six Million? If so, must it be horizontal or vertical? (Question asked by Rabbi Bernhard N. Cohn, New York.)

ANSWER:

IF THIS WERE a complete Torah, then even if it were, for the present, unfit for public reading (*posul*) and needed correction, the proper place for it (if it was not buried in the cemetery) would be in the Ark, and certainly not in a museum case. The reason for this is as follows: In the presence of the Torah, people must comport themselves with dignity, even if the Torah is kept in a room of a private house (see *Berachos* 25b and *Yore Deah* 282:8). If there is a museum case in a vestibule where people go to and fro, it would be impossible to expect them to maintain a respectful

demeanor at all times. Therefore it is better that the
Torah be kept in the Ark if it is, as I say, largely an
intact Torah. See the responsum on this question in
Contemporary Reform Responsa, pp. 110 ff. Furthermore, as to whether a *posul* Torah should be placed in
the Ark (instead of being buried), see *Contemporary
Reform Responsa,* pp. 114 ff. (especially p. 116).

However, we are not dealing here with a *Torah* that
is *posul* but largely intact. We are dealing with a fragment. But how large a fragment? It is not quite clear to
me *how much* of the *Sefer Torah* is included in this
remnant. The inquiry says that it "consists of one *etz
chayim* surrounded by about an inch of parchment."
Does that mean that around the *etz chayim* there are
enough turns of parchment to make a cylinder with
the thickness of one inch? If so, this remnant is of considerable size. Nevertheless, considering the thickness
of a complete *Sefer Torah,* a cylinder of one inch is
very much less than one-fifth of the total girth and,
therefore, must be much less than one complete book
of the Five Books. But let us assume that it *is* a complete Genesis. If on the left-hand roller, it would be
the complete Deuteronomy. Yet even if there is a
complete book, this one book has not enough sanctity
for it to be read in the synagogue. The *Shulchan Aruch,
Orah Hayyim* 143:2, says that even a complete book
(of the five) may not be read in the synagogue. Only
all five books sewn together may be read. Therefore,
even if it is a complete Genesis or Deuteronomy, which
is improbable, there would be considerable freedom in
the handling of this fragment. But in all likelihood we

are speaking here of a small fragment around one of the rollers. So it is primarily the roller that is seen. The roller itself has the status of only "auxiliary holiness" (*tashmishey kedusha;* see *Mogen Avraham,* par. 14 to *Orah Hayyim* 153). An *etz chayim* may, for example, be cut up or it can be made into another synagogue object (see *Current Reform Responsa,* pp. 36 ff.). Since, therefore, we are dealing with an *etz chayim* and not more than a fragment of scroll, this may be put into a case, especially if the case is embedded in the wall near the memorial for the Six Million, where whoever visits the place will certainly conduct himself with dignified demeanor.

Now as to the question of whether it would be proper for this fragment to be placed vertically or horizontally in the case: There is an interesting analogy relevant to this question with regard to a smaller scroll, namely, the *mezuzah.* Rashi says, in his commentary to Talmud *Menachos* 33a, that the *mezuzah* should be placed in a vertical position on the doorpost. However, the great fourteenth-century German authority, Maharil of Mainz, reports that Rashi's grandson, Rabbenu Tam, says that the *mezuzah* should be affixed *horizontally.* Then Maharil says that we ought not to contravene either of these great authorities. Therefore we should put the *mezuzah* diagonally (as we do today) in order to defer as much as we can to the opinion of both Rashi and Rabbenu Tam (see *Minhage Maharil,* the section on "Mezuzah," near the end of the section). At all events, if the *mezuzah* were affixed in a horizontal position, it would have the justification of one great authority at least, Rabbenu Tam. But besides the analogy with the *mezuzah,* we have more direct evidence as to the placing of the Torah. The Talmud, in *Megillah* 27a, discussing the relative sanctity of the Torah, the Prophets, and the Hagiographa, gives the general principle that the scroll of lesser sanctity (say the Hagiographa) may not lie on top of the scroll of greater sanctity (say the Prophets or the Torah). The Talmud continues by saying that one Torah may lie on the top of another. This indicates, of course, that the Torah can be kept horizontal. As a matter of fact, although today it is our prevalent custom to keep the Torahs standing vertically in the Ark, there were times when the Torah was kept in a series of pigeon-holes lying horizontally (see the end of the article by Ludwig Blau in the *Jewish Encyclopedia,* "Scrolls of the Law").

To sum up: If this were an intact *Sefer Torah* or a complete one of the Five Books, then if not buried (as it may be), it should be kept in the Ark, not in a museum case in the vestry where people walk to and fro. But since this is a smaller fragment, and the most conspicuous part of it is an *etz chayim,* which is in itself of secondary holiness, it may certainly be kept in an exhibition case, especially if the case is near the memorial, where the demeanor will always be dignified. As for the position of the Torah fragment, there is no real choice as between horizontal or vertical except perhaps that our modern custom is to have it vertical. But if for some artistic reason it is preferred to place the Torah fragment in a horizontal position, there is no Halachic objection to so doing.

17

RELIEVING PAIN OF DYING PATIENT

QUESTION:

A dying patient is suffering great pain. There are medicines available which will relieve his agony. However, the physician says that the pain-relieving medicine might react on the weakened respiratory system of the patient and bring death sooner. May, then, such medicine be used for the alleviation of the patient's agony? Would it make a difference to our conclusion if the patient himself gave permission for the use of this pain-killing medicine? (Asked by Rabbi Sidney H. Brooks, Omaha, Nebraska.)

ANSWER:

LET US DISCUSS the second question first, namely, what difference would it make if the patient himself gives permission for the use of this medicine, though he knows it may hasten his death? There have been some discussions in the law, in recent years, of the difference it would make if a dying patient gave certain permissions with regard to the handling of his body after death. For example, he might ask for certain parts of the usual funeral ritual to be omitted; and some authorities say that he may permit autopsy. If I remember rightly, this permission was given by the late Rabbi

Hillel Posek of Tel Aviv. But all these statements giving the dying man the right to make such requests deal with what shall be done with his body *after* death, but not any permission that he may give for hastening his death. After all, for a man to ask that his life be ended sooner is the equivalent of his committing suicide. Suicide is definitely forbidden by Jewish law.

However, we are dealing with a person who is in great physical agony. This fact makes an important difference. A person under great stress is no longer considered in Jewish law to be a free agent. He is, as the phrase is, *onuss,* "under stress" or "compulsion." Such a person is forgiven the act of suicide; and the usual funeral rites, which generally are forbidden in the case of suicide, are permitted to the man whose suicide was under great stress. The classic example for this permissibility is King Saul on Mount Gilboa. His death (falling on his sword) and the forgiveness granted him gave rise to the classic phrase, in this case, *onuss k'Shaul.* Thus, in many cases in the legal literature, the suicide was forgiven and given full religious rites after death if he was under great stress in his last days. See the various references given in *Recent Reform Responsa,* pp. 114 ff., especially the example of the boys and girls being taken captive to Rome who committed suicide (*b. Gittin* 57b); the responsum of Jacob Weil, 114; of Mordecai Benet, *Parashas Mordecai, Yore Deah* 25; and the other responsa given in *Recent Reform Responsa.*

However, a caution must be observed here. The law does not mean that a person may ask for death if he is in agony, but that it is pardonable if, in his agony, he *does* do so. In other words, we must apply the well-known principle in Jewish law, the distinction between *l'chatchillo,* "doing an action to begin with," and *b'di'avad,* "after the action is done." In other words, we do not say that "*l'chatchilo* it is permissible for a man to ask for death, but *b'di'avad,* if under great stress he has done so, it is forgivable."

So far we have discussed the situation from the point of view of the action of the patient. Now we must consider the question from the point of view of the physician. Is a physician justified in administering a pain reliever to a dying patient in agony when the physician knows beforehand that the medicine will tend to weaken his heart and perhaps hasten his death?

Jewish traditional law absolutely forbids hastening the death of a dying patient. It requires meticulous care in the environs of the dying patient, not to do anything that might hasten his death. (All these laws are codified in the *Shulchan Aruch, Yore Deah* 339. See the full discussion in *Modern Reform Responsa* pp. 197 ff.) If, therefore, this were definitely a lethal medicine, the direct effect of which would be to put an end to the patient's life, the use of such medicine would be absolutely forbidden. But this medicine is not immediately, or intentionally, lethal; its prime purpose and main effect is the alleviation of pain. The harmful effect on the heart of the patient is only incidental to its purpose and is only a possible secondary reaction. The question, therefore, amounts to this: May we take

that amount of *risk* to the patient's life in order to relieve the great agony which he is now suffering?

Interestingly enough, there is very little discussion
in the classic legal literature, beginning with the Talmud, about the relief of pain. Most of the discussion
deals with the theological question of why pain is sent
to us and how we are to endure it and our attitude to
God because of it. As for the paucity of reference on
the *relief* of pain, that can be understood because, after
all, in those days they had very little knowledge of opi-
ates or narcotics. However, the Talmud does mention
one pain-killing medicine which could be used in the
ceremony of piercing the ear of a slave (*Kiddushin*
21b). This is the basis of all modern legal discussions
as to whether an anesthetic may be used in circumcision. See *Current Reform Responsa,* pp. 103 ff. It
should be noted in that responsum that most of the
scholars agree to the permissibility of the relief of pain,
at least in that ceremony.

But in the case which we are discussing, it is more
than a question of relieving the pain of a wound or an
operation. It is a question of relieving pain at the risk
of shortening life. Now, granted that it is forbidden to
take any steps that will definitely shorten the life of a
patient (as mentioned above), may it not be permitted,
in the case of a dying patient, to take some *risk* with
his remaining hours or days if the risk is taken for his
benefit?

This question may be answered in the affirmative.
The law in this regard is based upon the Talmud
(*Avoda Zara* 27a and b). There the question is

whether we may make use of a Gentile physician (in that case, an idolater). What is involved is enmity on the part of an idolater toward the Israelite and the fact that the physician may, out of enmity, do harm to the patient. It makes a difference in the law whether the man is an amateur or a professional. The latter may generally always be employed. Also, the present state of the patient's health makes a difference, as follows: If the patient is dying anyhow, more risks may be taken for the chance of his possible benefit. The phrase used for these last dying hours is *chaye sha'a,* and the general statement of the law is that we may risk these fragile closing hours and take a chance on a medicine that may benefit the patient. (cf. *Shulchan Aruch, Yore Deah* 154). See *Modern Reform Responsa,* p. 199, and especially the classic responsum on this subject by Jacob Reischer of Metz, *Shevus Yaacov,* III, 75. In other words, this is the case of a *dying* patient, and the law permits us, in such a case, to risk the *chaye sha'a* for his potential benefit.

However, this does not quite solve the problem. The law permits risking the last hours on the chance of *curing* the patient. But may we conclude from that permission the right to risk the last hours, not with the hope of curing the patient, but for the purpose of relieving him of pain? Interestingly enough, there is a precedent in Talmudic literature precisely on this question (see the references in *Modern Reform Responsa,* pp. 197 ff.). The incident referred to is in *Ketubos* 104a. Rabbi Judah the Prince was dying in great agony. The rabbis surrounded his house in concerted prayer for his healing. But Rabbi Judah's servant (who is honored and praised in the Talmud) knew better than the rabbis did how much agony he was suffering. She therefore disrupted their prayers in order that he might die and his agony end.

In other words, we may take definite action to relieve pain, even if it is of some risk to the *chaye sha'a,* the last hours. In fact it is possible to reason as follows: It is true that the medicine to relieve his pain may weaken his heart, but does not the great pain itself weaken his heart? And may it not be that relieving the pain may strength him more than the medicine might weaken him? At all events, it is a matter of judgment, and in general we may say that to relieve his pain, we may incur some risk as to his final hours.

18

WOMAN DOCTOR AS MOHEL

QUESTION:

Women in increasing numbers have entered the medical profession, and many of them are obstetricians and gynecologists. Since it is a growing custom among Jewish parents (especially non-Orthodox parents) to have their baby boys circumcised in the hospital by the obstetrician, this raises the question whether, according to Jewish tradition, a woman (and even a Gentile woman) is eligible to perform the operation of *milah.* (Asked by L.S.F.)

ANSWER:

THE GENERAL QUESTION of who may circumcise was discussed in *Reform Responsa,* responsum #24, p. 105. Since, however, the above question adds an entirely new element, it seems worthwhile to review, first of all, the general background as mentioned in that responsum. The law as it stands is given in summary in *Shulchan Aruch, Yore Deah* 264:1. It begins with the general statement that "all are eligible to perform circumcision, even a minor, even a slave, even a woman; and even an uncircumcised Jew, provided there was a medical reason [i.e., hemophilia] for the circumciser not being circumcised."

This general statement is followed by exceptions,
mostly made by Isserles, who ends up with the statement that "a man should seek around for the best and
most pious *mohel.*" Nevertheless, it must be pointed
out at the outset that a *mohel* is not in any sense an
official functionary of the community. A rabbi or a
cantor must be appointed formally by the community.
A *shochet* must get a special certificate from the rabbi
(*kabbala*) attesting to his knowledge of the laws of
shechita and his skill, but there is no license, no appointment, required for a man to be a *mohel.* Anybody who is skilled can perform the function (of
course, with the exceptions referred to above). The
father himself is, in fact, expected, if he is able, to circumcise his own child; if not, he can pick anybody who
is skilled to do it for him. That is why Isserles says one
should "look around for a skilled and pious person."
In other words, the *mohel* is not a functionary. Anybody who is suitable and capable can serve.

However, there is a difference between this general
legal permissibility and the strong preference of pious
people. For truly Orthodox Jews, the various permissi-
bilities in the law are of no importance. What matters
is to find a truly pious (and, of course, skilled) *mohel.*

This preference was expressed most strongly by
Rabbi Eliezer Silver (Honorary President of the Agu-
das Harabonim), quoted in *Taharas Yom Tov* by Yom
Tov L. Deutsch, Vol. VIII (see *Hamoar* for Elul
1957). He said: "I have forbidden physicians, most of
whom are not observant Jews, to circumcise, but have

permitted only skilled *mohelim* who are religious to approach the fulfillment of this commandment."

This is, of course, a strict decision beyond the actual requirement of the law, but still it is a permissible one. The rabbinical authorities may always make extra-cautionary decisions, forbidding what may actually be permitted, in cases where they feel the religious situation requires such strictness. These extra prohibitions generally apply for the time of the emergency and in the city of the rabbi's authority. That is why Rabbi Silver continues: "Thank God, in my city [i.e., Cincinnati] and in my area they listen to me, and they do not permit just any physician to perform the circumcision." However, aside from this local, extra strictness, our concern is: What is the actual state of the law?

1. There is no question that a Jewish physician who is himself circumcised may legally perform the ritual circumcision. The only question about a Jewish physician arises from the concern expressed by Isserles (ibid.) as to a nonbeliever. Isserles says that a man who rejects the entire Torah or rejects the idea that circumcision is a Divine commandment (i.e., a *mumar*, one who turns aside or rebels against the Torah), such an irreligious doctor may not legally circumcise. This question has been discussed by many modern authorities, and the tendency of their decision is to be lenient on the matter. The question of the irreligiousness of the Jewish physician is fully discussed by David Hoffmann in his *Melamed L'ho-il* (*Yore Deah*, responsum #80), and he shows that most authorities are lenient

on this matter, and even those who are inclined to be strict and agree with Isserles (that a nonbelieving doctor is ineligible) nevertheless grant that if no other *mohel* were available, he would be acceptable. There is, therefore, no question that a religious Jewish doctor may circumcise and that even a nonreligious one is acceptable when no other is available.

2. May a Gentile doctor perform the operation? The laws which forbid a non-Jew to circumcise were based upon the fact that in the early days every non-Jew was an idolater, and there was fear that the idolater would harm the child (see *Tosefta, Avoda Zara,* 3:12). However, even an idolater was permitted if others were present or if he were a professional. So Israel of Kremsier (14th cent.), in his *Hagahos Asheri* to the Rosh, b. *Avoda Zara* 27a, says: "All prohibitions against using Gentile physicians [in general] apply only if the healing by a physician is done by an amateur and without pay, but if done by a professional and for pay, it is absolutely permitted." Of course, in the spirit of the law, if a Gentile doctor is to do the circumcision, the family should be present, and, of course, the ritual prayers, etc., should be recited by a rabbi or a member of the family.

3. The question of whether a woman may circumcise is based upon the discussion in the Talmud (*Avoda Zara* 27a) between Rav and Rav Yochonon. The debate centers upon the question as to which is the crucial verse in the commandment given to Abraham when he is given the command to circumcise himself and his family. Rav says that the crucial verse

is "Thou shalt keep my covenant" (Genesis 17:9), and Yochanon says that the crucial verse is "Let all born in thy household be circumcised" (17:13). From the analysis of these respective verses, Rav concludes that a woman may not circumcise, and Yochanon concludes that a woman may circumcise. The *Tosfos* (ad loc.) says that the law is according to Rav and that a woman may not circumcise; whereas almost all other authorities declare that in all disputes between these two scholars, the decision is according to Yochanon, and most of them agree that a woman *may* circumcise. Therefore she is listed in the *Shulchan Aruch* among those who may circumcise. But, of course, it is added that one should in preference look for a skilled man to perform the circumcision.

Let us say, then, that the situation of the law is as follows: Orthodox Jews, out of the natural desire to avoid such changes in practice as may affect Orthodox life, will always prefer a pious *mohel*. Other people, less Orthodox, will have the physician perform the operation whether he is personally religious or not, and when no Jewish doctor is available, will have a Gentile obstetrician perform the operation; and if the obstetrician is a woman, she will perform the operation. As to all these choices by non-Orthodox Jewish families, it can be said that they are going counter to Orthodox preference; but it cannot be said that such choices are violative of Jewish law.

19

FUNERALS FROM THE TEMPLE

QUESTION:

At present there is no clear rule as to which funerals may be held in the main sanctuary of the temple and which in the chapel, etc. This uncertainty can, and sometimes does, create difficulties for the families involved and for the temple also. When a family is waiting to complete funeral arrangements, and the temple needs time to decide whether the service may or may not be held in the main sanctuary, this delay often adds to the sorrow of the bereaved family; and if, for some reason, the request for the use of the temple auditorium is denied, this may create ill will for the temple. Is there a clear rule of procedure in this matter which is in consonance with our religious tradition? (Asked by Vigdor W. Kavaler, Executive Secretary, Rodef Shalom Temple, Pittsburgh, Pennsylvania.)

ANSWER:

ON THE FACE OF IT, the problem would be easily solved if the temple simply permitted the use of the main sanctuary to any member family which asks for it. However, this simple suggestion is contrary to both the letter and the spirit of the Jewish legal tradition on this matter. If we are to find a solution for the

problem, it should be in consonance with the spirit of
Jewish tradition. What, then, is the traditional point
of view as to funerals taking place on the synagogue
premises?

Basically, the traditional law is opposed to any
funeral at all taking place in the synagogue! This law
is derived by clear implication from the statement in
the Mishnah (*Megillah* 4:3) which declares that even
when a synagogue is in ruins, it still retains its inherent
sanctity, and therefore no funeral service may be conducted there. Thus it is clear that all the more is it
prohibited to hold funeral services in a sanctuary that
is still in use for public worship. However, there are
notable exceptions which are made to this general prohibition. The *Tosefta* (*Megillah* 3:7) takes the law to
mean that no *private* funeral services may be held in
the synagogue, but *public* funeral services may be held
there. In his comment on *Megillah* 28b, Rashi, the
prime authority, explains this distinction as follows:
Only such funerals may be held in the synagogue as
involve a public obligation of the community to participate in the mourning. That is to say, a great scholar
or communal leader may be buried from the synagogue
because a large place is needed so that the entire community can gather and fulfill its obligation of mourning for the deceased leader, or teacher (see further
references on this decision in *Reform Jewish Practice,*
Vol. II, pp. 55 ff.).

Of course, in the earlier centuries "community" and
"congregation" were identical terms. The whole community was organized into one congregational unity,

even though there may have been a number of synagogue buildings. But nowadays, when there are separate and independent congregational units in every
large city, the terms "community" and "congregation"
are no longer identical. Therefore the historic law must
be interpreted as follows: Only such funeral services
shall be held in the sanctuary at which the entire *congregation* owes the duty to attend; in other words, the
services for the leaders of the congregation.

The question now is: Who are to be deemed "the
leaders of the congregation" that would fit into this
category? It is important that such a definition be clear-
cut and definite because the whole purpose of this inquiry is to avoid uncertainty and discussion when a
family is bereaved.

It would, therefore, be in consonance with the mood
of tradition to adopt the following rule: The right to
hold a funeral in the main sanctuary should be given
to the rabbis and officers and board of trustees of the
congregation. Of course, since the presidents of the
three subsidiary organizations, sisterhood, men's club,
and junior congregation, are members of the board,
they are included in the above rule. This rule should
apply to rabbis, officers, and trustees, past and present.

Are the spouses of the above to be included in
this regulation? Again, here, tradition gives us some
guidance. Of all the authorities who discuss this question, only one includes the privilege of synagogue
burial to the spouses, namely, *Yore Deah* 344:19.
However, all other authorities disagree with this extension of the law and insist that only the scholar or

leader himself shall have this privilege. Of course, in
the older law that meant only men, but in Reform
Judaism, which declares as a basic principle the religious equality of men and women, the rule shall apply
to the leader or trustee whether a man or a woman.
But in accordance with the weight of legal opinion, the
spouse (husband or wife, respectively) of the leader,
shall not be included.

All this applies only to the main sanctuary. However, the chapel (our Josiah and Carrie Cohen Chapel)
is in a different category. There is a general principle
in the legal tradition that if, at the time of the building
of a synagogue or a chapel, a permissive precondition
is made, then many prohibitions, because of this preliminary condition, may be bypassed. Our Josiah and
Carrie Cohen Chapel was built and given to Rodef
Shalom with a precondition, namely, the understanding that its use be not confined to regularly scheduled
services, but that the chapel should be made available
at all times to all who wish to enter to meditate and
pray. This condition allows us to open the chapel for
funeral services to any member of the congregation
who requests its use. In fact, it has become an established custom with us, and with many other metro-
politan Reform congregations, to allow the chapel to
be used for the funeral service for any member family
which requests it.

However, this practice of our congregation and
others may sometimes involve a difficulty. When the
deceased had many friends or the family is large, then
the family may say that the chapel is too small and

will request a larger auditorium, preferably the main sanctuary itself. It would be logical, therefore, for the congregation to decide that if a family is not eligible by rule to use the main sanctuary, this family, if it finds the chapel too small, may use the J. Leonard Levy Hall. This hall also has the mood of a sanctuary. It has an Ark, and services are frequently held in it during the year. The fact that the J. Leonard Levy Hall is *also* used for school purposes does not detract from its status as a sanctuary. On the contrary, a school (*bes ha-midrash*) under certain circumstances is deemed to have a sanctity equal to that of the synagogue sanctuary (*bes ha-knesses*). (See *Shulchan Aruch, Orah Hayyim* 151:1, which groups synagogue and study-hall in equal sanctity.)

Since, therefore, it is important to have a consistent rule as to the use of the temple premises and thus avoid uncertainty and possible unhappiness, and since tradition gives us fairly clear guidance in developing such a rule under our modern conditions, the practice should be as follows: rabbis, officers, and members of the board of trustees, past and present, are in the category of "leaders of the congregation" to whom the entire congregation has some obligation of mourning. For these, therefore, the large sanctuary may be used. All other members of the congregation may use the chapel and, if they request it, the J. Leonard Levy Hall. This rule is in accordance with the spirit of tradition and, if accepted, should be made known to the entire congregation.

20

TWO COFFINS IN ONE GRAVE

QUESTION:

> Space in the cemetery is becoming scarcer every year. The question has therefore arisen whether or not we may bury one coffin above another in the same grave. (Asked by Sidney Kluger, Executive Director, Temple Sherith Israel, San Francisco, California.)

ANSWER:

IT IS OBVIOUS that to open a grave and put another coffin above the one already there is not desirable, and most of the scholars who deal with the question say that this should not be done. But all of them, after saying that it should not be done, nevertheless find a reason to permit it after all. For example, the great Chassidic scholar of the last century, Chaim Halberstam, in his *Divre Chaim* (*Yore Deah* 136), says simply that it should not be done; but then he adds that if it is an established custom in the community to do so, then it should be permitted to continue. Similarly, other scholars dealing with the question indicate that whatever the strict letter of the law may be in this matter, it is a widespread custom in many communities to do so. Thus, for example, see the responsum of Jacob

100

Reischer (d. in Metz, 1733) in his *Shevus Yaacov* II:95. It is not surprising, therefore, that when the *Shulchan Aruch* states the law, it also exhibits this same double attitude. In *Yore Deah* 362:4, the law is given at first bluntly as follows: "We may not bury one coffin above another." But then the law continues: "But if there is six handbreadths of earth between the coffins, it is permitted." Thus we might say, the general attitude of the law is ambivalent, namely, that such superimposed burial is not desirable but it is not forbidden.

It would be desirable to trace the development of the law, especially this ambivalent attitude in it, since the various elements involved may help each congregation to make its decision on the matter. Basically, the law involving the distance between one buried body and another is based upon the Mishnah in *Baba Bathra* 6:8. The discussion there revolves around a cave and how many burial niches may be dug in it, in what direction, and how close to each other. The Mishnah then is discussed in *Baba Bathra* 101 ff., and most later discussions base themselves upon this passage.

The Gaon Hai is cited in the *Tur* (*Yore Deah* 363) to the effect that each grave is entitled to three handbreadths of earth around it (*tefisas ha-kever*). Joel Sirkes (*Bach* to the *Tur*) explains the fact that some authorities say that there ought to be six handbreadths, and some authorities say only three handbreadths, intervening. Sirkes explains it as follows: Each coffin is entitled to three handbreadths of its own. Hence, between the lower coffin and the upper coffin, there

should be six handbreadths (three for each coffin).
Even this amount of space is not insisted upon by all
authorities. The fullest discussion of the whole matter
is by Abraham Danzig in his *Chochmas Adam* in the
section *Matzevas Moshe*, #10. He says (on the basis
of some text variation) that it may be possible to have
the width of only six *fingers* of earth between the
coffins.

The justification for such a small intervening amount
of earth came up in connection with the questions
which arose in the city of Paris in the seventeenth century. At that time the Jews of Paris were not permitted
to have a cemetery of their own. They buried in some
city lots, and the question, therefore, of coffin above
coffin immediately arose. They asked a question of
Aryeh Lev of Metz (see the second volume of his
Sha'agas Aryeh [Vilna edition, 1873], p. 120, responsum #17). He told them that they might bury in this
way, but to be sure to have six handbreadths between
coffins.

Those who would permit superimposed burial with
less than six handbreadths (as Danzig does, requiring
only six fingers) base themselves generally upon the
statement of Simon ben Gamaliel in the Mishnah cited
above, who ends the discussion in the Mishnah by saying that it all depends on the rockiness of the soil. This
is understood to mean that if the soil is firm and would
not disperse easily, even less than six handbreadths
would be sufficient. So, for example, Zvi Ashkenazi
(*Chacham Zvi*), in his responsa #149, is dealing with
a situation in the cemetery of Amsterdam where the

soil is loose and thin. There he would require even more than six handbreadths. However, Isaac Schmelkes of Lemberg, in his *Bes Yitzchok* (*Yore Deah* 153), says that in Paris they put a slab of stone between the graves and that, even if it were an inch only, it is sufficient to separate coffins.

In fact, Abraham Danzig cites *Toras Chesed,* in which the statement is made that all these laws as to how much intervening earth there must be were based upon the earlier custom of burying the bodies without coffins; but that nowadays, when we bury in coffins, we do not need to consider the necessity for intervening earth at all.

In fact we may say that if, as is frequently the custom nowadays in some cemeteries, the coffin itself is enclosed in a cement casing, then the top of the casing of the lower coffin and the bottom of the casing of the upper coffin could fulfill completely the requirements of even the strictest opinion. Moses Feinstein (*Igros Moshe, Yore Deah* 234) believes that even with cement intervening, there should be an interval of three to six handbreadths.

Frequently, in the discussion of this question, the authority will say that all the laws of intervening earth were meant for the time when we had plenty of room and therefore could leave sufficient earth between each coffin. But nowadays our land is crowded, and so the custom to bury closely side by side and one above the other has become widespread and must be deemed permissible. See especially the statement of Jacob Reischer of Metz cited above.

To sum up, then: Nowadays cemetery space is becoming scarce. We bury in coffins and sometimes even with cement casing around the coffins. This is to be considered sufficient to fulfill the requirement of the strictest authorities. Yet it must be stated, in explaining the double attitude of the law, that it would be preferable if we had the space for each coffin to have its own grave.

21

PERPETUAL LIGHT ON A GRAVE

QUESTION:

A family in the congregation is considering the installing of a perpetual light on the grave of a newly deceased member of the family. Would such an installation comport with Jewish traditional law and sentiment? (Asked by Vigdor W. Kavaler, Pittsburgh, Pennsylvania.)

ANSWER:

THE PERPETUAL LIGHT has had a well-established place in Jewish tradition from its very beginning. In the laws governing the Tabernacle in the wilderness, there is a mandate that there shall be a perpetual fire on the altar, never to be extinguished (Leviticus 6:6). Also, in the Tabernacle and later in the Temple in Jerusalem, the Menorah which stood before the sacred curtain burned perpetually. The idea of perpetual flames or light was carried over to the synagogue itself as the heir to the Tabernacle and the Temple. Thus to this day all synagogues have an Eternal Light burning in front of the Ark.

In the home, lights were always kindled as symbols of the sanctity of the Sabbath and Chanukah. Later, in the Middle Ages, the light came to be used in personal life in connection with the memory of the dead. Thus the custom developed to bring to the synagogue, on Yom Kippur Eve, a candle to be lit during the service in memory of the departed (see Isserles, *Orah Hayyim* 610:4). Then, still later, possibly about three centuries ago, the memorial light was kindled in the home of the bereaved. This light, now a present custom, was lit during the seven days of mourning (*shiva*). Possibly the idea of these two types of memorial light was inspired by the verse in Proverbs (20:27): "The soul of man is the lamp of God."

However, these two late light-customs, the Yom Kippur memorial candle and the candle of mourning in the home, were, of course, not perpetual lights at all. They burned for one evening on Yom Kippur and for seven days during mourning; and moreover, they are only a late development in Jewish custom and have no strong foundation in Jewish law.

As to an eternal light in the cemetery, that has no foundation at all in Jewish law or tradition. The first mention of such a light that I heard of was when I was asked by a midwestern congregation, four or five years ago, as to whether an eternal fire might be lit in the cemetery of the congregation in memory of the six million martyred Jews of Europe. It is certain that the idea of a perpetual light in the cemetery suggested itself to the congregation as a fitting memorial because of the eternal light burning under the Arch of Triumph in Paris in memory of the dead French soldiers (see *Modern Reform Responsa,* p. 249). The question of a perpetual memorial for the martyred Jews concerned one single light for the entire cemetery. The present question does not apply equally to the entire cemetery, but only to an individual grave. Perhaps the present request was suggested by the light that is kept burning by the Kennedy family on the grave of the martyred President, John F. Kennedy.

As far as I know, there is no mention anywhere in Jewish tradition of an eternal light burning in the cemetery, neither one general light for the entire cemetery, like the memorial for the six million martyrs, nor an individual light at a single grave. Of course, the fact that there is no precedent at all in Jewish tradition does not necessarily mean that we may not start a new custom. The question, then, is whether such a custom is desirable and comports with the general mood of Jewish burial practice and attitude toward the cemetery.

From the point of view of the mood of the tradition with regard to the cemetery, the suggested innovation is objectionable for two reasons, first, from the point of view of conspicuousness, and second, from the point of view of distinctiveness. First, as to conspicuousness: The mood of our cemeteries, from the very beginning, has been subdued, and objections were always raised to too much adornment or conspicuousness of a grave.

Many congregations, therefore, guard against the setting up of too large or too ornate a tombstone, or perhaps too much noticeable flowering of plants or trees around the grave. An effort is made that each grave comport with the subdued mood of those who come there for the burial of a dear one or return at a later time to pray at the grave. Therefore, nothing—tombstone, planting, or whatever else—should be other than quiet and subdued.

As for the second consideration, distinctiveness: While it is true that not all graves need to be arranged alike, and there are allowable differences between shapes of tombstones and plantings, care was always taken that no grave should be outstanding as exceptional. Sometimes, of course, the grave of some honored, saintly rabbi had a small hutlike structure over it. This special arrangement was allowed because people came from many communities to pray at the grave of this righteous man, and the grave had to be distinctive so that the pilgrims could find it. But other than that, care was taken that no grave should be outstandingly different from others. In fact, many European communities had special committees to watch over the tombstones, not only as to their size, but to see to it that the inscriptions on them be not too flowery, overpraising the departed (see *Kol Bo Al Avelus,* p. 380, citing Joseph Schwartz in *Hadras Kodesh*). Generally the term "partnership" (Maharam Schick, *Yore Deah* 170) is used concerning the cemetery. We are all equal partners in the cemetery, both the deceased and the living, and therefore no one grave should stand out as an exception.

All this is not a matter of strict law, but of the mood and spirit of the tradition. If, for example, it were already an established custom to have perpetual fires on many graves, that might be endurable, although of debatable propriety. But to begin a new custom of having a perpetual light on one especial grave would mean taking a step which not only has no basis in Jewish tradition, but which certainly is contrary to the historic mood.

22

THE BELATED FLOWERS

QUESTION:

> The family of a deceased woman ordered a blanket of pink roses for the casket and the grave. The flower-blanket arrived at the home too late for the funeral service. The family wanted to bring the blanket to the grave but was told that they should not return to the grave until the thirty-day period had passed. Should they disregard this injunction and lay the flowers on the grave themselves, or should they have some functionary do it for them? (Asked by Rabbi Philip S. Bernstein, Rochester, New York.)

ANSWER:

ORTHODOX CUSTOM objects altogether to having flowers on the coffin and the grave. The objections are summarized by the famous Hungarian authority Elazar Spiro ("Der Muncaczer") in his responsa, *Minchas Elazar*, IV, 61 (see *Contemporary Reform Responsa,* pp. 284 ff.). Therefore, if the family intended to have a blanket of flowers on the coffin and the grave, and the rabbi intended to officiate at the funeral, it is evident that we are not dealing with an Orthodox family and an Orthodox funeral. But although the family is not Orthodox, it was told not to visit the cemetery until the thirty days of mourning are past. Evidently this instruction to the family was based on the understanding that the prohibition of visiting the cemetery before the thirty days of mourning have passed is so strict and well established a prohibition in Jewish law that even a family that is not strictly Orthodox should, in deference to a strong tradition, obey the injunction.

But, in fact, is such a prohibition well established in Jewish law? In the early days people were expected to go to the cemetery the first three days after the burial to watch, or guard, the grave. This custom was not maintained because, as Joshua Falk, in the *Perisha* to *Tur* (*Yore Deah* 394), explains it, in those days they buried the bodies in niches and therefore the body could be examined (against premature burial). But now that we bury in the earth, that old custom has lapsed. However, the *Tur* cites a Gaonic responsum to the effect that when a scholar died, people went to the cemetery on the third, seventh, and thirtieth days after his death to visit his grave. Joseph Caro, in his *Bes Joseph* (ad loc.), says that the source does not mention the third day, but does mention the visit to the

cemetery on the seventh and thirtieth days. So in his
Shulchan Aruch (*Yore Deah* 344:20), he gives it as
a law in general that the grave is visited on the seventh
and thirtieth days. This, too, is a well-established Ashkenazic custom, not only for great scholars, but for all
honored departed. The *Kol Bo,* which is a prime source
of our Ashkenazic customs, gives it as a rule that on
the seventh day of mourning, the mourners go to the
synagogue and, after the synagogue service, to the
cemetery (he adds, however, that if the seventh day
happens to be on the New Moon, they do not go). As
a matter of fact, there was a long-established custom
among the Sephardim for the mourners to leave their
home during *shiva* and go to the synagogue every day
for worship (see Joseph Caro in *Bes Joseph* to *Tur,
Yore Deah* 393, in the *Bedek Ha-Bayis.*) Of course the
established custom is that the mourners do not leave the
house to go to the synagogue except on the Sabbath
(see *Mishmeres Shalom,* Laws of Mourning, p. 44b).

As for visiting the cemetery, it is perfectly clear that
even by the strictest Jewish law there is no prohibition
at all to visiting the cemetery before the thirty days
are over, and the authorities who speak of cemetery
visitation specifically mention the visitation on the seventh day.

However, it may well be that the person who in-
structed the people not to go to the cemetery had another objection in mind. The blanket of flowers is now
in the house of mourning, and there is a widespread
idea that nothing is to be taken out of the house of
mourning once it was brought in. This popular idea

has no firm basis in Jewish law. Joseph Nordlinger, in his *Joseph Ometz,* p. 192 (which, with the *Kol Bo,* is a basic source of Ashkenazic customs), mentions the custom not to take anything out of the house of mourning during the seven days of *shiva.* He warns against an increase of restrictions of this kind, and he reminds us of the rabbinic principle that in cases of mourning we should not add restrictions to those already made by the sages. As for this particular restriction, he says that he learned from his teacher, (Maharil) that there is no basis for the prohibition. He speculates on the origin of this popular notion. There is a custom, he says, that if a man borrows a shirt to wear during the funeral, he may not return it until after *shiva.* It may be that the people have extended this custom to an avoidance of taking *anything* from the house till after *shiva.* However, Akiba Eger (1761–1837) believes that the popular prohibition *should* be followed because there is a spirit of ritual uncleanliness (*ruach ha-tuma*) on all objects in the house of mourning. Hershkowitz, in his book on customs, *Ozar Minhage Jeshurun* (p. 302), strives to find a more rational explanation and says that if people were allowed to take things from the house of mourning, the heirs of the deceased might be deprived of what belongs to them (see *Reform Responsa,* p. 178). Greenwald, in his *Kol Bo* (p. 264:14), repeats the statement of *Joseph Ometz* that there is no basis for the prohibition.

Thus, even if this were a strictly Orthodox family, they could not be prohibited from going to the cemetery on the seventh day, a visit which, indeed, some authorities actually recommend. Also, there is no real objection to taking anything out of the house of mourning. Since this is not a strictly Orthodox family, they may certainly leave the house at the end of *shiva* to visit the grave if they wish. But since the flowers would have withered by that time, there can be no possible objection against some functionary taking them from the house earlier and placing them upon the grave in order to honor the dead. Much is permitted in Jewish law for the purpose of honoring the dead.

23

BURIAL OF CREMATION ASHES

QUESTION:

A Conservative Jewess in Delhi, India, married a Hindu, Colonel Khosla, twenty-five years ago. She is still residing in Delhi. Recently her daughter Bella, aged fourteen, received accidental burns in her kitchen. She was hospitalized and, after four days, died in the hospital. She was cremated according to Hindu rites. The Jewish community refuses to bury her ashes. (Inquiry through Rabbi Joseph Glaser, New York.)

ANSWER:

IT IS NOT QUITE clear from the letter what is asked of us here. The letter contains the following statement: "At the last Executive Meeting of the Committee it was decided to approach the Chief Rabbinate in U.S.A." This seems to indicate that the small Delhi Jewish community (which, as the letter states, is divided as to whether to bury the ashes in the Jewish cemetery or not) has decided to inquire of the Chief Rabbinate of the United States. There is no Chief Rabbinate in the United States. So, possibly since the mother is described as a Conservative Jewess, the inquiry is being directed to various religious groups in the United States, and to us among them.

Of course if we are asked for the Reform point of view (since the mother is not Orthodox), it is very clear that we have a firmly established custom in Reform Judaism to bury in our cemeteries the ashes of the cremated. As a matter of fact, our Conference decided (as published in our *Yearbook*, 1892, p. 43) that we will never refuse to officiate at a funeral at which a cremation is to take place. I presume we passed that resolution because the Chief Rabbinate of England had decided to permit the burial of ashes in the Jewish cemeteries, but *not* to officiate.

But it may be that the inquirer wants more than our Reform point of view. Let us, therefore, discuss the matter from the point of view of Jewish tradition. There is no question that the child who died is a Jewish child, since she has a Jewish mother, and therefore under normal circumstances could be buried in the Jewish cemetery. In fact it is a mandate to bury the body of a Jew. However, her body was cremated, and therefore the community is divided as to whether to bury the ashes or not. I have already discussed the question of cremation rather fully a number of times in the past (see *Reform Jewish Practice*, I, p. 133; also *Modern Reform Responsa,* pp. 269, 278, 237; also *Contemporary Reform Responsa*, p. 169). It is, therefore, sufficient here to mention the main elements involved in the problem. Besides, the specific questions involved here are different from those discussed in the past.

There is no doubt at all that cremation as a practice is contrary to Jewish law, although it must be mentioned that when the men of Jabesh-gilead (I Samuel 31:11–13) captured the bodies of Saul and Jonathan from the Philistines and burnt them and then buried the ashes, they were described as "valiant men." The only question that is at all debatable is not the cremation itself, but the burial of the ashes in the Jewish cemetery. Rabbi Meyer Lerner of Altona published a whole book of responsa that he gathered from the Orthodox rabbinate of Europe (*Chaye Olam*), the aim of which was to prove that the ashes of the cremated should not be buried in a Jewish cemetery. However, at the same time, contrary Orthodox opinions were published, among them the permission to bury ashes given by Azriel Hildesheimer of Berlin.

There is, however, a full discussion on the question of the burial of the ashes by David Hoffman of Berlin (in a sense a successor of Hildesheimer at the Orthodox Seminary). After a complete and detailed discussion, he concludes that the mandate to bury the dead does not apply to the ashes of the cremated. Yet though there is no *mandate* to bury the ashes, there is also no *prohibition* against it. In other words, the ashes *may* be buried in a Jewish cemetery, although he prefers that it not be done.

Aside from the central question of the permissibility of the burial of the ashes, there is an additional consideration here, in this specific case, which would strengthen the case for permitting the burial. Jacob Emden of Altona (one might say a sort of predecessor of Meyer Lerner), in his responsa (Vol. II, 169), proves that there is no question as to the ashes of bodies burnt by *accident* (in conflagrations and also the bodies of martyrs burnt at the stake). It is certainly a duty to bury these ashes in the cemetery. David Hoffmann, in his responsa referred to above, accepts the opinion of Jacob Emden and repeats the permission for the burial of such ashes. This has some relevance to the case described in the letter. There is no evidence that the mother committed the sin (from the Orthodox point of view) of ordering the cremation. It was the hospital that did it, following the usual practice in India. Therefore we may well say that this was a burning *b'oness* (i.e., under compulsion), and therefore the ashes may certainly be buried in a Jewish cemetery.

To sum up: There are enough mitigating circumstances in the case described to follow the permission indicated in the summation by David Hoffman, namely, that while the burial is not a duty, as normal burials would be, it is nevertheless permitted, especially in this case, where the mother did not order the cremation.

24

MOTHER'S NAME ON SON'S TOMBSTONE

QUESTION:

A young chaplain-rabbi was killed in Thailand. His family belong to the Hartford Reform Congregation, Beth Israel. His mother is an active National Sisterhood board member. She asked that the Hebrew inscription on her son's tombstone should include her name as mother of the deceased. The local funeral director said that this request is improper, that only the father's name may be used with that of the deceased. Is this correct? What traditional law is involved in this matter? (Asked by Rabbi Harold S. Silver, Hartford, Connecticut.)

ANSWER:

THERE IS VERY LITTLE firm law governing tombstones. Even the latest works that specialize in these matters have comparatively little to say. Greenwald, in his *Kol Bo,* has only a few pages, beginning with p. 379, and Shalom Schachne Cherniak, in his *Mishmeres Shalom,* has only a few columns. The reason for the paucity of the law on the matter has some bearing on this discussion.

The main purpose of having a tombstone had changed in the passing years. Originally the stone was meant merely to mark the grave as a warning to Kohanim to know what spot to avoid, a warning which would be especially necessary if the grave were in some open field. Later this purpose for the tombstone changed since cemeteries (and not scattered graves or caves) developed, and the Kohen could simply avoid the cemetery. Now the purpose of the tombstone is not so much to be a warning to the Kohanim to keep away, but as a guide to the family, to tell them where to come to honor the dead or to pray. In other words, the tombstone is now for the benefit of the family. See, for example, the responsum by Isaac Glick (*Yad Yitzchok*, III, #38), who says that the tombstone is for the benefit of the living to know where to come and pray. This change of mood as to the purpose of the tombstone should indicate to us, in our specific discussion, that the feelings of the bereaved family deserve sympathetic consideration in all the discussions about the tombstone.

The discussions that *have* arisen in recent law about the tombstone usually involve three questions: (1) whether it is permitted (as is the custom in certain Orthodox cemeteries) to have a photograph of the deceased on his tombstone (cf. Greenwald, p. 380, n. 1); (2) whether the secular date may be used on the tombstone; (3) whether the tombstone may be used for the benefit of the living (for example, to sit down and rest upon it). The third question has more meaning in the Orient, where the tombstones are not vertical, as with us, but are laid horizontally, somewhat elevated, like a bench over the grave.

As for the answers to these questions, the photograph on the tombstone is generally frowned upon as a practice. The secular date is reluctantly permitted if it is at least accompanied by the Hebrew date. As for sitting on the tombstone, that question has some bearing on our question because what is involved is the question of whether or not the tombstone is, also, for the benefit of the living, as mentioned above. Generally that is answered in the affirmative. So, as mentioned above, the desires of the living should have consideration in the discussion of the tombstone.

Now as to the specific question: May the tombstone giving the name of the deceased give his name as the son of his mother rather than, as is generally the usage, as the son of his father? Of course the funeral director (or the rabbi who advised him) would be quite correct if he had merely said that the general *custom* is to cite a man's name with his father's name, as "Moses the son of Amram." This is the way a man is called up to the Torah, and thus is his name used in the *get* and other formal documents.

Nevertheless the question must be raised, as it is raised here in this comparatively rare question, whether the general custom of using the father's name is more than custom but is actual *law*. Is it *wrong* to use the mother's name, describing the man as "Moses son of Yocheved," instead of "Moses son of Amram"? The answer goes to the heart of our question. The Bible records the name of a well-known Biblical character as the son of his mother and never as the son of his father. King David's chief general (and his nephew) was Joab ben Zeruah. Zeruah was David's sister (I Chronicles 11:6). Also in the Talmud there is an Amora whose name was Rab Mari ben Rachel (*Yevamos* 92b).

In fact, the great authority of two centuries ago, Ezekiel Landau, in his commentary to the *Shulchan Aruch* (*Dagul Mirvava* to *Even Hoezer* 129:9), speaking of the divorce document, in which the proper rendering of each name is vital, says that in the case of a proselyte we should use his mother's name instead of his father's name, and cites the precedent of the rabbi mentioned in the Talmud, Mari the son of Rachel. As a matter of fact, the *Pische Teshuvah*, at the end of par. 26 to the same divorce section, says that if a man is better known by his mother's name than by his father's name, that should be used in the *get,* and he says that it is obvious that if it is written thus, the *get* is valid.

This permissibility with regard to the divorce document, in which the names have to be precise, is crucial in all discussion of the specific matter involved here. As a matter of fact, there were communities which actually had an established custom of using the mother's instead of the father's name on the tombstone. One such community (and it could hardly have been the only one) wrote to David Hoffmann telling of their established custom and wanting to know whether it is correct. He answers (*Melamed L'ho-il, Orah Hayyim* 23) and says that the tombstones which he had seen of all the great rabbis gives the father's name and not the mother's. Nevertheless, if it is an established custom in the community to use the mother's name, the custom should be continued, or at least not be objected to.

Now, why should such an Orthodox authority as David Hoffmann permit the custom of using the mother's name, when he himself says that the tombstones of the great rabbis that he saw had the father's name? The answer clearly must be that although most tombstones have the father's name, this is because that is the usual way of referring to a man, but it does not mean that the mother's name may *not* be used. In fact, in his responsum he gives some examples in which the mother's name is used *exclusively*. In the prayer before the taking out of the Torah on holidays (*Rebono Shel Olom*), the supplicant refers to himself by his mother's name. Also, in the regular text of the *Yizkor* on holidays, the deceased is referred to as child of the mother. (In our *Union Prayer Book*, we merely say "father" or "mother" or "brother," and do not use the personal name at all, but in all the *Machzorim* where the personal name of the deceased is used in the *Yizkor,* it is always as the child of the mother.) Also, as he correctly points out, it is a well-established custom, when we pray for the sick, to refer to the sick person by the mother's name only. This custom is based upon the verse in Psalms 116:16, where the supplicant says: "I am Thy servant, the son of Thy *handmaiden*."

For all these reasons and established precedents, David Hoffmann, in spite of the fact that most of the tombstones he had seen used the father's name, nevertheless was unwilling, in those communities where the custom of using the mother's name on the tombstone was established, to recommend that the custom no longer be followed.

To sum up: The tombstone is not a matter of strict detailed law but largely of custom. What legal disputes have occurred emphasize the benefit that it brings to the living. Hence their feelings must be consulted and considered. The liturgical literature has many examples in which the mother's name is used to the exclusion of the father's name, and there are communities (or there *were* in Europe) in which the mother's name was used regularly on the tombstone.

In this specific case, therefore, we can say that there is no real objection to the son being called the son of his mother. In fact, we might follow the decision of Greenwald (pp. 380–81) with regard to the use of the secular date on the tombstone, namely, if the secular date is used together with the Hebrew date, the use of both dates would be permissible. So here, too, we might say that if the mother would consent to having the name of both parents, hers and her husband's, there could be no objection at all. But if with her husband's consent (as the inquirer states) her name alone is used as the parent, there is no real ground in the law for objection.

25

THE RENTED HEARSE

QUESTION:

> At a recent funeral, the bereaved family learned that the hearse used by the Jewish funeral director was rented from a Gentile funeral director (or that both of them use it in a sort of partnership). They strongly objected, insisting that there should be a hearse used only for Jews. Is there any traditional background and justification for this objection on the part of the family? (Asked by Rabbi Murray Rothman, Newton, Massachusetts.)

ANSWER:

BEFORE GOING INTO the question, I inquired whether it is a widespread practice for Jewish and Gentile funeral directors to use the same hearse. I learned that funeral directors who have very many funerals may have their own hearse, but in general, since livery is expensive nowadays, most funeral directors rent their hearses as they rent their limousines, and so the same hearse is, indeed, used for both Jews and non-Jews.

I also inquired from funeral directors whether the objection of the Jewish family you referred to has been heard in their cities, and I found that this objection is not at all widespread. However, the fact that the objection is not widespread does not make the question less important, because it is in the psychology of bereaved families to add new restrictions on themselves, being eager to do "the right thing" for their departed one. Thus restrictions, observances, and prohibitions multiply even when there is little basis in the legal tradition to justify them. Since, therefore, this objection to the rented hearse may well increase and spread, it would be worthwhile, at least at this early stage, to see what there is in the tradition that led people to this protest.

First, it must be understood that the use of a hearse is itself new as a method of transporting the dead from the home to the cemetery. Up to about a century ago, the bodies were carried on the shoulders of pallbearers. This custom is traced back to the burial of the patriarch Jacob, whose body was carried by his sons to his grave in the cave of Machpelah (Genesis 50:13): "His sons *carried* him into the land of Canaan and buried him in the cave in the field of Machpelah." It was only in comparatively modern times, when the cemeteries in the large cities were at a great distance from the Jewish homes, that it became virtually impossible for the bodies to be carried all the way. Since it became impossible to do without transportation, the authorities were compelled to permit it.

An interesting form of the question is found in the responsa of Maharam (Moses Schick), *Yore Deah* 35. The inquirer said that the people feel that the honor of the dead (in the eyes of the Gentile community) would suggest that when the body is transported to the cemetery, it be transported in a hearse similar to the ones which the Gentiles use. Moses Schick permits the use of a hearse but suggests that the Jewish community make its hearse look different from the one the Gentiles use.

The same question is discussed by Eliezer Deutsch of Bonyhad, a leading Hungarian authority, in his *Dudoye Ha-Sodeh,* #25. The question came to him from Rabbi Klafter in New York, where the Jewish neighborhoods are far from the cemeteries. Deutsch says, of course, that the preferred transportation is by pallbearers ("shoulders"). Next to that, an automobile-drawn hearse is preferable to a horse-drawn hearse since horses are unclean animals. Then he gives the same caution as did Moses Schick, namely, that the hearse should be so constructed as to look different from the Gentile hearse so as to avoid the sin of imitation (*chukas ha-goy*).

Of course it is clear that both authorities speak of hearses owned by the Jewish community and so in actual fact only Jewish bodies would be transported in them. But that does not mean necessarily that if a hearse had at one time or other been borrowed from the Gentile community, the rabbinical authorities would object to its use, on the ground that Gentile bodies were transported in it. After all, they were describing the situation that prevailed in Europe, where there were no Jewish funeral directors conducting funeral-directing as a private business. All the funeral paraphernalia were owned by the community, and these authorities take that fact for granted, and therefore they said that the community-owned hearse should look different from the one owned by the Gentile community.

But would they have ground for objecting to a borrowed or rented hearse if such were possible in Europe? Of course, where a hearse was not used and the body was carried on shoulders, the pallbearers would come into direct contact with the coffin, and one can see at once why there would be objection in those days to Gentile pallbearers. As a matter of fact, just such an objection is recorded with regard to the funeral of the patriarch Jacob. Jacob had Gentile grandchildren. In the listing of the children of the patriarchs (Genesis 46:10 and Exodus 6:15), there is mentioned, among the sons of Simeon, "Shaul, the son of a Canaanitish woman." According to the Midrash, Jacob on his deathbed asked his sons not to permit any of his Gentile grandchildren to carry his coffin (see Genesis R. 100:2): "Be careful that no uncircumcised shall touch my bier so that the Shechina shall not depart from me."

This Midrashic statement about Jacob is nowhere codified as law; but certain Chassidim—for example, the Lubavich Chassidim—object to any non-Jew driving the hearse. The local funeral director, to satisfy their scruples, has a Jewish driver for the hearse, and at the cemetery only Jewish men open the doors of the hearse to remove the coffin. But this objection against any contact of the body by Gentiles has never been codified into law and is based solely upon the Midrashic narrative of the patriarch Jacob.

As a matter of fact, not only is it not the law that
Gentiles may not conduct a Jewish funeral, there is
even a definite requirement in the law that necessitates
their taking an active part in it. The law clearly states
(*Orah Hayyim* 526:1) that if a man dies on the first
day of a holiday, Gentiles must attend to the funeral
arrangements. This does not refer to intimate contacts,
such as washing the body. It refers to such laborious
work as digging the grave and filling it up and making
the shrouds; according to some authorities, even the
transportation of the body in the public domain must
be the work of Gentiles (see especially the opinion of
Rabbenu Tam to the *Tur,* ibid.). In fact, it is forbidden to wait until the second day in order for Jews
to perform these functions. This law of Gentile participation in the funeral goes back to the Talmud
(*Beza* 6a).

On Sabbath and on the Day of Atonement, a body
may not be moved or transported at all, and, as the
law puts it (*Shulchan Aruch, Orah Hayyim* 526:3):
"Even *Gentiles* may not move it." This clearly implies
that other than on Sabbath and the Day of Atonement
Gentiles *may* transport the body, i.e., on the first day
of the holidays, Passover, Shavuos, and Succos. Of
course, according to the *Shulchan Aruch* (*Orah Hayyim* 526:1), on the first day of these holidays Jews
also may move the body.

Perhaps the objection of this family has some vague
connection with the laws of ritual uncleanliness;
namely, they imagine that the fact that Gentile bodies
have been carried in the hearse somehow makes the

hearse ritually unclean (*tuma*) for the use of Jews. But, first of all, it must be understood that all the laws of ritual uncleanliness through contact with the dead (*tumas ha-mayss*) are no longer applicable except to Kohanim. Kohanim are still forbidden to go to cemeteries or to be in the same room with a dead body, except for certain close relatives. If the family which raised the objection was a family of Kohanim, then one could understand their extra sensitiveness on this matter. But even so they are mistaken. It is a general rule in the law that the bodies of Gentiles are ritually *clean*. In other words, they would not defile a priest ritually as the body of a Jew would do. The only way in which the body of a Gentile would be ritually unclean for a priest would be if he came into tactile contact with it. The body of a Jew is unclean for a priest not only by tactile contact but by "enclosure" (*ohel*). The priest may not be in the same enclosure, in the same room, with the body of a Jew not his close relative. But the law is clear that a Gentile body is ritually clean by enclosure (see Maimonides, *Hil. Avel.* 3:3); therefore a priest may even walk in a Christian cemetery, although the *Shulchan Aruch* (*Yore Deah* 372:2) tells him to be careful about doing it.

Therefore, even if a non-Jewish body were still in the hearse, the hearse would not be ritually defiled as an enclosure. Certainly the fact that a non-Jewish body was in the hearse yesterday has no effect on the usability of the hearse for a Jewish body.

To sum up, then: These popular notions with regard to burial tend to multiply and therefore must be

carefully watched and analyzed. The transporting of
the dead by auto-hearse is comparatively new. The
scrupulousness of Jacob that no Gentile should touch
his body goes back to the time when bodies were carried by pallbearers. Nevertheless, the participation of
Gentiles in funerals, as on the first days of holidays, is
required in the law (of course, for certain parts of the
funeral). The past presence of a Gentile body does
not affect the usability of the hearse since it is clear in
the law that the bodies of Gentiles are clean ritually
by enclosure (*ohel*).

26

SELLING PART OF THE CEMETERY

QUESTION:

> A congregation is planning to sell the unused part of its
> historic cemetery. Is this sale in accordance with the
> enactments or spirit of traditional Jewish law? (Asked
> by Louis J. Freehof, Sinai Memorial Chapel, San Fran-
> cisco, California.)

ANSWER:

THE ORIGINAL BURIAL places in the land of Israel were
in caves, in the walls of which niches were cut to receive the bodies. These caves were generally privately
owned by a family, and so there is very little public
law with regard to them. But after the permanent set-

tlement of the Jews in Babylonia, where rocky caves were not available in the sandy soil, bodies were buried directly in the ground in cemeteries. As a result, Jewish law began to discuss cemeteries as a matter of social and public policy. Since those days, a large amount of Jewish law has developed governing cemeteries, as to the ownership of cemeteries by various communities, the buying of individual graves by families or individuals, the relationship of the Kohen to the cemetery, the handling of the graves and the tombstones, etc.

In all the vast amount of law that has accumulated, I have never found a single reference to the selling of part of cemetery land. Eliezer Deutsch of Bonyhad, Hungary, one of the leading Hungarian authorities of two generations ago, and his son-in-law, Joseph Schwartz, devoted a great amount of study to cemetery questions. They became, as it were, the authorities on these matters, and many questions of cemetery law were addressed to them. Now it happens that in Eliezer Deutsch's book *Dudoye Ha-Sodeh,* which deals almost entirely with cemetery matters, the index has been amplified by Joseph Schwartz to include a listing of all the cemetery matters discussed in all of the other books of Eliezer Deutsch and also in all of the books of Joseph Schwartz himself. (By the way, Joseph Schwartz wrote a book, *Hadras Kodesh,* devoted entirely to the laws governing the *Chevra Kadisha.*) This index, which lists about 360 questions on burial, cemetery, mourning, etc., is certainly the most complete index to Jewish law on the matter. After I was asked the present question, I went through the entire list and did not find even a single passing reference to questions dealing with the sale of cemetery property. A more recent collection which deals with cemetery matters, *Mishmeres Shalom* by Shalom Cherniak, also does not have a single reference to the sale of cemetery land. This is a remarkable fact since such a vast variety of subjects in this field are discussed in the law.

Why is there not a single reference to the sale of cemetery property? One cannot argue that this is because it just never happened or, if it happened, never was recorded. With Jewish law in this matter ranging from Babylon for seventeen centuries down to our day, with Jews living in different countries under varying circumstances, sometimes at peace, sometimes forced into exile, certainly it is conceivable that in a Jewish community under oppression, or in financial straits, or forced into exile from its homes, some would entertain the idea of selling their cemetery land. Yet not a single instance of such an act is recorded. Evidently it was not recorded because it never happened. It was clearly inconceivable that a Jewish community should ever sell its cemetery, or part of it.

Besides this historical evidence, which, after all, is negative, there are many indications which point to reasons why cemetery land was not and should not be sold. In the first place, Jewish communities went to great efforts to own and maintain cemeteries of their own, and very often, when they were unable to purchase the land outright, they were greatly grieved at the fact. Authority after authority urged that cemetery land be purchased outright and not merely on a lease. This was the decision of Ezekiel Landau of Prague (*Noda B'Yehuda,* I, *Yore Deah* 89). In fact, Cherniak, in his collected code, *Mishmeres Shalom,* cites Isaac Elkanan Spector (*Ayn Yitzchok, Yore Deah* 34) to the effect that he would never consent to a burial unless the cemetery were owned outright. Often Jewish communities had to struggle against the prince or duke of the land who, for example, wanted to run a road through the Jewish cemetery. See the responsa of Samuel, the son of Ezekiel Landau, on this matter (*Shivas Zion* #62; also Moshe Feinstein in *Igros Moshe, Yore Deah* 247).

The land, once owned, was treated with great reverence. While there is no ancient law for formally dedicating cemeteries, the custom developed in recent centuries to do so; and, of course, this dedication, being a religious ceremony, added to the sanctity of the cemetery. As to respecting the cemetery, the law (*Shulchan Aruch, Yore Deah* 368) is emphatic that the cemetery must be treated with decorous behavior and great reverence. One may not commit a nuisance even outside the walls of the cemetery (see *S'day Chemed, Avelus* #134). In fact, the authorities, speaking of the attitude of respect one must have for the cemetery, compare it to the attitude of respect one must show to the synagogue itself (see Menachem Azariah Fano, a leading Italian rabbi, 1548–1620, responsum 56).

This respect for the cemetery is not confined to those parts of it in which there are graves. Even the

parts of the cemetery in which no bodies are buried
are to be respected. This is clear from the following
three instances:

1. The law in the *Shulchan Aruch* which requires
respectful demeanor in the cemetery is based on the
Talmud, *Megilla* 29a. The Talmud there speaks of not
using the grass which grows in the cemetery for cattle-
feed, for this use of it would dishonor the dead. The
grass must be burned on the spot. To this Talmudic
statement, Asher ben Yehiel, the twelfth-century authority, says that this reverent treatment (of not using
the grass for cattle-feed) applies not only to the parts
of the cemetery where the graves are, but even to parts
not used.

2. Menachem Azariah Fano (in the responsum cited
above) says very clearly that even the parts of the
cemetery that are not yet used for burial partake of
"the sanctity of the synagogue."

3. Finally, as to the sanctity of the total cemetery,
used and unused, the great Hungarian authority Moses
Sofer discusses a case in which the wall of the cemetery
needed repairs, but the prince would not permit the
wall to be rebuilt unless the community built it farther
into the cemetery, thus using up part of the cemetery
land. He urged, of course, the community to make
every effort to prevent losing land from the cemetery,
although in this case there were bodies to be disinterred. The description of the cemetery as having
the sanctity of the synagogue, with the sanctity ex-
tending not only to where the graves are but to the
whole cemetery, is clearly stated by Moses Sofer in

his responsum 335, in which he speaks about the fact that one may not sleep in the cemetery as one may not sleep in the synagogue, and he says it has the sanctity of the synagogue, and he continues: "Even not upon the grave itself but the whole place set aside for a public cemetery, [irreverent action] is forbidden with the sanctity of the synagogue." This decision of Moses Sofer is repeated in the *Pische Teshuvah* to *Yore Deah* 368, par. 1. Menachem Fano explains that the unused parts of the cemetery are deemed equally sacred with the used parts because the land was set apart by the community for the *purpose* of burial and so must be treated with respect even when there are no graves in it.

Of course, if a congregation buys a large tract of land, intending to use all or part of it for a cemetery, and the whole tract has not been in any way dedicated for cemetery purposes or specifically declared to be for cemetery purposes, then, of course, before the land is actually a cemetery, part of it can be sold and the rest dedicated as a cemetery. But if it is land already used for a cemetery by the congregation, and especially one used for generations, it is land which has "a sanctity like that of a synagogue." See also Hoffmann (*Melamed L'ho-il, Yore Deah* 125), who expressly forbids selling part of the cemetery.

To sum up: The efforts made by hundreds of Jewish congregations to protect their cemeteries against inroads and to purchase the land outright as a permanent possession, and the remarkable fact that, as far as I know, there is not a single reference in the law to any congregation selling part of its cemetery, all this would indicate the following: While there is no statute specifically prohibiting selling cemetery land, such a sale is clearly against the mood of the tradition. It is as if one would sell a room or two in the synagogue for some secular purpose.

Addendum

Since writing the above, I have come across an actual case of the sale of part of a cemetery by a Jewish community, but this case reinforces our conclusion. It is found in *Bes Yitzchok* (*Choshen Mishpot* #61), the great responsa collection of Isaac Schmelkes, rabbi of Lemburg. The incident is as follows: In the historic community of Buczacz in Galicia, the *Chevra Kadisha* sold part of the cemetery. A dispute arose on the ground that a certain member of the *Chevra* was not present and was not consulted, and therefore the sale was void. This question came to Isaac Schmelkes, who was the leading rabbi of Galicia in the year 1904. After discussing the question of whether the sale was valid or not because of the absence of this important member, he concludes definitely as follows: the cemetery can never be sold. *Magen Avraham* (Abraham Gumbiner), in his commentary to *Orah Hayyim* 153, end of par. 12, seems to indicate that while a community may not sell a synagogue in a large city, it may sell the cemetery or part of it, basing this permission upon the well-known Turkish rabbi Moses Trani (Mabit), in his responsa, III, 143. But Schmelkes indicates that the right to sell mentioned by Gumbiner, citing Mabit, refers only to the right to sell for the purpose of Jewish burial and not for nonreligious purposes—except, of course, under the same circumstances as when a synagogue itself can be sold, which is rare. Generally a synagogue in a large city may not be sold, on the ground that Jews from all over the world have contributed to it. However, Abraham Gumbiner permits the sale of such a synagogue when it is no longer used for worship. In the same way, if the cemetery were no longer used for burial, he would give permission to sell that too, with the unanimous consent of the community. But that is rare. We have no record of any old cemetery being sold, even when filled up or when Jews were exiled. So the fact remains that other than this debatable sale in the city of Buczacz, I have found no mention of any sale of cemetery land anywhere in the literature.

27

QUARRELING FAMILY AND SHIVA

QUESTION:

The deceased had lived in his sister's house. Before the funeral, a dispute arose between his sister, with whom he had lived, and his married daughter. Each insisted that the undertaker should announce that the *minyan* and the *shiva* would take place in her house. The sister based her claim on the fact that her brother had lived with her, and the daughter based her claim on the fact that she had paid for her father's funeral. Which of these two has the right to have the *minyan* and the *shiva* in her house? (Asked by Rabbi M. Robert Syme, Detroit, Michigan.)

ANSWER:

NOWADAYS, IN MANY households, Reform and also Conservative, the traditional seven days of mourning, the *shiva,* is no longer fully observed. Instead of the family remaining home for the full seven days for *minyan* services and to receive the condolences of friends, most *"shiva"* nowadays lasts for one or two days; sometimes (in fact increasingly) the family receives visitors before the funeral at the undertaker's parlor, and that is all. Thus it is somewhat surprising, what with *shiva* being observed less and less strictly, that there should be family disputes as to where it should be held. Nevertheless, I am informed that such family disputes occur with some frequency, and therefore the matter has to be gone into rather fully from the point of view of tradition. Is there any guidance in the traditional law or custom as to what is the proper locale for the *shiva?*

It is clear from the discussion in the Talmud (*Shabbas* 152a) that the proper place for the seven days of mourning is in the house of the deceased. The Talmud says that if a man dies and his survivor has no relatives left to comfort him, then ten men shall be appointed to go to his house to comfort him. Rashi says more specifically: "to the house where the man had died." This Talmudic statement is repeated as law in the *Shulchan Aruch* (*Yore Deah* 376:3), which adds that they should come to the house for the seven days of the mourning and that other people also come. Evidently, then, in case a man had no relatives, these ten members of the community were assigned for this special task, thus to ensure that there should not fail to be seven days of prayer in the house of the deceased. Isserles, in his note, says that the assigning of ten worshipers applies where a man has no close relatives to mourn for him, but if he has relatives (and friends), then of course this committee of ten is unnecessary. Then Isserles cites Maharil (the chief source of our Ashkenazic customs) to the effect that it is the established custom to have prayers with a *minyan* of ten all the seven days at the house where the deceased had died. (See also *Aruch Hashulchan, Yore Deah* 376:7, and Isserles, *Yore Deah* 384:3.)

This clear statement of the established custom, that the *shiva* and the *minyan* take place in the house where the deceased had died, is therefore referred to by Greenwald in his well-known compendium on funeral and mourning rituals, *Kol Bo* (p. 261). However, in his note (#13) justifying this custom, he refers to sources that give a rather mystical explanation of why the *minyan* and the *shiva* should take place in the house of the deceased. This mystical explanation has its roots on the same page of the Talmud, that records the custom of a fixed *minyan* in the house of the deceased. Rav Chisda comments on the following verse from Job (14:22), which speaks of a man who has died as follows: "His flesh grieveth for him and his soul mourneth over him." Although the text of the Talmud quotes only the first half of the verse, it is clear that Rav Chisda's comment is based upon the second half of the verse. He says: "The soul of a man mourns for him for seven days." The idea that a man's soul mourns for him for the seven days of *shiva* is elaborated by Samuel Edels (Maharsha, s.v. "Misabelles") in his compendium to the Talmud (ad loc.). The idea is still clearer in the legal compendium of Abraham Danzig, *Chochmas Adam* (sec. 165, par. 11), who says that the grieving soul hovers in his house for seven days; then Abraham Danzig adds that the only consolation that comes to the unhappy spirit of the departed is that prayers are recited in his house for seven days, three times a day. Substantially the same statement was made in the sixteenth century by Joshua Boaz in his Anthology of Halacha to Alfasi (*Shilte Hageborim,* at the end of chap. 3 of *Moed Katan,* p. 18 of the Vilna edition).

Of course this mystical idea of the unhappy spirit of the departed hovering in his home for seven days has a rational, psychological basis, namely, that it is in the home where the man has lived among his familiar surroundings that we are most conscious of his hovering presence, and hence this is the appropriate place for the *shiva* and the *minyan.* Thus law and folklore both agree that the *minyan* should take place in the family home of the departed.

This guideline was quite sufficient in the past, when it was generally in their own home that people died. But today it is no longer a helpful guideline since it is rather exceptional for a person to die in his home, although of course that does occur. Generally a person who dies, dies in a hospital or in a nursing home or in an old folks' home. What, then, could it mean today that the sense of his presence hovers in the house where he died? Of course if there is still a family home and if the family is still living in it, one may say that the spirit of the tradition would indicate that even though the deceased did not actually die there, the sense of his presence is still there, and it is there that the *shiva* and the *minyan* should take place.

However, there are other elements in the traditional law on this matter that must still be considered. The Talmud (*Moed Katan* 21b–22a) discusses the counting of the seven days of mourning. This count may vary, depending upon the question of when the be-

reaved relatives had heard of the death. It often occurred, when close relatives lived in different cities,
that the report of the death might come five or six
days after the burial. When the relative hears of the
death, even though it is, let us say, five or six days late,
he observes the *shiva* in his place, beginning from the
day that he heard the news. But suppose he travels to
the city where his relative had died, and there *shiva*
is already advanced three or four days before the *shiva*
which he had already begun at home, does he follow
his own counting of the seven days, or theirs? This,
the Talmud says, depends upon where the "head of the
household" (*godol ha-bayis*) is, or in the *Shulchan
Aruch* (*Yore Deah* 375:2), "the head of the family"
(*godol ha-mishpocho*). The "head of the household"
generally (there are complicating exceptions) deter-
mines the count of the *shiva*. Therefore, besides the
house where the deceased died, the presence of the
godol ha-bayis is an element to be considered in the
determining questions of the *shiva* (see also Eliezer
Deutsch, *Dudoye Ha-Sodeh* #31 and #32, par. 3).

The question, then, is exactly what is meant by
"head of the household"? This question is discussed
frequently and fully in the legal literature. One of the
latest Halachic compendia, *Mishmeres Shalom* by
Shalom Schachne Cherniak, has at least twenty-five
separate paragraphs defining the identity of the "head
of the household." All the discussions ultimately rely
upon the defintion given by the twelfth-century Spanish
scholar Isaac Ibn Gayyat in his *Sha'are Simcha* (*Avel
#268). He says that the head of the household is the

one upon whom the household depends and whom everybody follows. It may be a man or a woman. It may even be a young man, as long as he is over thirteen. Whoever is the effective leader of the household, he or she is the head of the household. The Spanish scholar Solomon ben Aderet, in his responsum #532, follows Ibn Gayyat and comes to the same conclusion. Therefore, there can be no question where the *shiva* must take place if both these criteria coincide, as they often do—namely, the house in which the deceased has died (or has lived), and the presence there of the effective head of the household. (See also the full discussion of the determinatory presence of the "head of the household" in *Aruch Hashulchan, Yore Deah* 375:9 and 10.)

However, in the specific problem mentioned in the question here asked of us, there is a special difficulty: The house in which the deceased had lived is the house of his sister, but the daughter, having paid for the funeral, must feel that, practically speaking, she could be considered the "head of the household" and therefore the *shiva* should take place in her house. Unfortunately, these conflicting claims cannot be adjudicated easily. We do not know to what extent the sister, with whom the deceased had lived, was actually the head of the household, or whether the deceased had maintained the household. Nor do we know to what extent, if any, the daughter had helped maintain her father during his lifetime. Therefore, as to this specific problem, with all the vagueness involved in it, we can only come to the following conclusion: It often happens when a family is scattered (generally in separate cities) that *shiva* is observed in a number of places simultaneously. Therefore there is no harm if our modern partial *shiva* is observed here, too, in both places. Let the undertaker not announce any specific place for the *shiva*. The close friends of the sister will call on her, and the close friends of the daughter will call on her.

While this specific case, because of the various unknown factors involved, cannot be given a definite answer, our study of the question provides an answer for more average situations. The *shiva* should take place in the deceased person's home, if there is still such a home and the family is still living in it. Otherwise (or in addition), where the effective "head of the household" is, there the *minyan* should take place.

28

GENTILE FUNERALS ON THE SABBATH

QUESTION:

Is it permissible for a Jew to participate in a Gentile funeral on the Sabbath? (Asked by Rabbi Steven L. Jacobs, Birmingham, Alabama.)

ANSWER:

YOUR QUESTION as to whether it is proper to participate in a funeral of a Christian on the Sabbath is an interesting one because it involves a balancing of positive and negative factors. First the positive factors: Is it proper for a Jew to participate in the funeral of a Christian? The answer is definitely yes. The Talmud, in *Gittin* 61a, says that we are in duty bound to visit the sick and bury the dead and comfort the mourners of Gentiles. This is confirmed as law in *Yore Deah* 151:12 and 367:1. See the whole discussion in *Current Reform Responsa,* p. 175.

The second positive factor is as follows: Granting that a Jew may participate and, in fact, is urged to help Gentiles bury their dead, etc., may he, however, go to the Gentile cemetery? One might say he could fulfill his duty at the funeral parlor or the home. To this second question the answer is also yes. The Talmud, in *Taanis* 16a, speaks of visiting the cemeteries on fast days in order to achieve the mood of penitence, and Isserles (in *Orah Hayyim* 579:3) says that on fast days, if no Jewish cemeteries are available, we may visit Gentile cemeteries.

Now as to the negative factor: What about visiting the cemetery on the Sabbath? First of all, it must be clear that it is forbidden to have the funeral of a Jew on the Sabbath. The *Tosfos* to *Baba Kama* 81a top says that the reason we may not have the funeral of a Jew on the Sabbath is because it would be shameful to the dead to violate the laws of the Sabbath in his behalf. See also *Kol Bo Al Avelus,* p. 197, par. 38. But a Gentile is not required to observe the Sabbath. Therefore there is no objection to his funeral taking place on the Sabbath. The only question is of the Jew violating the laws of the Sabbath. Strictly speaking, a Jew may not violate the Sabbath for *any* reason unless, of course, danger to life is involved. But if, for example, the cemetery were within walking distance, there would be no objection to the Jew going to the cemetery. With most less Orthodox Jews who do ride on the Sabbath, this riding would hardly be considered a sin.

One might add the question of *Oneg Shabbat,* the joy of the Sabbath, which might be marred by attending a funeral. However, if it is a close friend, the sorrow of his death is already there, and attending the funeral might even be a bit of consolation. If it is a public personality who is not a close friend (and the refusal to attend his funeral might harm the community), then no violation of the joy of the Sabbath is involved.

To sum up: Aside from the question of the Sabbath, it is a *mitzvah* to join the Gentile friends and participate in the funeral and also to go to the cemetery. If, however, the funeral is on the Sabbath, certainly an Orthodox Jew who refrains from riding on the Sabbath should not go. But as for others who do ride on the Sabbath, it would be illogical to avoid this gesture of friendship.

29

SYNAGOGUE FROM FUNERAL PARLOR

QUESTION:

Is there any objection in Jewish law to converting a building which was a funeral parlor into a synagogue? (Asked by Rabbi Sidney Wolf, Corpus Christi, Texas.)

ANSWER:

IT MIGHT MAKE some difference, if only minor, if the funeral parlor were a Gentile one, not a Jewish one. In Jewish law, one might possibly entertain a more serious objection if the funeral parlor were Jewish than if it were non-Jewish. This may seem strange; one would imagine the reverse, but the fact is this:

If the objection is based upon *tuma,* the ritual uncleanliness of the dead, then the fact is, as far as a Kohen is concerned, that Jewish bodies are unclean for him by "enclosure." That is to say, a Kohen may not go into a house that contains a dead body. But Gentile bodies are *not* unclean by enclosure, only by contact. In other words, a Kohen can go into a morgue which contains only Christian bodies, but not into one that contains Jewish bodies.

But all this assumes the actual presence of bodies in the building. Such a question as to whether a synagogue may be built or a building be used as a synagogue where there are actually bodies present has arisen in England and created a whole series of responsa.

An old church was bought and converted into a synagogue. It was discovered that in the basement of the church, going back to the days when England was still a Catholic country, the bodies of monks and others were buried in what we would call the basement. And the question arose as to whether a *shul,* a synagogue, may be in a building in which all these ancient bodies are underneath it. There were varied opinions because in that particular case, the bodies or their bones were still there.

But the case that you are asking about is one in which there are no longer any bodies, Jewish or Gentile, on the premises. So your question amounts to this: Is the fact that once there *were* bodies in the building a reason for not permitting the use of the building?

This question can be answered definitely by analogy. The law gives us a clear analogy in the case of a building used for idolatry. The question is put in this way: If idols were present and were worshiped in a building (or a room), may it be used later as a synagogue? This question, before we mention the answer, could arise in modern times and, in fact, is a modern question. The reason for it being a live question is this: While the Christian religion is not considered to be idolatrous in Jewish law, nevertheless, certain objects, such as the crucifix, would be deemed idolatrous objects. Therefore the modern form of the question is this: Suppose a room or a large enclosure contained crucifixes and was used in Christian worship, can such a room be used as a synagogue after the crucifixes are removed? The answer to this question is generally yes, because it is only the objects which are dedicated to the non-Jewish worship, but not the room or the house itself. Therefore when the objects are removed, the house or the room may be used for Jewish worship. Of course, if the building is actually dedicated, that might be another question.

Therefore, we may say that since the question of ritual uncleanliness of bodies is much less important than idolatry, if a room may be used after an idolatrous object is removed from it, then all the more is it permissible, if the bodies are removed from the building, for the building to be used as a synagogue.

30

OMISSION OF COMMITTAL SERVICES

QUESTION:

> A custom is originating in certain western congregations
> to change the form of the traditional funeral service.
> There is no funeral service in home or chapel before the
> body of the dead is removed, either for interment or
> cremation. At the cemetery (in the case of burial) there
> is no service at all. On the day of burial, or sometimes
> a few days later, a memorial service is held. This memo-
> rial service is the only funeral ritual that is observed.
> Is this custom justified by tradition? Should it be en-
> couraged?

ANSWER:

IT IS NOT TOO suprising that such a custom can arise
nowadays. There is, in many quarters, a desire to sim-
plify the entire funeral ritual and to have less and less
contact with the dead. The old tradition of the family
sitting *shiva,* seven days of mourning, and then following thirty days of half-mourning and, for a parent, a
full year of partial mourning—all this is being increasingly set aside. Many now receive the consolation of
their friends in the funeral parlor. This is, in itself,
basically unobjectionable, except that in some families

it supplants the *shiva* entirely and leads to the neglect of the whole ritual of mourning.

The avoidance of any chapel or burial ritual at the time of death will easily lead to further avoidance. If the bereaved do not participate in any cemetery ritual at the time of the funeral, they will certainly not visit the grave in later times; and if such visitation is consolatory, as it must have been, since the custom is prevalent, then these bereaved are deprived of that consolation too. And as for the departed, the bitter lament of the Psalmist is fulfilled: "I am as forgotten as are the dead from the heart" (Psalm 31:13).

The new mood of the avoidance of contact with death and bereavement may or may not be harmful. It is, of course, for the psychologists to decide whether or not this constitutes a running away from an inescapable reality. After all, the complete Jewish ritual of mourning, the full Orthodox ritual, is meant to avoid exaggerated or unmeasured grief: "The law is to diminish mourning" (*Moed Katan* 26b). On the next page in the Talmud it is stated that if a man mourns immoderately, God Himself rebukes him and says: "Are you more merciful than I am?" In fact, it is stated as a law in the *Shulchan Aruch* (*Yore Deah* 389:5) that when a man's friends rebuke him for excessive mourning, he should cease his mourning ritual. Thus it is clear that our tradition has in mind a fixed, and therefore limited, ritual of mourning and the avoidance of excess. This certainly seems to be psychologically sound. The bereaved face the fact of death, do honor to the departed as tradition requires, and when the ritual is finished, the mourner, having thus expressed himself, can now be consoled and go on with the business of living. It is a question, therefore, for psychologists to decide, whether a bereaved person who avoids all ritual of mourning does not suppress his own grief thereby and actually delay his consolation.

As far as the tradition is concerned, the present laws and customs are the result of the evolution of various observances. Originally there was a special ritual at the very moment of death. The law was that whoever was present when a person died had to make a tear in his garment (*keriah*). This was changed because it was feared that the people present at the bedside of a dying person (especially if they were not relatives) would want to avoid tearing their garments and would therefore go away and leave the dead to die in loneliness. So for that reason the *keriah* was shifted either to the graveside or to the funeral service. So the various prayers ("Blessed be the righteous Judge . . . ," etc.) which were originally said at the moment of death in the presence of the man just deceased were, likewise, moved to the funeral service or the graveside.

Just as these rituals (tearing the garments and the prayers) were always to be in the presence of the dead (first at the moment of death and later at the service), so, too, the eulogy is to be in the presence of the dead (see *Yore Deah* 344:12 and 17).

So definite was the tradition on having the various rituals in the presence of the dead that even in the case of sinful people the ritual was carried out. Basically the law (stemming from *Semachos*) was that wicked people, those who abandoned the community and those who committed suicide, were to be given no ritual at all (*eyn misaskin,* "We do not engage ourselves with them"). But even in the case of these individuals the law gradually changed, and we are required to bury them, of course, and provide *Kaddish* and shrouds. See the references on this particular matter in *Recent Reform Responsa,* pp. 118–19:

> The strictest of all codifiers is Maimonides ("Hilchos Avel") who says that there should be no mourning rites, and so forth, but only the blessing for the mourners. The Ramban, in "Toldos Ha-Adam" says that there should be tearing of the garments. The next step is taken by Solomon ben Aderet, the great legal authority of Barcelona (thirteenth century) in his responsum 763. He says that certainly we are in duty bound to provide shrouds and burial. Later authorities, as for example, Moses Sofer, in his responsa, Yore Deah 326, says that we certainly do say Kaddish; and further, he would permit any respectable family to go through all the mourning ritual, lest the family have to bear innocently eternal disgrace if, conspicuously, they failed to exercise mourning.

Thus it is clear that our Jewish tradition was rather insistent that a definite amount of ritual be carried out in the presence of the departed. Of course a memorial service in the absence of the body of the departed is proper and traditional in a case when the body is lost at sea or for some other reason cannot be found. Nor is there any objection in the tradition to a memorial service taking place after the funeral, especially in the case of honored scholars, when it was a tradition to hold memorial services in various cities, therefore obviously in the absence of the body. Also, at the end of the thirty days of mourning or on the anniversary of the death, such memorial services were held. But all these memorial services were never meant to be a substitute for the actual funeral service at the time of death.

As to the question we have raised above, namely, whether the avoidance of these rituals is sound psychologically, we may now say rather positively that the observance of these rituals *is* psychologically sound. A recent book by Jack D. Spiro, entitled *A Time to Mourn,* states the following (p. 114):

> *Expressing Grief.* Through various laws, the mourner is required to remind himself of the death of his loved object, not only for the purpose of facing reality but also to help in giving vent to his feelings. Mourning is basically an affective process which operates to relieve the tension of frustrated love impulses. But it does so only if the mourner is capable of expressing the related emotions. As Lindemann points out, one of the most serious obstacles to accomplishing the work of mourning is that "patients try to avoid the intense distress connected with the grief experience and to avoid the expression of emotion necessary for it."
>
> When an emotion is denied expression, it is not destroyed but only pushed down into the unconscious. The pressure builds up and may manifest itself in some disguised, unwholesome form. By giving vent to the affective tension caused by the frustration of his love impulses, the mourner moves on his way toward severing his emotional ties to the deceased. The dynamic energy itself, which had been consumed in the love

relationship, seeks satisfaction. Through the expression
of grief this energy is used, thus bringing emotional
relief to the mourner and gradually allaying the affec-
tive force of the love relationship. The mourner thereby
becomes capable of detaching himself from the deceased.

It is evident, therefore, that this new practice of
avoiding committal services entirely, or avoiding the
family presence if there *is* a committal service, is contrary both to tradition and to sound mental health, and
should, therefore, be discouraged.

31

THE USE OF THE CORNEA OF THE DEAD

QUESTION:

Physicians in recent years have developed a technique
of transplanting the cornea from the eyes of people
recently dead onto the eyes of the blind and thus, in
many cases, restoring their sight. Is this procedure permitted by traditional Jewish law? (Asked by Rabbi
David Wice, Philadelphia, Pennsylvania.)

ANSWER:

THIS QUESTION has received considerable discussion in
Jewish legal literature during the last two or three
years. There have been a number of articles on the
question in the Orthodox rabbinical magazine *Ha-*

Pardes, and also a full discussion of it by the late Rabbi L. Greenwald, in his *Kol Bo Al Avelus,* p. 45.

It is necessary, first, to state the general attitude of Jewish law as to the use of normally forbidden objects —blood, *trefe* meat, etc.—in case of sickness. The law is in the fullest sense liberal, and is codified in the *Shulchan Aruch, Yore Deah* 155:3. An invalid who is not in grave danger may make use in healing of all forbidden things which are forbidden by rabbinic law, but not of such as are forbidden by the stricter law of the Pentateuch itself. An invalid who is in imminent danger (*choley sheyesh bo sakanah*) may make use for his healing even of objects which are forbidden by the strictest Pentateuchal law. A man who is blind in one eye would be considered an invalid not in immediate danger, but one who is blind in both eyes would be considered one who is in imminent danger. Therefore, there is no question that a person totally blind, or in imminent danger of becoming totally blind, may make use of *anything* that may bring him healing—in this case, vision.

There is no question that the *invalid* is permitted by Jewish law to make use, therefore, of the cornea of the dead. But the question which concerns the Orthodox writers on this matter is not whether the blind man may use it, but whether *we* have the right to provide it. This is another and more complicated matter. There is, first of all, the question of *tumah,* "uncleanness." Part of the body of the dead makes unclean by contact, and since it is the procedure to have that part of the body available, the touching of it makes unclean. This part

of the question need not delay us long, since uncleanness nowadays applies only to Kohanim, priests, and
the question of uncleanness would come up only if the
doctor himself were a Kohen. But even in his case it
is not sure that he would become unclean by contact
with the cornea or the eyeball. The doubt about uncleanliness pertains to the size of the object. Does an
amount as small as this make unclean? All of those
who discuss the matter count this amount as "less than
an olive," their usual measurement for the amount that
makes unclean. If, then, human flesh less than an olive
must be buried, then it does make unclean if not buried,
the two considerations being related to each other.
Does less than an olive require burial? This is debatable. The *Minchas Chinuch* #537 (Joseph Babad)
says that even such a small amount needs to be buried;
but the authoritative commentator to the *Yad,* namely,
the *Mishne L'Melech* (Judah Rosanes), at the end of
Hilchos Avel, the second paragraph before the end of
his comment, says it need *not* be buried. Thus this is a
question which can be decided either way.

But something further is involved. If only the cornea
itself were removed from the body of the dead, it would
be easy to decide the question permissively, but the
practice is not to take out the cornea alone, but to remove the entire eyeball and keep it under refrigeration
until needed for the operation. If it *were* the cornea
alone which is removed, then the cornea, being, as its
name implies, horny, skin-like material, does *not* make
unclean by contact. The law is clear that the skin of a
dead human being without flesh does not make un-

clean, but that (practically or "rabbinically") we
merely treat it as unclean lest it be used irreverently
(Talmud, *b. Nidda* 55a). The Talmud states this pic-
turesquely: "Lest a man make floor coverings of the
skin of his parents." But essentially the cornea per se
(being skin or horn) does not make unclean and does
not need to be buried.

However, in practice the whole eyeball is taken
out and kept. The question, therefore, depends upon
whether the eyeball of the dead needs to be buried. If
it does, then not burying it involves the sin of *bal solin,*
"Do not delay the burial of the dead," and also uncleanness. Even if the whole eyeball may be considered by
measurement as being below the mandated amount that
some authorities require to be buried (i.e., less than an
olive), Greenwald in his discussion says it should be
buried for another reason. It is an *ever* (limb) of the
body, and the limbs should be buried whatever their
size. However, even that is doubtful because it is not
sure that the eye is counted among the "limbs" of the
body. The only clear indication in the older law that
the eye *is* to be counted as a "limb" which requires
burial is based upon an Aggadic statement in *b.
Nedarim* 32b. There we find an Aggadic discussion as
to why God called the patriarch first "Abram" and
then later "Abraham." The name Abram totals the
number 248, the number of the "limbs" of the body.
The Aggadic explanation of the difference is that God
referred (by the second name) to five more "limbs"
of the body, and these five are then enumerated, the
two eyes being counted among them.

But directly contrary to this Aggadic statement that the eye is to be considered a "limb" which must be buried is the Halachic implication of the Mishnah in *Oholos* 1:8, in which the limbs of the body which defile are enumerated, and the eyes are *not* enumerated among them. It is, therefore, debatable in the law whether the eye is to be considered a "limb" which requires burial.

How then can we decide when the following crucial facts are doubtful? Does a small amount less than an olive defile, and is it required to be buried? Is the eyeball to be counted legally a "limb" (*ever*) which, whatever its size, is required to be buried? The decision can only be made on the basis of general attitude to the law. An Orthodox rabbi like Greenwald, who in his introduction mentions the modern use of the cornea as another evidence of the laxity of our age, and who, therefore, feels obligated to guard against further laxities by being doubly strict, will decide all these doubts on the stricter side (*l'chumra*). Whereas a more liberal teacher, more concerned with making the law viable for our changing age, will decide these doubts leniently (*l'kula*).

My decision, therefore, which has adequate justification as seen above, is as follows: Because the *general spirit* of the law is to allow the dangerously sick to use anything otherwise prohibited, and since there is justification in the law for not even being required to bury that which is "less than an olive," and since it is doubtful whether the eye is one of the "limbs" which must be buried, and since, at all events, we have become accustomed to permit autopsies in which even limbs of the body are not buried for a while, we are justified in deciding that even though the entire eye is taken out and kept under refrigeration, the cornea may be used to restore the sight of the blind.

(This responsum was originally written for the *Central Conference of American Rabbis Yearbook,* Vol. LXVI, 1956.)

32

FUNERAL AND BURIAL AT NIGHT

QUESTION:

I have been informed that nowadays in Israel there are, rather frequently, funerals and burials at night. Is this justified in Jewish tradition? Should it be followed in the United States? (Asked by Louis J. Freehof, San Francisco, California.)

ANSWER:

WE MAY PRESUME at the outset that if the report is correct, and the funerals at night in Israel were conducted by the regular pious *Chevreh Kadisha,* the practice must surely have justification in the law and tradition. A study of the sources reveals the fact that although the matter of funerals at night has been fairly widely discussed in the legal literature, no clear-cut answer has been arrived at. Nevertheless, it can be stated that the weight of opinion, or at least of preference, is that no funerals be held at night.

Interestingly enough, the first relevant references to burial at night come from a nonrabbinical Jewish source, namely, the historian Flavius Josephus. Since he lived at the time of the destruction of the Temple, his statements reveal some of our earliest practices and attitudes. There are two relevant references from Josephus' *Antiquities*. In Bk. 4, chap. 8, par. 24, he speaks of the evil son who is put to death and adds: "Let him be buried at night, and thus it is that we bury all who are condemned to die." In other words, it was criminals who were buried at night. The second reference from Josephus is from *Antiquities,* Bk. 5, chap. 1, par. 14, speaking of the sinful Achan in the time of Joshua. He says of him: "He was immediately put to death and attained no more than to be buried at night in a disgraceful manner, as was suitable to a condemned malefactor."

Clearly, then, the older Jewish practice, at the beginning of the first century, was that criminals were buried at night. Therefore, to bury a decent person at night might involve implications as to the person's sinfulness and that there was something shameful about his life.

As far as I know, nothing further on the subject is found in the earlier rabbinic literature, in Mishnah or Talmud, except, of course, that the general law is based on Deuteronomy 21:23, and therefore the negative commandments 536 and 537 forbid the keeping of a Jewish body overnight. A person who dies must be buried the same day, as is still the Orthodox Jewish custom. The law forbidding holding the body over for the next day uses the Biblical phrase in Deuteronomy: "Thou shalt not keep him overnight" (*lo solin*), which might be understood to imply that since a person is to be buried the day he dies, and may not be kept *over-night*, it would be perhaps preferable, if he died rather late in the day, to bury him that night if there were no time sooner. Thus the law against "keeping him *over-night*" would not be violated.

But there are many objections cited in the law against burial at night, even though such burials would prevent the violation of the commandment not to keep him overnight. In *Yore Deah* 401:6, Isserles discusses the question as to whether the regular prayers for the dead, the *Tzidduk ha-din* and the *Kaddish,* should be recited if there is a funeral on the half-holidays and Succos, and at the end of that statement he says: "There are some who say that if you bury the dead at night, you may not say *Kaddish* or *Tzidduk ha-din.*" When Isserles says "There are some who say" (*yesh omrim*), it is not a mere reference to a chance observance. The phrase has some force of law and is generally taken by scholars as the preferable practice. Moreover, his statement that no *Kaddish* or *Tzidduk ha-din* (i.e., funeral service) can be said at night comes from the *Kol Bo,* a prime source of older Ashkenazic practice. Greenwald, who discusses this subject in his handbook *Kol Bo Al Avelus* (p. 188), mentions also that not only may *Tzidduk ha-din* and *Kaddish* not be said at night, but also a eulogy (*hesped*) may not be spoken at night. So if neither *Kaddish* nor *Tzidduk ha-din* nor a eulogy may be said at the night burial, the service becomes surreptitious and hasty, as if there were something to be hurried up and done with, just as in the case of the criminals who, as mentioned by Josephus, were surreptitiously buried.

The second reference in the *Shulchan Aruch* is in *Orah Hayyim* 420:2, in which, again, Isserles quotes the *Kol Bo* that *Kaddish* and *Tzidduk ha-din* are not said if there is a burial at night. Isserles's careful statement in *Orah Hayyim,* namely, "if there is a burial at night," indicates, of course, that burials *may* take place at night—that they are not absolutely forbidden. For example, Jacob Reischer of Metz (d. 1733), in his *Shevus Yaacov* (II, responsum #26), speaks of a situation in which a man died on the first day of a holiday. The second day of the holiday was a Christian holiday, and it was, therefore, impossible to bury him then. Rather than keep the body over for three days, it would be permitted to bury him at night, and so Jacob Reischer says: "If there is some special need, it is *permitted* to bury at night."

It may well have been that some communities followed the practice of permitting funerals at night. Meir Arik, the honored authority of the last generation, in his responsa work *Minchas Pittin* (*Yore Deah* 263), referring to the opinions of Isserles which recommend that no funeral be held at night, says that Isserles made his decisions having in mind those communities which do not have an established custom to permit burial at night.

To sum up: It cannot be said that it is *prohibited* by Jewish law and tradition to have funerals at night, but it is evident that there was a strong preference against such a practice. The established custom in the early days, mentioned by Josephus, that criminals were buried at night must have left the feeling that there was something shameful about such a practice. And, indeed, some of the sources mention the fact that people are less likely to come to the cemetery at night, which, again, would diminish the honor due to the dead. Also, the established custom of not saying *Kaddish* or *Tzidduk ha-din* or a eulogy at night would make the service seem hasty, secret, and not comporting with the honor due to the departed. Nevertheless there are special circumstances (calendar, etc.) which would make it necessary for such a burial to take place. In other words, under special necessity, night burial is permitted, but under ordinary circumstances, it should be avoided.

33

REMOVING THE DEAD ON SABBATH

QUESTION:

A man died on the Sabbath. The physician demanded that the body be removed at once (from the hospital?). The Jewish undertakers came and took the body to their establishment. Then an objection was raised that it is forbidden to do so on the Sabbath. What is the law on the matter?

ANSWER:

THERE IS CONSIDERABLE law on the matter of moving the dead on the Sabbath. The law is complicated in many ways. First, the question of removal involves the various premises—"private premises," "public premises," and neutral premises (*karmelis*). The strictest prohibition against moving objects on the Sabbath is from private to public premises. Then there are differences as to methods of removal: (1) by sliding the body from bed to bed—a sort of unintended moving (*min ha-tsad*); or (2) by putting a loaf of bread or a child with the body—a sort of incidental moving; or (3) by asking Gentiles to move the body. Then there is a variety of possible reasons for moving the body on the Sabbath: (1) if it is in the sun and is decomposing;

or (2) if it is in a fire and may be burned; or (3) if it is
in a shameful place; or (4) if it is in a place where it
hinders worship.

All these complications preclude a simple answer to
the question of whether it is permitted to move a body
on the Sabbath. Nevertheless, a study of the development of the law shows an increasing tendency, on the
part of the authorities, to be permissive in this matter.

The source of the law is in the Talmud (*b. Sabbath*
43b), where the method is given as to how to slip the
body (from bed to bed) out of the sun into the shade.
Then follows a discussion of what to do in case a body
is caught in a fire. Rashi, commenting, concludes that
in case of fire the body may be moved completely, i.e.,
from private to public premises. Asher ben Jehiel
agrees with Rashi (cf. his statement ad loc. and *Piskey
Horosh*). Asher's son, Jacob ben Asher, quotes his
father's opinion in the *Tur* (*Orah Hayyim* 311). Zedekiah Ha-Rofeh (13th cent., Italy), in his famous legal
work, *Shibboley Ha-Leket* (end of sec. #118), says
that if the deceased is lying in indignity in public or in a
place of ruins, he may be removed by a Gentile. If he
is not in public, but in a semi-public place (*karmelis*),
he may be removed even by Jews, because of the respect due to human beings (*mipne k'vod ha-berios*).
The fifteenth-century Germano-Italian authority Jacob
Landau ("Agur," Laws of Removal on Sabbath, p.
38a) adds an element of permission and says: If the
body is clothed, then no loaf or child is needed as ac-
companiment to the removal. Then he gives an actual
case in which Eliezer of Metz (12th cent.) permitted

the body of a Jew to be removed by Gentiles from jail (where he had died) to the house of his relatives.

From here on the law seems to grow steadily more permissive. Jacob Moellin of Mainz (14th century, responsum #65), after discussing the various restrictions, concludes, in general, that even for the needs of the living (i.e., not only for the honor or protection of the dead) the body may be moved; and that this is the prevailing custom. Moses Isserles to *Shulchan Aruch* (*Orah Hayyim* 311), where the laws are gathered, says, on the basis of earlier authorities, that you may tell a Gentile to remove the body. Eliakim Getz (rabbi in Hildesheim in the 17th cent., *Even Hashoham* #31) says that if (on a Sabbath) a man falls from a house and the body is covered with blood, he may be moved (with a loaf of bread). Solomon Kluger (cited by Greenwald, *Kol Bo,* pp. 61 ff.) permitted a body to be removed from the bathhouse on the Sabbath so that the women could take their ritual baths. His contemporaries agreed with his decision. Eliezar Spiro, the famous rabbi of Muncacz, in his notes to *Orah Hayyim* 311, permitted the body of a Jew to be removed from a hospital on the Sabbath, for fear that the doctors would perform an autopsy. He declared this decision to be the law for future procedure (*halacha l'maaseh*).

Greenwald himself (cf. *Kol Bo,* p. 61 note) wrote a responsum on this matter to the rabbi of Oklahoma City. He was asked about moving a body on the Sabbath in the summer (when the body might decompose). He permitted it to be moved. Also, if it is in the hospital, where the authorities insist that the body be removed, he permitted it to be moved. Then he added a strange, cautionary restriction—when moved, it should not be taken to the Jewish undertaking parlor, lest Jewish undertakers do the embalming on the Sabbath. Of course, we need not be concerned with the latter caution, since the undertakers can be prohibited from embalming on the Sabbath. The body can be put on ice by Gentiles.

In general the law has developed in the way that Greenwald himself describes at the beginning of his discussion: "The later authorities have frequently permitted the removal of the body on the Sabbath if there is a serious need for it." We conclude as follows:

1.   The body should preferably not be moved if there is no need to do so or no authoritative demand for it.
2.   The body may be moved if there is need, such as the summer heat, or if it was badly hurt in an accident, or if it is where it is disgraceful for it to remain, or if the medical authorities demand it.
3.   Jews may move it, but in general it is preferable that Gentiles move it.
4.   When the body is taken to the undertaking parlor, no postponable work be done on it on the Sabbath.

34

ASHES OF CREMATION IN A
TEMPLE CORNERSTONE

QUESTION:

We are in the process of erecting a temple building in Hollywood, and a question has arisen regarding the placing of an urn containing the ashes of a former member of our congregation in the cornerstone of the sanctuary or the religious school building. Is this permissible? (Asked by Rabbi Samuel Z. Jaffe, Hollywood, Florida.)

ANSWER:

THIS QUESTION has come up in different form in the law. In fact, it was the theme of a bitter discussion more than thirty years ago in England. An old church building was bought and converted to a synagogue. Later it was discovered that in its basement vault, in past centuries, there were some Christian tombs. Could this building be used as a synagogue?

The answer is based upon the question of the ritual uncleanness of the dead (*tumah*). Jewish dead are unclean in two ways: (1) if touched (*nagah*), and (2) by being in the same enclosure (*ohel*). Thus, for example, a Kohen to whom these laws apply nowadays not only may not touch the corpse of a Jew, but may not be in the same room or building with it. A Gentile body is considered unclean by touch, and therefore, for example, Kohen could not be an active pallbearer for a Gentile friend. But a Gentile body does not make unclean by enclosure; that is to say, a Kohen could be in the same room or building with the Gentile dead. Rabbi Daiches of Leeds (the grandfather of the present literary critic) gave permission to use the building as a synagogue, but only on the ground that the bodies of non-Jews are not considered as defiling with the defilement of the dead. If it had been a vault in which *Jews* had long ago been buried, there would have been no question. The building would have been unusable as a synagogue because the remnants of Jewish bodies make unclean even by being in the same enclosure (*m'tam'in b'ohel*). In other words, if Jews had ever been buried in that place, it would be utterly unusable as a synagogue.

There is, in fact, an older responsum than this one, which deals with the subject which you raise. The famous rabbi in Prague, David Oppenheim, wrote a responsum which is published at the back of the responsa collection of Jair Bachrach, rabbi of Worms two centuries ago. The question was this: They were excavating for a synagogue and they found bones. If these had been bones of Jewish dead, the land would have been unusable.

While it is doubtful whether the ashes as such bring ritual uncleanliness to a Kohen as a dead body would (cf. *Melamed L'ho-il, Yore Deah* 114), nevertheless, in a building in which the ashes of a Jew are permanently entombed, a Kohen might well hesitate to enter, because the building would seem to him to be like a cemetery. Therefore there is no doubt at all that deliberately to put the residue of a Jewish body in the cornerstone of a synagogue would be repugnant to the spirit of Jewish law. It should not be permitted.

35

PHOTOGRAPHING THE DEAD

QUESTION:

> A request was made by someone closely bereaved that the face of the dead be photographed and the photograph be sent to relatives who live too far away to come to the funeral. Is this procedure proper according to Jewish law and tradition? (Asked by Louis J. Freehof, San Francisco, California.)

ANSWER:

THE QUESTION is bound up with the broader question of whether it is proper to look at the face of the dead. In general, the law, as developed in the last century or so, is opposed even to looking upon the face of the dead. The question is comparatively new because it is only in recent years, when Jews have come into greater contact with non-Jews, that the custom of "lying in state" was borrowed by Jews. The rabbis, knowing that this is a new custom, and that it was borrowed from the Gentile environment, were, of course, opposed to it, first, by their general feeling of opposition to any novelty in old customs (Moses Sofer said: "New things are forbidden by the Torah"), and second, and more specifically, because this was clearly an imitation of Gentile practice, which is in itself a sin, a violation of the Biblical command: "Thou shalt not go in the way of their practices" (Leviticus 18:3). In this specific case, however, the rabbis opposing "lying in state" had at least two Talmudic statements on which to rest their case, and these two statements have bearing on your specific statement about photographing the dead. One statement is in *b. Horayoth* 13b, in which it is said that the mind of the beholder is badly affected (i.e., his memory weakens) if he looks on the face of the dead. The other is from *b. Moed Katon* 27a, in which the Talmud says that the faces of the corpses of the poor were covered because their suffering made the faces ugly. "Then," the Talmud continues, "they covered the faces of all [the dead] out of honor to the dead." Clearly the Talmud considers it a violation of the honor or dignity of the dead that people should stare at their faces. At all events, the custom of covering the faces of the dead is recorded as law in the *Shulchan Aruch* (*Yore Deah* 353:1).

Joseph Schwartz, who edited a rabbinic magazine, *Vay'laket Joseph,* in which many practical questions are discussed by various rabbis, chiefly Hungarian, deals precisely with your question of photographing the face of the dead. In Vol. 8, #57 and (in the next issue) #80, the question is dealt with. In #57 he raises the question himself. In #80 Rabbi Isaac Weiss of Karlberg gives his opinion. Schwartz himself, in #57, raises the general objection of the law against the living getting any benefit from the dead (*hanoas ha-mayss*). Then he raises the doubt whether mere *looking* is to be deemed a benefit (*hanoa*) to the beholder; but, he adds, the professional photographer who gets paid for doing the work is getting a benefit from the dead. Therefore a Jewish photographer should certainly not do the work if it is to be done at all. Rabbi Isaac Weiss is more definitely against the practice, and he speaks of the fact that when the great Hungarian rabbi, Judah Assad, died, a photograph was taken of his face to be distributed and sold. This was a wrong action which he properly denounces. In general, then, he is opposed to the practice.

Based upon what there is in the law on the matter, I would say as follows: The mood of the law is clearly against it, although the arguments (benefits from the dead, etc.) which are cited are not very strong. These arguments may be weak, but the feeling is strong that it ought not to be done. If, then, the person had never been photographed before, and there is no picture of him as a remembrance, there might be some justification for photographing the face of a corpse, but nowadays this is highly unlikely. Let them keep the picture of him taken in life, not the pathetic picture of the dead face; or as Rabbi Weiss said at the end of his responsum, "Let them remember his words and his good deeds." In short, while I would not forbid the practice, I would discourage it as much as possible.

BURIAL OF A SECOND WIFE

QUESTION:

> A woman in her seventies was the second wife of a man
> who died recently at the age of eighty-four. The man had
> been married before and had children by his first wife.
> At the request of his children (and evidently with the
> consent of his second wife), he was buried beside his
> first wife. Now his second wife says that she and her
> husband had twenty-five good years together and she
> also wants to be buried by his side. Should this be
> permitted? (Asked by Rabbi Philip S. Bernstein,
> Rochester, New York.)

ANSWER:

WHAT OUGHT TO BE a straightforward situation is
somewhat complicated by the need for further facts.
For example, it would make a difference whether the
second wife had been married before and had or did
not have children with her first husband. Also, it would
make a difference whether the second husband, about
whom the inquiry is now being made, was buried in a
family plot in which there are still vacant graves, or
whether he was buried in a small plot—for example,
a double grave, or in a row where one space had been
reserved for him when his first wife died. If he is not

buried in a good-sized family plot where there is vacant space, then the request of the second wife would involve disinterment, which creates further complications in Jewish legal tradition. Let us, therefore, take up the question systematically.

First of all, the more general question: Is there objection in Jewish tradition to men and women being buried side by side? Some Orthodox cemeteries nowadays follow the custom of separate rows for men and women, but the custom of separate rows has no firm basis in Jewish law. See the whole discussion in *Modern Reform Responsa,* pp. 260 ff., especially on p. 262, where Rabbi Elazar Margoshes reports that in all the historic Jewish cemeteries, in Lemberg, etc., men and women *are* buried side by side.

The second basic question is this: Does Jewish law consider that a man who marries a second time still has a family relationship with his deceased first wife (as to whether or not he should be buried by her side)? This is a moot question in Jewish law. In fact, the great Hungarian authority, Moses Sofer, says that when a man is remarried, his relationship to his first wife no longer exists. But this is not the majority opinion. The weight of legal opinion is that the first relationship still exists; that he should, for example, keep her *yahrzeit* (but not at home in the presence of his second wife). As for burial, the custom is fairly well established that he should be buried with his first wife if he had children with her. This is what was done in the case about which this question is raised, and it may be deemed to have been a proper procedure. See the specific discussion of this question in *Reform Jewish Practice,* Vol. I, p. 147. (By the way, the reference there is given to Greenwald's *Och Letsoro,* p. 145. This book of the late Rabbi Greenwald was displaced by his later and improved *Kol Bo Al Avelus.* There the question is discussed on p. 188.)

Now the specific question asked here is whether the second wife should also be buried with the deceased husband. If the second wife had been married before and had children by her first husband, then custom (though not necessarily the law) would require that she be buried with her first husband, especially if her children by her first husband request it. But if she was not married before, or had been married before and had no children by her first husband, there would be no objection to her being buried by the present husband's grave.

But one more matter is involved here: If there is no room for her to be buried by his side unless he be disinterred (which would also involve disinterring his first wife), then this cannot be permitted. In general, disinterment is frowned upon by Jewish law (as, by the way, according to civil law also, it is to be avoided). In Jewish law, disinterment may be permitted only under four conditions: (1) if the first burial was conditional, i.e., if it was carried out with the understanding that the body was to be moved later; (2) to bury a man in an already existing parental plot; (3) if the present burial place is unsafe; (4) to rebury in the Holy Land (see *Shulchan Aruch, Yore Deah* 363:1).

The answer, then, to the question should be conditionally as follows: If the woman had no children by her preceding husband, and if the burial will require no disinterment, then there is no objection in Jewish law and tradition for her to be buried by her husband's side, even though his first wife is already buried by his side.

37

DISINTERMENT FROM A CHRISTIAN CEMETERY

QUESTION:

A Jewish lad of eighteen, killed in an automobile accident in a small town in Louisiana, was buried in a Catholic cemetery with Catholic rites. The family has now moved to a city (Greenville, Mississippi) where there is a Jewish congregation and a Jewish cemetery. They are desirous of disinterring their son's body and reburying it in a Jewish cemetery. If they do this, is there any particular ritual which should be observed at the reburial? (Asked by Rabbi Allen Schwartzman, Greenville, Mississippi.)

ANSWER:

FIRST OF ALL, it is necessary to make clear that the Jewish status of this boy is not at all affected by the fact that a Catholic priest officiated with Catholic rites at his funeral. Hundreds of thousands of men and women in Spain, Marranos, were married by Catholic priests and buried by Catholic priests in Catholic cemeteries. Yet when the Marranos escaped to Jewish communities, even centuries after, their Jewish status was unquestioned as long as their mothers were Jewish. The Catholic rituals can have no status in Jewish religious law. The Jew remains a Jew. This is confirmed by scores of responsa. Therefore, in coming to their decision, the parents need not lend any weight to the fact that the boy was buried by Catholic rites in a Catholic cemetery.

Now the question is whether his body should be disturbed by disinterment. There is a large amount of accumulated law on this matter, going back to the opinion of Rabbi Akiba in the Talmud (*Baba Bathra* 155a), and the laws have reached codal form in the *Shulchan Aruch* (*Yore Deah* 363). In general, Jewish tradition is averse to disinterment. The reason for the disinclination to disinter goes back to the Talmud, where Rabbi Akiba forbade the disinterment of the body of a young man in order to settle some financial question. What was involved was whether the deceased boy was adult enough for a certain sale of property in which he had participated to be valid. Rabbi Akiba said that one must not "deface the body" for such purposes. This objection does not apply here as it did in the old days, when they buried *without* a coffin; the body would certainly have been disfigured when it was taken out of the grave. Here, the whole coffin is removed and the body is not disfigured This argument, that moving the whole coffin does *not* involve what

Rabbi Akiba called "disfiguring the dead," was used by the great authority, Chacham Zvi Ashkenazi (rabbi of Amsterdam and Hamburg, 18th cent.). There is also another objection to disinterment, but it does not apply here either, and since it is folkloristic, there is no need to go into it.

Now, from the more positive side: Is it *right* to disinter and rebury the body? The *Shulchan Aruch,* after giving its general objections to disinterment, immediately gives a series of valid exceptions under which it is proper, and even obligatory, to disinter and transfer the body. A number of these permissions apply quite directly in this case. If, for example, the family intends to have a family plot in the cemetery in Greenville, then we can say that the reburial can be permitted, because a man may be disinterred to be buried with his family. Of course, some strict Orthodox authorities would not consider it a family burying place unless the parents, for example, were *already* buried there; but we can interpret that liberally and say that he would be in the midst of his family some day. Of course, if there were close relatives of his already buried in the Greenville cemetery, even the strict Orthodox objections would fall away. As a matter of fact, Chacham Zvi Ashkenazi, whom we have cited above, deals precisely with this question (disinterring a Jew buried in a Christian cemetery) in his responsum #50, and chiefly for the reasons mentioned above, considers it a *duty* to remove the body from a Christian cemetery to a Jewish one.

As for services at the reburial, none are really required. In the very last section of the *Shulchan Aruch* which speaks of these matters (*Yore Deah* 403), it does not mention any service ritual. There is some requirement of mourning (*keriah,* etc.) for an hour, at the time when the disinterment takes place; but even with regard to this ceremony, there is no justification for requiring that it be done. The great Hungarian authority, Moses Sofer, had a decision to make with regard to *wholesale* disinterment from a cemetery which was, I believe, confiscated by the government. He actually forbade anybody to tell the various relatives when the disinterment would take place so that they should not be required to mourn. As for prayers and *Kaddish,* etc., all these are primarily for the honor of the dead and are not too strictly required. If, for example, a man would ask before his death not to have these prayers, there is considerable ground for omitting them. So they are not indispensable and are not required at reburial. Of course, if you judged that some prayers—a psalm and *Kaddish,* for example—would be of consolation to the living, there would certainly be no objection to reciting them.

To sum up: The fact that he was buried with Catholic rites in a Catholic cemetery has no bearing on the Jewish status of the deceased. The objections to disinterment based upon the danger of defacing the body (*nivvul ha-mayss*) do not apply when the body is in a sealed coffin. It is considered by Chacham Zvi, who was a great authority, that to rebury from a Christian to a Jewish cemetery is a righteous act. Finally, since in the Jewish cemetery there is a greater likelihood of his being at rest near the graves of his kin, it is certainly proper to rebury him. As for services, they are not *required,* but, if helpful, there is no objection to them.

38

DISINTERMENT OF A JEW FROM JEWISH CEMETERY FOR REBURIAL IN CHRISTIAN CEMETERY

QUESTION:

A Jewish man was married to a Catholic woman, who remained a Catholic. They have a child, who has been raised as a Catholic and is a Catholic. The man died a number of years ago, and he was buried in the Jewish cemetery in the plot of his family. His Catholic widow lives in a suburb. She is considering asking permission to have the body of her Jewish husband disinterred from his family plot in the Jewish cemetery, in order to have him buried in a Catholic cemetery in the neighborhood in which she lives. Is such disinterment permissible in Jewish law or custom? (Asked by Vigdor W. Kavaler, Pittsburgh, Pennsylvania.)

ANSWER:

THE LAWS OF THE Commonwealth of Pennsylvania (and possibly of other states also) give to a widow the right to determine in which cemetery her husband should be buried. This widow, four years ago, had decided that her husband, being Jewish, should be

buried as a Jew in the Jewish cemetery, and in the
plot of his family in that cemetery. Now she has
changed her mind and is thinking of having his body
disinterred and reburied in a Catholic cemetery. Upon
inquiry from a prominent lawyer, I have ascertained
that the law is as yet not quite clear as to whether the
legal right of a widow to determine the cemetery in
which her husband should be buried is a lifelong right
of hers, and that, therefore, she may decide to disinter
him and move him as often as she pleases; or whether,
on the other hand, having once exercised her right at
the time of his death, and having buried him in one
place, her authority over the body has now ceased.
Whichever way the law is, or will be decided at some
later time, it is certain that the courts will take into
consideration the regulations and laws of the cemetery
in which he is now buried. It is, therefore, of importance
to the courts to be aware of the regulations and laws
of the Jewish cemetery.

As a general principle, Jewish law and custom
strongly object to any disinterment at all. The body,
once buried, must be left undisturbed. This is clear in
the *Shulchan Aruch, Yore Deah* 363, which is headed:
"The prohibition of removing the dead or his bones
from their place." The first paragraph states the law as
follows: "We may not move the dead or the bones,
neither from one honored grave to another, nor even
from a less-honored grave to a more honored grave,
and certainly not from an honored grave to a less
honored grave." This basic objection is, however, modified by certain special exceptions. If, for example, the

body has been buried in one cemetery with the clearly announced intention of later removing it to another cemetery, such disinterment would be permitted. Also, it is permitted to move the body to a grave in the plot where his family is buried if the body had been buried in a separate grave, as the *Shulchan Aruch* says: "It is pleasing to a man to rest with his ancestors." It is also permitted to move a body if it is now in some neglected place where the body might carelessly be disturbed. Such a body may be disinterred in order to be moved to a cemetery which is protected. It is always permitted to disinter a body in order to rebury in the sacred soil of Palestine. Likewise, the great authority Z'vi Ashkenazi, cited in the *Pische Teshuvah* to this passage, declares that it is to the honor of the dead to be disinterred from a Gentile cemetery to a Jewish cemetery.

All these are specific exceptions to the firm general principle forbidding disinterment. Certainly, since it is deemed an honor for a Jew to be buried in a Jewish cemetery, it would not be permissible to remove him from a Jewish cemetery in order to be buried in a Gentile cemetery. Furthermore, since it is particularly "honorable" in a Jewish cemetery for a man "to rest with his fathers," and since this man is already buried in the family plot "with his fathers," it is certainly prohibited to disinter him, even to rebury him in some other Jewish cemetery. Therefore, the request of the widow to move her husband from the family plot to a Christian cemetery is contrary both to the spirit and the letter of Jewish law and custom, and it cannot be permitted.

39

HALTING FUNERAL AT SYNAGOGUE

QUESTION:

> The custom is growing in our city of detouring the funeral procession to pass the synagogue. The procession is halted at the synagogue door, and often *El Mole Rachamim* is recited there. (Asked by Rabbi Morris M. Tosk, Bayonne, New Jersey.)

ANSWER:

YOUR INQUIRY includes a number of interesting questions. Let me answer your last question first. You ask about the propriety of holding funerals in the synagogue. I have already dealt with the matter rather fully in *Reform Jewish Practice* (Vol. II, pp. 54 ff.) and have included nearly all the material.

Your other question concerns the custom of the funeral procession making a detour in order to pass the synagogue where there is often the recitation of *El Mole Rachamim*. This is a well-known practice. I have heard of the custom, although I have never participated in this type of funeral procession. Since, however, it is so well known, I thought it would be an easy matter to find a discussion of it, either in the Codes or in the books of *minhagim*. To my surprise, there is *no*

182

mention anywhere in any of the sources, as far as I could find, describing a funeral procession stopping in front of the synagogue. Why should such a well-known custom not be recorded? The only possible explanation, it seems to me, must be that the custom is not as well known or as widespread as we thought. Sometimes a custom is local in origin and therefore is not recorded. Then for some mysterious reason it becomes widespread, and one looks in vain for the expected description of the observance.

The diffusion process of a custom is exemplified in the supposed prohibition of burying a woman next to a man not her husband. The prohibition was completely unknown or disregarded in the great communities of Europe, but was followed in the province of Bukowina. Then it spread into wider observance; but you will seek in vain for a clear-cut reference to it in the codes or in the books of *minhagim*. So it may well have been with the custom of circuitous funeral processions arranged to pass the synagogue or synagogues. It spread from a local custom and has not yet had time to be permanently recorded.

Since there is no record of the widespread custom of halting the funeral procession at the synagogue, it seemed possible that this was a non-Jewish practice, or a folk practice, which found its way into Jewish life. But I inquired of two veteran undertakers, one Jewish and one Christian. The Jewish undertaker assured me that as far back as he remembers, at least half of Orthodox families ask that the procession be halted at the synagogue, and about half of them wanted the *El Mole*

Rachamim recited there. The Christian undertaker told me that he knew of no Christian custom, Catholic or Protestant, to stop the procession at the gates of the church, except, he said, for Chinese families. It is evident, then, that this custom was not learned or did not seep into Jewish life from Gentile sources, but must somehow come from Jewish sources, if only in a folkloristic way.

However, although the circuitous funeral procession seems not to be recorded as such, it has some sort of authentic origin. First of all, the law required (*Yore Deah* 343, 4) that all work in the city cease when there is a funeral. The purpose of the cessation of work was that people might accompany the funeral procession, which was an important *mitzvah*. Now, of course, if there were a regular *Chevra Kadisha* in the city, or if the city were especially large, the duty of stopping work and accompanying the funeral was eased. These laws had specific reference at the funeral procession of a rabbi or teacher. His students had to cease their work, namely, their studies. Thus the school was closed. If the deceased was a chief rabbi of the city (*av bes din*) and presumably also teacher in all the schools, all the schools in the city were closed (*Yore Deah* 444:18).

Now a rabbi's funeral should take place in or inside of the synagogue; in fact, sometimes in the synagogue itself (or at least in the *beth ha-midrash*), as will be seen in the article in *Reform Jewish Practice,* Vol. II, pp. 54 ff. (*Yore Deah* 444:19). We pass over the dispute as to whether the body of the rabbi should actually be brought in or merely that the eulogy be given

REFORM RESPONSA FOR OUR TIME

in the absence of the body. The fact remains that the funeral of a scholar was in one way or another connected with the synagogue building.

Now add to the fact that the study house, the *beth ha-midrash,* was part of the synagogue building, and since the work of study had to cease at the teacher's funeral, it is obvious that the students would participate in the procession itself or utter prayers when the procession came to the synagogue (or more specifically, to the *beth ha-midrash,* the school). So the custom was primarily to bring the body of the teacher by the school (*beth ha-midrash*), where the students were obligated to quit their studies and participate in the service.

We must take into account the fact that there is a general tendency to democratize funeral practices in Jewish life (beginning with the Talmudic decision of Rabbi Gamaliel that all shrouds should be simple). This tendency can be seen in the matter of ceasing work in the city so that the dead can be adequately attended to. At first the law was that work needed to cease only for a scholar, and then it is noteworthy that Isserles (in *Yore Deah* 361:1) says that nowadays there is not a single Jew who has not studied Scripture and Mishnah, and therefore all deserve the cessation of work and a eulogy.

Because of this desire to equalize the status of the dead, there developed in America the custom of burying more and more of the nonscholarly dead from the synagogue sanctuary itself, a practice which was bitterly objected to by the *Chochmas Adam* (158:18) and by Yudelevitch in *Bes-Ov,* V, at the end of the volume (cf., also, *Divre Malchiel,* II, 93). Perhaps because people wanted to avoid that much equalization which was against the law, namely, to have more and more funerals conducted from the synagogue itself, they were contented with at least riding by the synagogue and in some cases having a prayer recited at the door of the synagogue.

A minor spur to the development of the custom was the tradition to go to the cemetery by a roundabout way anyhow. This is based on the fact that Jacob's children took his body from Egypt to bury him in Hebron. They went by the way of the threshing floor of Attad, which was far out of the way (cf. *Minhagey Yeshurun*). Furthermore, there was an old custom to halt the coffin a number of times (although this halting took place in the cemetery), and that made it easier to develop a custom of pausing at the synagogue. For all these reasons, the custom of halting at the synagogue developed, although, as I have said, I have found no single mention of it in any of the Codes or in the books of *minhagim*.

Your final question involves the use of the prayer *El Mole Rachamim*. This prayer is entirely new (perhaps a hundred years old) but is spreading greatly in popularity. Greenwald, in his *Kol Bo Al Avelus,* says (p. 221): "The prayer *El Mole Rachamim* has greatly spread among all circles of Jews, and no one knows who is its author. It is not mentioned in any of the books of *Reshonim*." So we are dealing here with a comparatively new but beloved prayer-song, and there is no accounting for how it may have spread, nor definite requirement for when it must be sung or recited.

40

VISITING ANOTHER GRAVE AFTER A FUNERAL

QUESTION:

A number of people told me that they were told that it is improper to visit another grave after attending a funeral. Is there any basis in Jewish law or established custom for such a prohibition? (Asked by Rabbi Kenneth I. Segel, Pittsburgh, Pennsylvania.)

ANSWER:

ON THE FACE OF IT, it seems unlikely that such a rule should be well founded in Jewish law or custom. The reason is that the tendency in Jewish law is in the reverse direction, namely, not to put restrictions on the visiting of graves, but, on the contrary, to encourage frequent visits to the graves in order to pray at the graveside. The custom is recorded in the Talmud. Especially on fast days, people would go to the cemetery to pray (*Taanis* 16a), and we are also given a classic example of prayer at the grave, namely, that Caleb prayed at the grave of his ancestors to be saved from the scheming of the ten spies, who wanted to bring a derogatory report about the land of Canaan (*Sotah* 34b). Of course the rules developed that there were certain days that were preferable for visiting the graves, such as fast days, the eve of New Year and Yom Kippur; and contrariwise, to avoid going to the cemetery on happy days, such as Sabbath and holidays. Nevertheless, the *Mishmeres Shalom,* quoted by Greenwald in his *Kol Bo* (p. 166), says that if someone has a sick person in the house in whose behalf he wants to pray, he may go to the cemetery even on a Sabbath or half-holiday (*chol ha-moed*). In spite of this general permission to visit the graves for prayer, the people on their own accord have developed certain curious restrictions.

It so happens that I have answered this question before. It is found in *Reform Responsa,* p. 176. The following is the essence of that response:

> There are a number of popular ideas about visiting graves. Many of them have no validity in the law, and the scholars who discuss them, when a question is asked, usually brush them aside as without justification. For example, there is the popular belief that after the burial the grave must not be visited within a period of twelve months. This is not so. The *Tur* (#344) speaks of visits made on the seventh and the thirtieth days after burial, etc. Another idea is that if one has not visited a grave for twenty years (as could easily happen when a man emigrates to another country), it is wrong for him ever to visit that grave again. Some popular opinions hold that if one has not visited a grave for ten years, he should never visit it again. These popular opinions are brushed aside as invalid (see *Dudoye Ha-Sodeh,* 38, where other references are found).
>
> Where such ideas come from is hard to say. The one you ask about is not even referred to in any questions

that I have seen in the literature. There may be some
scholar who has dignified this popular notion with a
question, but I doubt it. Therefore it is not even widespread. I have a theory as to how this particular idea
arose. First, at a funeral you may not *step* on another
grave (*Yore Deah* 364, to the Shach, at the end of #2).
Hence, it may be that the people were discouraged from
wandering away from the grave lest they tread on other
graves. Second, there is a law (*Orah Hayyim* 224:12)
that he who sees graves must pronounce a blessing, but
that blessing must not be pronounced again if he sees
other graves within a period of thirty days. This would
seem to the people to be a discouragement from seeing too many graves in too short a time. Also, much
folklore is involved. People were afraid of "the spirit
of uncleanness," "evil spirits"; therefore they rushed
from the cemetery, pulling up grass, throwing it over
their shoulders, and washing their hands of uncleanness when they got home. So they hurried out after a
funeral.

To that responsum I might add the following source
as a possible reason not to visit other graves. In some
editions of the *Sefer Chassidim* by Judah He-Hasid,
there are appended two pages known as the will of
Judah He-Hasid. This is a collection of folkloristic be-
liefs; for example, never to build a house on land on
which no house had ever stood before; not to marry a
woman whose name is the same as your mother's name,
etc. This booklet had a very wide influence, even though
some scholars said that the "will" was meant to apply
to Judah's own descendants, not to the rest of Jewry.
Nevertheless, this folkloristic collection of customs ap-
pealed, and the booklet has had a very wide influence

on Jewish folk customs. One of the regulations in this
booklet is that one should not visit the same grave twice
in one day. This regulation was perhaps extended to
mean that one should not visit another grave after having
been to an interment.

Another possible source for this folk notion is the
rule, dating back to the Mishnah (*Berachos* 3:2) and
recorded in the *Shulchan Aruch* (*Yore Deah* 354:1;
see also Baer, *Totz'os Chayim,* p. 75), that after the
interment the people present should stand in rows to
comfort the mourners as they walk away from the grave.
Perhaps people came to feel that if they left immediately
after the interment to visit other graves, they would not
be staying at the graveside of the person just buried and
thus would be failing in their duty to comfort the
mourners. In other words, the regulation evolved to
keep the people from scattering to visit the graves of
their own relatives immediately after the funeral just
concluded.

Any or all of these may explain this custom, which,
after all, seems to have no foundation in Jewish law or
even established *minhag*. Even *Mishmeres Shalom*
(Shalom Schachne Tcherniak), who gives all the latest
laws and customs as to mourning, etc., makes no mention
of this supposed prohibition (as far as I can find)
where he discusses in great detail the laws and customs
of visiting the cemetery (V, 26–32).

41

REFORM MARRIAGE FORMULA

QUESTION:

In order to express the equal status of bride and groom
in the wedding ceremony, I have used a variation of the
traditional formula used by the groom. The groom
says, *Haray at,* etc., and the bride says, *Haray ata
mekudash,* etc. But on reflection this double use of the
formula seems to create Halachic difficulty. For example,
if according to the bride's formula the groom is now
taken by the bride, as the bride is taken by the groom,
then if a married man commits adultery, the child would
be a *mamzer,* just like the child of a married woman with
a man not her husband. Is there a way out of this
difficulty or, also, what formula could be used which
would obviate such difficulties, and yet indicate clearly
the equal status of bride and groom? (Asked by Rabbi
Mark Cartun, B'nai B'rith, Stanford University, California.)

ANSWER:

LET US IMAGINE that we would ask this question of a
leading Orthodox authority. We might ask it of Moses
Feinstein, the author of the many-volumed work on
responsa, *Igros Moshe.* Moses Feinstein is perhaps the
chief Halachic respondent nowadays in America. In
one of his responsa (*Even Hoezer* #76) he was faced

with the problem of a Jewish woman who was divorced in the courts and could not obtain a Jewish *get*. In order to spare this woman from the unfortunate status of *agunah*, he inquired about her original marriage. He discovered that she was married by a Reform rabbi. Thereupon he declared that the Reform marriage was not a Jewish marriage at all (chiefly because there were no kosher witnesses at the recitation of the formula and the giving of the ring). Since, therefore, the woman was not legally married by Jewish law, she did not need a *get* at all, and she was free to marry. A rabbi who will make so shocking a decision certainly is strict enough. If, then, we ask Moses Feinstein what are the Halachic implications of having a bride recite the formula *Haray ata,* he would laugh at the inquiry and brush it aside. From his point of view, the question has no meaning. He would consider the formula recited by the woman as a foolish invention, totally contrary to Jewish law, since by Jewish law the husband takes a wife and the woman is "acquired" (*nikniss*) of course with her consent. Therefor, if he had to give an answer at all, he would say that the question is meaningless. A formula that has no legal validity cannot possibly have any meaningful legal consequence.

In a somewhat different sense, we Reformers also tend to brush such a question aside, but from a motive different from that of the Orthodox rabbi. An outstanding example of a formula or a decision whose Halachic consequences we brush aside is in the crucial matter of divorce. We accept the full validity of civil divorce, and a woman so divorced may marry again without a Jewish *get*. This action is analogous to the situation in the question that is asked here. It, too, involves a declaration of the legal equality of men and women. In Jewish law only the man can divorce a wife, and if he is not available to do so, the woman is an *agunah,* "chained" forever. By our radical action we brought freedom to countless thousands of Jewish women all over the world.

But our action has involved grave Halachic consequences. According to Orthodox law, a woman divorced only in the courts is not truly divorced; if she marries again she is an adulteress, and the children from the second so-called marriage are *mamzerim*. Now consider how many tens of thousands of people are children of a remarriage of a woman without a *get* from her first husband. The Orthodox rabbinate could declare the entire Reform community as being under the taint or suspicion of illegitimacy (*ch'sach mamzerus*), and not only could the Reform part of Jewry be so denounced, they could do that also to Conservative Jewry, whose *get* they do not accept as valid. And as a matter of fact, there are also uncounted thousands of Jewish women who are not affiliated with Reform or Conservative Judaism who have remarried without a Jewish *get*. It is theoretically possible (if the Orthodox rabbinate dared to do so) to declare a vast section of Jewry as being under the taint of illegitimacy. Indeed, one member of the chief rabbi's *Bes Din* in England threatened to do something of that kind, but he never actually did it. Perhaps the hesitation is due to the statement in the Talmud that all Jewish families are presumed to be legitimate (*b'chezkas kashrus*) unless their status is disputed (*kiddushin* 76b and *Shulchan Aruch, Even Hoezer* 2:2). Evidently, then, they find it too embarrassing or disturbing to dispute the legitimacy of so great a section of modern Jewry.

All these deeply disturbing consequences are the result of our decision to allow a woman to remarry without a *get*. In making this decision, we have not only incurred the possibility of the unhappy consequences mentioned above, but have brushed aside the vast section of Jewish law that deals with divorce. Yet we brush all these laws aside without hesitation because there is a matter of conscience involved. We insist upon the equal status of men and women, and are willing to put aside a large section of the law and face possible unpleasant consequences.

The same situation can apply to the question asked here. Since it is a matter of conscience with us that the bride be of equal legal status with the groom, and if we use a formula to express that equal status, then if the formula possibly involve such Halachic difficulties as mentioned here in the question, then, just as in the case of the *get*, we must be willing, for the sake of conscience, to brush aside the possibilities of these Halachic consequences.

However, the questioner finds it difficult to take so outright a step and remains concerned with the possible unpleasant Halachic consequences of the use of the Hebrew formula by the bride. Perhaps this sensitiveness, this unwillingness to brush aside Halachic consequences, although a matter of conscience is involved, is due to a change in the mood of our Reform movement. Today there is a greater interest than in the past in Halacha, and therefore a greater desire to conform to it as much as possible. Hence we involve ourselves in inevitable contradictions. Here we are eager as a matter of principle to prove the equal status of bride and groom. Our declaration of their equality is totally against the Halacha. Then, when we do violate the Halacha for the sake of principle, we worry about the Halachic consequences of our action. Clearly we should do with the Reform marriage formula as we do with the Reform divorce action. We declare and live by our principle and face the Halachic difficulties involved therein.

Perhaps the difficulties mentioned in the question would be at least partially avoided if we did not attempt to use a Halachic-sounding formula (*haray ata*) for a non-Halachic action. I myself, in many hundreds of weddings (and I believe most of my colleagues too in their marriages), make no attempt to use a Hebrew Halachic-sounding formula, but instead proceed as follows: The groom recites (after the rabbi) the traditional formula, *Haray at,* etc. The bride then says (after the rabbi) the following English sentence, "Be thou sacred to me as husband according to the law of God." Thus we are not troubled by sounding Halachic when we are really in this case contra-Halachic. This procedure is also the one suggested in the *Rabbi's Manual.*

42

MARRYING A TRANS-SEXUAL

QUESTION:

> Two young men converted to Judaism. Then one of
> them underwent a trans-sexual operation, and the state
> now accepts him as a woman. May the rabbi officiate
> at the marriage of this couple? (Asked by Rabbi Gordon
> Gladstone, Middletown, Ohio.)

ANSWER:

THE INQUIRER STATES that the person who took the
operation is accepted by the state as a female. Just
what does that mean? Does it mean that the state would
issue, or has already issued, a marriage license to this
pair as a male and female couple, permitted to marry
under the laws of the state? If the state did issue a
license, or indicated that it would issue a marriage
license, to this pair, then there might be some possible
consideration for permitting the marriage or perhaps,
even, for the rabbi to officiate. But if the state has not
issued a license, then the rabbi cannot legally officiate,
and we are saved from dealing with this uncomfortable
and unpleasant matter.

Whether or not a license has been issued, let us see
what guidance tradition might offer on this trouble-

196

some question. There have been statements in the past in the Jewish tradition and the laws which deal with persons of dubious sex. There is much discussion of the *tumtum* and the *androgynous* (i.e., hermaphrodite) and also of the *ailonis,* a woman of such masculinity that she cannot be expected to bear children. There is, in fact, a whole chapter in the Mishnah (the fourth chapter of the tractate *Bikkurim*) which deals with the *androgynous,* and there are mentions in the literature of operations or changes in these various forms of incomplete sexuality, but there is no reference at all to any operation to change a person by artificial means from one sex to another. Of course the *tumtum* was an incomplete male already. This *androgynous,* or hermaphrodite, had organs of both, and the *ailonis* was primarily a female. One especially interesting reference to a sex change is cited by Abraham Ibn Ezra. In his commentary to Leviticus 18:22 (the verse forbidding homosexuality), Ibn Ezra cites Rabbenu Chananel, who says: "There are some who can make changes in the body to have the male look like a woman, but this is not possible in nature." Aside from this citation from Rabbenu Chananel, there is no real reference in our past literature to an effort toward artificial sex change. What references there are refer to persons who by *nature* are imperfect in the sexual parts of their body, or else to the mutilated (*sariss*).

However, in modern times, because of the sex-transformation operations which have been taking place recently in America, discussions have arisen in Israel dealing with the Halachic problems raised by such operations. In the latest volume of *Noam* (Vol. 16, p. 152) there is a full discussion by Abraham Hirsch on the matter. The discussion revolves around a situation somewhat different from the one in our discussion. It deals with the Halachic problems involved if, *after* a couple has lived together as husband and wife, one of the members undergoes a sex-transformation operation. In that case there are apparently two women, or two men, living together as husband and wife. The question is discussed in the article, then, whether a *get,* a divorce, must be issued. Hirsch cites an earlier author on the question, who says that the divorce must be issued because the parties are now of the same sex. But Hirsch refutes this as follows: The sex transformation is not really what the name indicates it to be. The outer body of a man may be changed to look like that of a woman, but the person is not now a woman in any essential sense. There are no womb and ovaries, and it is impossible for the so-called woman to conceive and bear children. This is a fact confirmed to me by a leading gynecologist.

Therefore the question before us, namely, whether a rabbi should officiate at the marriage of such a pair, is essentially the following: Is the new "woman" really a woman? If "she" is physically, as it is clear, only superficially a woman, then this marriage would be a marriage of two men, a homosexual marriage, to which a rabbi dare not give the honored term *kiddushin,* "sanctification," i.e., to a homosexual relationship, which Scripture calls "an abomination" (Leviticus 18:22).

However, there may be another and a more lenient way of looking at the question. This new "woman" (with internal male characteristics) may be described in the term used in the Halacha, *ailonis,* namely, a masculine woman, a woman who is masculine in voice and bearing and is unable to have children. The Talmud (in *Ketubos* 101b) describes an *ailonis* as "a woman and not a woman," a description which could fit this ex-male. As for the *ailonis,* the law is clear. A marriage between a man and an *ailonis* is absolutely valid in the law. The Mishnah on which the Talmudic discussion is based (*Ketubos* 11:6) says that if a man marries an *ailonis,* knowing she is an *ailonis,* the marriage is valid in every way. So Maimonides decides in *Ishus* 4:10. If, then, this new woman is to be deemed an *ailonis,* a marriage of a man to her might be deemed valid in Jewish law.

Therefore we have two opposite lines of guidance: one that this marriage may be considered homosexual and therefore forbidden; the other that the new woman could be considered merely a mannish woman, *ailonis,* and the marriage permitted.

How, then, shall we decide this dilemma? It would be wise to let the decision be based upon the reaction of the community to such a marriage. If the community, including the larger general community, would be outraged or cynical or derisive at a rabbi officiating at this marriage, then the Jewish community would be hurt by his action. How can the community attitude be determined? Perhaps as follows: If the state decides to issue a wedding license to the couple, then we can say that the general community fully accepts this marriage, and the rabbi may safely officiate. If, however, no wedding license is issued, the rabbi cannot officiate legally anyhow, and also has saved the community from ugly repercussions in a miserable situation.

43

MARRIAGE WITHOUT RABBI OR HEBREW

QUESTION:

> There are a number of young people these days who, for a variety of motives, prefer to compose their own marriage ceremony and also to be married without a rabbi officiating. Is a Jewish marriage valid if no rabbi officiates and no Hebrew at all is used? (Asked by Rabbi Philip Bernstein, Rochester, New York.)

ANSWER:

ONE MIGHT IMAGINE that the question of the indispensability of Hebrew in Jewish ceremonies would have been settled long ago. Yet, interestingly enough, it has been an on-going discussion from the very beginning of recorded Jewish law and continuing down to our days. Yehiel Epstein, author of one of the latest authoritative codes, *Aruch Ha-Shulchan,* (published in Vilna, 1923), makes this statement in *Orah Hayyim* 62:4: "The great teachers for the last eighty years have decided that nowadays it is forbidden to pray the

Shema and the *Tefilla* and recite the various blessings in any language except in Hebrew." Surely it is strange that in a legal tradition as ancient as ours, such a decision should have been arrived at only eighty years ago. A hundred and fifty years ago, when the Hamburg Reform Prayerbook was published, Moses Sofer, the great Hungarian Orthodox authority, forbade the use of any modern language in prayer by saying (in *Eleh Divre Ha-Bris*): "It is utterly impossible to translate the precise meaning of the Hebrew into any other language. Therefore if we recite the words exactly as the Men of the Great Synagogue ordained them [i.e., in Hebrew], then, even if we do not know their meaning, our prayer will be favorably received. This is not so if we pray in any other language."

Moses Sofer refers here to the opinion of some scholars that prayers in the vernacular must be thoroughly understood, but prayers in Hebrew need not be. However, his argument is a curious one and can only be understood against the background of the situation. He was attacking Reform, of which he was one of the great opponents, and he had to face the difficulty that the reciting of prayer is actually quite valid in any language. The law, as stated in the Talmud in *Berachos* 13a, is that we may recite the *Shema* in any language that we understand; and so it is with the *Tefilla* and all the blessings over food and the blessing preceding the *mitzvos* (cf. *Tosfos* to *Sota* 32a). This permissibility goes through all the Codes. In the *Shulchan Aruch* (*Orah Hayyim* 62:2; cf. especially *Be'er Hetev* and 101:4), it is clearly stated that all prayers and all blessings may be recited in any language. Judging, then, by the timing of the statements of Moses Sofer and Yehiel Epstein, the prohibition of the use of any other language was modern, and a reaction to Reform. But basically, any language that is understood may be used in every form of prayer.

Even the traditional marriage formula, "Be thou consecrated . . . ," need not be precise. The Talmud and the Codes (*Even Hoezer* 27:1–2) give many varieties of the marriage phrase uttered by the groom, and many of these varieties are quite valid. The *Be'er Hetev* (ad loc.) puts the situation clearly. He says: "It is our custom nowadays for the groom to say, *Haray at m'kudeshes,* etc., but it does not make much difference if the phrase is varied." Of course, the complete lack of Hebrew in a wedding ceremony deprives the ceremony of the beneficent effect of honored tradition, which unites the young couple with the marriage of their parents, their grandparents, and all of Israel. Much is lost if all Hebrew is removed from the ceremony, but it cannot be held that the marriage is invalid if the Hebrew is omitted.

As to whether a rabbi is indispensable as the officiant, this is also a matter which has gone through considerable evolution. Before going into the question of Jewish legal tradition on this matter, let us consider the situation from the point of view of secular law. I have made inquiries as to whether a man who is not a minister or a judge (a man who has not received permission from the state to officiate at weddings) has committed an offense against the law if he does officiate. The answer for the State of Pennsylvania is in the affirmative. He has violated the law and is fined fifty dollars for having officiated without permission of the state. However, the marriage at which he has officiated may nevertheless be valid as *common-law marriage*. The law may be different in other states, but before a man officiates at a wedding, it would be wise if he discovered whether in the state of his residence he is not violating the law and, also, to what extent the marriage is valid, if it is valid at all.

The situation, as far as Jewish legal tradition is concerned, is somewhat different, though actually analogous. The Mishnah and the Talmud and the later law are full of instances where valid marriage was contracted without any sort of religious ceremony at all. If a man gives a woman an object of value (more than one *peruta,* one penny) and asks her to accept this as a symbol of marriage between them, and she consents, and there are two valid witnesses present, the couple is fully and legally married according to Jewish law (cf. the references above). Therefore, basically, no officiant at all is necessary. When marriages were conducted with more ceremony, the blessings could be recited by any guest, or the recitation of them given as an honor to some special guest.

As a matter of fact, Max Grunwald, in his article in the *Jewish Encyclopedia* (Vol. VIII, p. 341), says: "Before the fourteenth century the presence of the Rabbi was not required; nor did he speak at the marriage ceremony." Unfortunately, Grunwald does not give a reference for this statement, but possibly he refers to the fact that Maharil, in the fourteenth century, in his section on marriage, describes a marriage ceremony in detail (in his city of Mainz) in which the rabbi plays a prominent part and recites the blessings. It may be that this fourteenth-century account is the earliest reference to the presence and participation of a rabbi at the ceremony.

However, in whatever century the participation of the rabbi first began, it was a natural development that this should come about. The Talmud (*Kiddushin* 6a and 13a) says that he who does not know all the details of marriage law should not have any dealings with the subject. This statement refers to the fact that the laws involved in marriage (such as forbidden degrees, periods of delay after a previous marriage, etc.) are so complex that no one but an expert should presume to answer the problems that may come up in any projected marriage. Since the rabbi was the expert in marriage laws, it was natural that he should play an important part in the negotiations preliminary to the marriage. Thus he came to participate in the ceremony itself. He recited the blessings and then, also, conducted the rest of the service.

As it was with the question of the necessity for Hebrew in the ceremony, so it is also a fact that the presence of a rabbi is not indispensable at the ceremony (except, of course, for the relevant provisions of the secular law as to the status of the officiant). Nevertheless, rabbis have been officiants at weddings for many centuries, and the Hebrew language has been used at weddings for many more centuries. Such a long tradition cannot be discarded without some spiritual or emotional loss. Certainly some of the sense of continuity with the past, which can add so much to the stability of the marriage, would be lost if a Jewish marriage were conducted without any Hebrew at all and officiated at by some friend who is not representative of the religious life of the community.

44

THE FERTILITY PILL

QUESTION:

> In recent years doctors have discovered a medicine in the form of a pill which is given to childless women and helps them to achieve fertility and even multiple births. Is such a pill, which seems to change the physical nature of the woman, permitted by Jewish tradition? (Asked by Rabbi Jonathan Brown, Harrisburg, Pennsylvania.)

ANSWER:

THE TALMUDIC LITERATURE has clear mention of medicines to prevent childbirth. They speak of "the drink of sterility" (*kos shel ikrin; Even Hoezer* 5:12), but I do not remember anywhere in the literature where there is mention of a medicine of the opposite effect, namely, a spur to fertility. Clearly such a medicine was not known to the ancients, since it is based on modern studies of glands and hormones, etc.

As to the general aim of these fertility pills, it is obvious that their purpose is in harmony with one of the central attitudes of Scripture. If there is any one blessing which God promises all through Scripture, it is the blessing of having many children. In Genesis (1:22) even animal nature, the fishes and the birds, are blessed by the Creator and mandated to "increase and multiply and fill the earth." And when Adam and Eve were created (1:28), they received the same blessing that animal nature had received, to "increase and multiply." The same blessing was given to Noah after the Flood. And when Abraham enters the land of Canaan, God's blessing to him is that his descendants will be numerous as the stars in heaven and the sands on the seashore (Genesis 22:17). When Jacob leaves home, his father, Isaac, gives him a similar blessing (28:3). In Leviticus 26:9, the awesome chapters of blessings and curses, the people of Israel is promised, if they obey God's commandment: "I will make thee fruitful and multiply thee."

Of course, it may be argued that these blessings had great meaning in the *early* days, when our earth was largely empty, but today, with the threat of overpopulation and relatively insufficient food supplies, the old blessing to "increase and multiply" might be deemed to be no blessing at all. This may well be so, but as far as the Jewish people is concerned, the situation is somewhat different than with the world population taken as a whole. Within our own lifetime, we have lost, through mass murder, six million of our brethren, almost half the Jewish population in the world. We are again a people that is "few in number" (Psalm 105:12). To us nowadays, every Jewish child is doubly precious. For us, surely, the Biblical blessing is still a blessing. For that matter, among all peoples and all religions, there are numerous families that have been unable to have children and long for children of their own. To them, in spite of the threat of world overpopulation, the Biblical blessing is a longed-for blessing, and the modern fertility pill can be the pathway to it.

All this is clear enough from the point of view of sociology, but from the point of view of Halacha, there is much to consider in the matter of the fertility pill. The commandment to "increase and multiply" is the first commandment given in Scripture. It is the first of the *mitzvos*. But strange as it may seem, it is a commandment incumbent upon *men* and not upon women (*m. Yevamos* 6:6; *b. Yevamos* 65b; *Shulchan Aruch, Even Hoezer* 1:13). This means that it is a sin for a man to remain unmarried. It is his duty to provide children. But it is no sin if a woman remains unmarried. A woman may, under certain circumstances, use preventatives against conception (*Nedarim* 35b). But it is almost impossible to permit a man to prevent his seed from being fruitful (cf. *Even Hoezer* 5:12). If a man has begotten a son and a daughter, he is considered to have fulfilled his obligation "to increase and multiply." However, even so, it is considered a sin for him not to continue to have children if he can afford to do so and is able to do so (*Yevamos* 62b and *Even*

Hoezer 1:8). But what if a woman is not fruitful? Generally the custom was, after ten years of childless marriage, for the man to divorce her and marry another (*Even Hoezer* 1:3 Isserles and *Even Hoezer* 1:14). This was indeed the custom, but it certainly was a source of sorrow. Why should efforts not be made to heal the barrenness of a woman, so that she can continue with her husband? We notice in Scripture that barren wives did not accept their fate calmly, but prayed that God would make them fruitful.

On this question as to whether a woman may resort to medical aid to become fruitful, there is some interesting discussion in recent law. Eliezer Wildenberg, in his responsa *Tsits Eliezer* (Vol. 11, pp. 105b ff.), has a long debate on this question. He cites the opinion of Menachem Mendel Paneth in his *Sha'are Zedek,* who says that barrenness is not a sickness involving physical pain, etc., for which she must seek medical aid. If a woman is barren, that is God's decree. It is part of her nature. But Wildenberg refutes this opinion (which *is* rather an exceptional one) and says, first of all, that it is an established custom in all the generations that even the leaders of the community sought the help of doctors to cure the barrenness of their wives so that they might live together and fulfill the commandment. Wildenberg cites the great Spanish scholar Solomon ben Aderet, who tells of his teacher, the physician Nachmanides, who cured Gentile women of their barrenness. It is clear that to seek a cure for barrenness (even though it is not necessarily a disease involving physical pain, etc.) is well within the approval of Jewish tradition and custom.

However, the very fact that the duty to "increase and multiply" is incumbent specifically upon the man may nevertheless make a difference in the possible permissibility of the fertility pill. Let us assume, for the sake of discussion, that there is some danger to the general system in the taking of the pill. Now if a fertility medicine were given to the man, one could say that since it is his *duty* in Jewish law to "increase and multiply," then he is justified in accepting some physical risk in order to fulfill the commandment. But since the woman is not at all mandated to "increase and multiply," why should she assume any risk at all to her general health to fulfill that which she is not commanded to fulfill?

As to the above question of danger involved, I have consulted Dr. Harold Cohen, Clinical Professor of Obstetrics and Gynecology at the University of Pittsburgh. From him I have learned the following: There is no such thing as a fertility pill given to the man (who by Jewish law is mandated to "increase and multiply"). The pill is given only to the woman (who by Jewish law has no such mandate). Furthermore, as a matter of fact, there *is* a physical danger to the woman that may be created by the fertility pill. Her ovaries may be enlarged, and there is later danger of the necessity for surgery. Therefore physicians, in every individual case, will need to balance the physical danger against the family benefit. So, too, there will

be considerable discussion in the Jewish legal literature, balancing the danger against the benefits.

So far I have found only one mention of the use
of this pill. In Vol. 16 of *Noam,* published by Menachem Kasher (p. 43 in *Kuntros Ha-refuah*), there is
mention of a *kadur heroyon,* i.e., a fertility pill. The
authority discussing this pill is concerned only with the
question whether or not it may be taken on the Sabbath. On the Sabbath, sickness involving pain or danger may receive all necessary healing. But fertility pills,
as also vitamin pills, do not involve physical pain
which requires a doctor's immediate attention—hence
the discussion of whether the fertility pill may be taken
on the Sabbath. But the very fact that the only question asked about the fertility pill was whether or not
it may be taken on the Sabbath is an indication that for
the present there is no general objection to it. On
principle there could hardly be any objection to it. The
idea of quadruplets or quintuplets was, at least on one
occasion, looked upon as a blessing. When Scripture
says (Exodus 1:7) that in Egypt "the Children of
Israel were fruitful and multiplied," the Midrash (cited
by Rashi to the verse, of *Exodus Rabba* 1:8, also
Yalkut Shimoni ad loc.) relates that "they gave birth
to six infants in one womb."

As the pill becomes more widely known, and the
discussion concerning the dangers that might be involved is dealt with, the dangers will be weighed against
the blessing the children may bring to family life. In
consideration of the fact that to "increase and multiply" is one of the premier blessings of Scripture, and

that the commandment to "increase and multiply" is a
man's primary *mitzvah,* it would seem that, although
the Talmud knows only of sterility medicine, the use
of the new fertility pill may win general, if grudging,
approval in the law. Of course, if the medicine is
someday so improved that it no longer has any harmful
side effects, then it would be acceptable to the Halacha
without any objection.

45

HYSTERECTOMY

QUESTION:

A young woman has had a hysterectomy and cannot bear
children. Her husband refuses to have intercourse with
her because this would be "spilling seed," prohibited in
the Torah. Can this actually be justified within *Halacha?*
(Asked by Rabbi Daniel Syme, New York.)

ANSWER:

THE YOUNG MAN is entirely mistaken as to the law in
this matter. First of all, while the general purpose of
marriage is to have children, nevertheless it is no longer
prohibited to a man to marry a woman who cannot
have children. See the clear statement of Isserles in
Even Hoezer 1:3. Now it would stand to reason that
if a man may marry a barren woman, it is understood
that he would have intercourse with her, and that the

intercourse in which the seed will be unproductive cannot be deemed sinful.

But we do not need to rely upon this inference, logical as it is. There is a clear statement in the law, first found in the *Mordecai* #3 to the sixth chapter of *Yevamos,* and stated with unmistakable clarity in the *Shulchan Aruch,* in the section of "spilling of seed" (*Even Hoezer* 23:5), as follows: It is permitted to have intercourse with a woman who cannot bear children (and it is not considered wasting seed) since the intercourse is conducted in the normal way. As long as the intercourse is normal, and there is no artificial barrier inserted into the womb before intercourse, there is no committing of the sin of "seed spilling."

There can be no doubt that the opinion of Isserles in *Even Hoezer* 23:5, which we have cited, applies clearly in the case of hysterectomy. This is confirmed by the chief Orthodox authority in America today, Moses Feinstein (in his responsa *Igros Moshe, Even Hoezer* #3). Rabbi Feinstein had received a request from a Chicago rabbi to endorse a permission by the Jewish court (*ma'aseh bes din*) allowing a certain man to marry another wife (without a *get* to his present wife). Rabbi Feinstein endorses the document for one of the various reasons given but rejects two of the reasons as irrelevant or invalid. One of the reasons which he rejects is that the wife has had a hysterectomy. Feinstein declares that this fact is no reason to void the marriage; and he cites precisely what we have cited from *Even Hoezer* 23:5 as proof that a man may continue to have sexual intercourse with his wife even after she has had a hysterectomy.

I cite Moses Feinstein not only because he is a prime Orthodox authority and has applied, as I did, the permission in *Even Hoezer* 23:5 to hysterectomies, but because he also gives two strong Talmudic proofs of the permission to remain married and have intercourse with a woman who has had a hysterectomy. His two proofs are as follows: The first is from the Talmud in *Yevamos* 42b. There the discussion is over the rule that a woman must wait three months after being divorced or widowed from one husband before she may marry a second. The purpose of this three-month wait is to distinguish (*havchana*) between a child of the first husband and a child of the second—in other words, to make sure of the paternity of the child. If she had waited only two months and given birth seven months after her second marriage, it would be uncertain whether the child is a nine-month infant from the previous husband or a seven-month baby of her second husband. Therefore she must wait three months between the two marriages. The discussion in the Talmud is whether or not she needs to wait the three months if she is barren. Rashi explains the word "barren" here as meaning if she has had a hysterectomy. Thus it is clear that a woman who has had a hysterectomy may (or may not) have to wait three months, but in either case, she may be married and live a normal sexual life.

The second proof cited by Moses Feinstein is also from Rashi. It is in *Ketubos* 60b. There the discussion is about the rule that a woman who is nursing a child may not remarry for twenty-four months (the period of lactation). Then a similar debate arises in the Talmud as in *Yevamos,* whether a woman who is barren must wait the twenty-four months. Rashi, evidently facing the unasked question as to how a woman who is barren can have a child and now be nursing him, explains the word "barren" as meaning that she had a hysterectomy. Therefore, whether or not she has to wait the twenty-four months, she may be married and live a normal life. Thus Rashi to the Talmud makes it clear that a hysterectomy must not prevent normal sexual relationships because in Jewish law a wife has the *right* not to be ignored in this regard.

Let me explain further the statement above that as long as the intercourse is normal, and there is no artificial barrier inserted into the womb before intercourse, there is no committing of the sin of "seed spilling." Even the rule in *this* matter offers some additional support to our conclusion with regard to a hysterectomy. Normally the law would prohibit the insertion of an obstacle (such as a diaphragm) before intercourse because that would result in what would be deemed "spilling the seed." But the law cited in a number of places (especially in *Yevamos* 12b) is that three classes of women—a minor, a nursing mother, and a woman already pregnant—*may* insert such obstacles before intercourse. In fact, Rabbenu Tam goes further than Rashi and says that these three women not only *may* use the obstacle, they *should* do so (cf. *Tosfos* ad loc.). So it is evident that there are many cases in which, during normal intercourse, the so-called spilling of seed is ignored. This applies clearly in a case of hysterectomy.

Fertilized Ovum Implant

The inquirer also asked about the new medical procedure whereby a fertilized ovum from one woman's body may be implanted in the womb of another woman. Is the host woman to be considered the mother of the child (and the child Jewish if the host woman is Jewish)?

The answer is that the status of the child depends upon the seed of his parents, the father and the mother. If there is no sin involved, the child follows the status of the father. If there is sin involved, it follows the status of the mother. (This is a rather rough statement of a more complicated rule.) Therefore, what this child is will not depend upon the host mother, who is a mere incubator, but on the status of the parents, male and female, who fertilized and provided the ovum. Artificial insemination is not the same thing because while in that case the sperm is inserted in the woman's womb, she supplies the ovum.

46

MARITAL RIGHTS OF A RAPED WOMAN

QUESTION:

If a married woman is raped, is the husband required to divorce her? What, in general, is the status in Jewish law of a woman who is the victim of a rapist? (Asked by S.S.)

ANSWER:

THE PROBLEMS, marital and legal, involved in the crime of rape are being discussed nowadays quite frequently and heatedly. This is true partly because of the general laxity of present-day morals and also because many social-minded people, and especially advocates of women's rights, protest the present treatment by the civil authorities of a woman who declares that she is the victim of rape. The charge is often made that the police question the woman in such a way as to imply that she was not raped at all but had consented to, or even encouraged, the sexual encounter. For all these reasons, it becomes rather important nowadays to analyze the status in Jewish law of a woman who is raped or who says that she has been raped.

The laws on this matter go all through Jewish legal literature, beginning with the Bible, continuing in the

Talmud, and finding permanent place in the Codes, such as the *Shulchan Aruch* and Maimonides. It becomes clear, even from a cursory reading of the material involved, that Jewish law has maintained an attitude which is precisely the opposite of that imputed to the legal authorities today. That is to say, Jewish law, from the very beginning, comes to the defense of the woman who is raped or who claims to be raped. The Bible, in Deuteronomy 22:29, says that if a man rapes an unmarried woman, he must pay a fine and then must marry her and may never divorce her. The Mishnah repeats this law in *Ketubos* 3:4. The Talmud, discussing the matter in *Ketubos* 39b, says that the rapist must pay for the pain and shame that he has caused, and must marry his victim even if she is blind or lame (or deformed). The *Shulchan Aruch,* in *Even Hoezer* 177:3, modifies this law as follows: The rapist must marry the girl provided the father and the girl both consent to the marriage. And the *Shulchan Aruch* continues that if he divorces her, he must be compelled to take her back again.

Of course, rabbinical courts today do not deal with such matters. They confine themselves to cases in civil law, such as contracts, debts, etc., but do not consider that they still have the right to deal with criminal law, such as murder, rape, etc. (see *Choshen Mishpot* #1). Nevertheless, it is the decision of the scholars that the rapist, while he can no longer be legally compelled to do so, should be pressured to marry her (of course, as the *Shulchan Aruch* says, if she consents to be married to him). (See article "Anussa" in *Ozar Yisroel*.)

All this applies to an unmarried girl who is the victim of rape. But what if the victim is a married woman? Is there any reason in the law for the husband to divorce her? The questioner has the impression that this is so. This impression has some logic since it is based upon a clear analogy, namely, that if a woman is voluntarily and definitely immoral, her husband must divorce her. The question asked here is therefore the following: Does this duty to divorce her apply to a woman who is the victim of rape? Definitely not! The Talmud in *Ketubos* 51b, discusses the matter and clearly states that if a wife is the victim of rape, she is permitted to continue as wife to her husband. The ground for this permission is the general principle in rabbinic law that a person under compulsion is forgiven whatever sin he may have committed (*onus rachmona patray*). In fact the Talmud says that if she is being raped but during the process yields and participates willingly, even then she is to be forgiven because her desire has overcome her.

So the *Shulchan Aruch,* in *Even Hoezer* 6:11, states as a law that a woman who is raped is permitted to remain married to her husband. See *Be'er Hetev,* ibid., who says it is *obvious* (*pashut*) that she is permitted to remain his wife. The *Encyclopedia Talmudis* (s.v. "Anussa") refers to some authorities who are in doubt as to whether the husband need divorce his wife. But actually their doubts concern only the question of whether the wife was really raped or not. Yet even as to such doubts, the presumption of the law is that her statement is generally to be accepted as true. Of course

if it is certain that she had been raped, then all authorities agree that the husband may keep her as his
wife.

The *Shulchan Aruch,* stating this law, adds, however, that if her husband is a priest, she is not permitted
to remain married to him. This exception is due to the
special laws of ritual sanctity that surround the priesthood. For example, it is not a sin for a woman to be
a divorcee, yet a priest may not marry a divorcee. In
other words, the priest must follow special laws of
sanctity which do not necessarily reflect upon the
character of a wife.

It is interesting that even with regard to a raped
woman and a priestly husband, there is a variation of
the law which indicates that the attitude of Jewish law
is exactly opposite to that which is imputed to present-
day authorities. This variation is found in *Even Hoezer*
6:13. If it is proved definitely that the woman was
raped, then, as has been stated, the priest may not
retain her as wife, just as he may not marry a divorced
woman. But if there is no proof, but she declared that
she has been raped, the priest *may* continue to keep her
as a wife, although after the priest dies his widow may
not marry any other priest because of doubt.

Also related to the above discussion is the question
of a captive woman. Here, too, the question rises of
Jewish women taken into captivity and the presumption
that they are raped as helpless captives. May the husband keep a captive woman after she is ransomed?
These questions are discussed in the *Shulchan Aruch,
Even Hoezer* 7, and it is clear that the slightest proof

that the woman has remained pure is accepted both for Israelite and priestly husband. See especially the famous responsum of Meir of Rothenburg in *Responsa Literature,* pp. 99 ff.

To sum up: Contrary to the alleged attitude of present-day civil authorities, Jewish law from the very beginning has always been on the side of the woman-victim. If she is unmarried, the rapist must marry her if she consents to the marriage. If she is a married woman, the husband may keep her, unless he is a priest, for priests are subject to special laws which do not reflect upon the character of the woman.

47

GENTILE MEMBERSHIP IN SYNAGOGUE

QUESTION:

The congregation in question is revising its constitution. The following statement has been proposed for the new constitution: "Any individual, not less than 18 years of age, of Jewish faith or whose spouse is of the Jewish faith, and of good moral character, shall be eligible for membership." This implies that a Gentile married to a Jew would be permitted to hold temple office as one of the rights of his membership and to participate as a voting member in all matters, including ritual. Should such a statement be included in the new constitution? (Asked by Rabbi Joseph Rudavky, River Edge, New Jersey.)

ANSWER:

I ANSWERED THIS question a number of years ago to Judge Joseph G. Shapiro, Bridgeport, Connecticut, and Rabbi Murray Blackman, Cincinnati, Ohio (see *Recent Reform Responsa,* pp. 63–66). If you lack this volume, we will gladly send you a photostat. However, it is clear that the question needs to be restudied since, as has been reported, a number of Reform congregations already have a similar provision in their constitutions. It becomes a question of considerable moment whether permission to a Gentile to become a full member is proper or not, to be encouraged or discouraged.

The very raising of the question reveals a dilemma in our American Reform Judaism as to the treatment of unconverted spouses of Jews. To Orthodox Jewry such a situation creates no difficulty. Not only would it be unthinkable in Orthodoxy that a Gentile should be admitted to membership in the synagogue, but even the Jewish spouse of an unconverted Gentile could hardly retain membership. There are many responsa which deal with the question of whether a *mohel* should circumcise the child of a Jew married to a Christian woman, or whether a person married to an unconverted Gentile should be buried in the congregational cemetery.

With us in Reform Judaism, we have long adopted the more liberal attitude to mixed marriages. We do not encourage them, of course, but we do not penalize them either. For example, the Gentile spouse of a Jew or Jewess may be buried in the family plot. We have even permitted, for further example, the father of a Gentile wife to be buried in the family plot.

As for the children of a mixed marriage, if the mother is Jewish, the children are Jewish by definition, but if the mother is Gentile, the children are Gentile. Nevertheless, even in this case, we do not require the Orthodox ritual of conversion for such a child, but we admit the child into our religious school and accept the child's confirmation as complete conversion. So, also, when a child is Bar Mitzvah, we allow the Gentile parent or stepparent to come up to the Torah.

But the dilemma is about membership. How is it possible for a non-Jew, who does not believe in Judaism and who may even be a practicing member of a Christian church, to be a member of a Jewish congregation? Would we admit any Christian, even one not married to a Jew, to join the congregation? This is not an imaginary situation. These are days of religious adventurism, in which people experiment with Buddhism, Guruism, etc. We would not think of admitting such people as members to the congregation and, thereby, into the family of Israel. Is, then, a Gentile to be rewarded with membership in the Jewish community because he has married a Jewess and remains a Christian? Can the prayers be recited sincerely by one who cannot possibly believe in the text of every blessing: "Who has chosen us," "Who has commanded us to obey" this and that commandment? For example, the membership blank of our congregation, to be signed by an applicant, reads as follows: "Believing in the liberal interpretation of Judaism and desiring to participate in the spiritual activities and purposes of a Reform Jewish Congregation, I hereby apply for membership in the Rodef Shalom Congregation." This, then, is our dilemma. We wish to be thoughtful and generous to a mixed family. We do not wish to break it up. We hope that the children will be raised as Jews.

Our concern for the *family* as a unit suggests the following provision, which you will notice gives no unacceptable privileges to a Gentile who does not wish to convert to Judaism, but protects the family of which he is a part and which we hope will be a Jewish family.

My suggestion is, therefore, that the provision should read: "Any member of the Jewish faith, born or converted to Judaism, may become a member of our congregation. In case of a mixed marriage, the family as a whole becomes a member and the membership shall be in the name of the Jewish spouse."

48

CONGREGATIONAL ABSENTEE VOTE

QUESTION:

> Many of the members of a congregation in Texas live as far as a hundred miles away from the city in which the congregation is located. These members cannot attend every congregational meeting. Often the local members call a meeting consisting of a quorum of ten or fifteen people and pass rules affecting the entire membership. This is certainly unjust to the out-of-town members. Is there not some basis in Jewish traditional law, permitting the use of the modern custom of absentee ballots, i.e., voting by mail? (Asked by Rabbi Josef Zeitin, Odessa, Texas.)

ANSWER:

METHODS OF ARRIVING at decisions in communal affairs are discussed, at least by implication, in the Talmud and in later law. The two places in the Talmud which speak of communal government are *Megillah* 26a and *Baba Bathra* 8a. Both passages speak of the right of the community (or its designated authorities) to pass laws governing the entire community. In both cases the community is designated by the term *b'nai ha-ir,* "The People of the City." There was also an administrative body called the *shiva tuvey ha-ir,* "The Seven Good Men of the City," much as we say in modern English and American law of a jury, "twelve good men and true." (Probably both phrases are influenced by the words used by Jethro to Moses, in Exodus 18:21, to describe the first governing body, "able men, men of truth," i.e., "good men and true.")

While we do not know what proportion of "the men of the city" had to be present at a decision or, for that matter, whether the leadership group needed to be unanimous, this much is certain: We know that most frequently the decision was by vote and the majority prevailed. A good example of this would be in the discussion in *Beza* 20b, where we are told that at first the members of the school of Shammai were a majority, and so they made certain decisions. Soon afterwards the members of the school of Hillel became the majority, and they made other decisions.

It is not clear how many members of the community constituted a quorum, but evidently there were times when the *entire* community needed to be present, *ma'amad anshe ha-ir.* This fact is clear from the case discussed in the Talmud (*Megillah* 26b) where Rabino asked permission from Rav Ashe to plant a crop on a site where there were some ruins of a synagogue building. He received the permission, but this decision was debatable since the sanctity of a synagogue still inheres in its ruins. However, the permission he re-

ceived to plant on the site was considered legally justified because it was given "by the seven worthies of the
city," "in the presence of the men of the city" (*ma'amad
anshe ha-ir*), which would indicate that in especially important matters no decision could be reached by any
designated administrative board without the consent of
the entire community. In fact, this is generally the view
of the law as it was developed. The *Mordecai* to *Baba
Bathra* (i.e., the passage referred to above, *Mordecai*
1:481) says that the administrators by themselves have
the right to make emergency decisions to prevent religious violations, but for all other matters they are not
permitted to make any new ordinance without the consent of all. A similar thought is expressed by Meir of
Rothenburg in his responsa (ed. Budapest, 1896; responsum #968).

The general question of majority rule or unanimous
rule is fully and ably discussed in Louis Finkelstein's
basic work, *Jewish Self-Government in the Middle
Ages*. The question we have referred to, namely,
whether the decisions by leaders or the community itself, whether by majority or unanimity, all this had to
be settled in behalf of the developing communities in
northern France and the Rhineland. See the early part
of Finkelstein's book. It seems that Rabbenu Gershom
advocated majority rule. Later Rabbenu Tam leaned
toward unanimity. And still later a compromise seems
to have been made that if the administrative board (the
seven worthies) was itself elected unanimously, then
it can make decisions without the community giving
its unanimous consent.

So it is clear from the Talmudic law, and especially from its development in the early Middle Ages, that considerable concern was felt for the rights and the voice of the entire community, although, of course, there were necessary restrictions to the requirement of unanimity, so that no one individual should be in the position to paralyze the legislation of the community by refusing to agree.

Since there is frequent reference to the *ma'amad anshe ha-ir,* the presence of the entire voting community, we may take it for granted that it is important to consider, as you felt in your letter, that we must give careful attention to the rights of the absentee members. To insist that those members who live far away must take the trouble to come to every meeting if they wish to participate is an unfair requirement and, in fact, violates the general principle of Talmudic law that "we may not make any decrees [i.e., regulations] for the community which the majority of the community cannot endure" (*Baba Kamma* 79b). In the light of the above, the motivation of the suggestion to make absentee voting possible can be considered justified by the spirit of the law.

How, then, in the spirit of Jewish practice should the principle of voting by mail be arranged for? It is possible to make enactments by unanimous or majority consent which shall govern the community. This is done by the process of congregational *haskama,* in other words, by an agreed upon ordinance. How the *haskama* works can be seen, for example, in a recently published book of responsa, *Zichron Shlomo,* the responsa of Jacob David Vilofsky (Ridbaz), a Palestinian authority of the past generation (responsum #1). The question was: Two generations ago, when the new immigration was still sparse, the community of Jaffa decreed by *haskama* that no matter how large the congregation might grow by immigration, no group in the congregation shall break off to form a separate congregation. The immigration then increased, and in spite of the *haskama,* a small group broke away and formed a separate congregation. The Ridbaz decided that the *haskama* was valid and the group had no right to establish a separate congregation. This is only one example of innumerable *haskamas* made by congregations and which are valid in governing the life of the congregation.

Therefore I suggest the following *haskama:* The rabbi and the officers (i.e., "the seven worthies") should be empowered to decide which congregational proposals are merely administrative (such as where to buy stationery, etc.) and which are actually substantive, such as deciding whether the men and women should sit together if they have hitherto been separate; whether or not to raise the dues, and by how much. In all such matters as are declared to be substantive, the entire congregation should be given an opportunity to vote by their presence at a meeting or, when necessary, by mail. This *haskama* should itself be adopted by a vote of the entire membership, present or by mail, and would be our adaption of the Talmudic principle of *ma'amad anshe ha-ir.*

49

OCCASIONAL GAMBLING AND STATE LOTTERIES

QUESTION:

What is the Halachic attitude to the man who gambles only occasionally? Also, what would be the Halachic attitude to the legalized off-track betting and lotteries instituted by the various states of the Union? (Question by Rabbi Jack Segal, Houston, Texas.)

ANSWER:

THE GENERAL TALMUDIC TERM for gambling is "those who play with cubes," i.e., dice; and the statement is made that such gamblers are not eligible to be witnesses in the Jewish court (thus the Mishnah in *Sanhedrin* 3:3 and in *Shevuos* 7:4). Of course there are other forms of gambling besides dicing; and all these other forms are meant to be included in the denunciation of gambling. It is interesting that Isaac Lampronti, the rabbi of Ferrara, Italy, in the eighteenth century, author of the great encyclopedia *Pachad Yitzchok*, discusses this question: Why do the Mishnah and the Talmud specify dicing, when they actually mean to include all other sorts of gambling? Remembering that Isaac Lampronti was also a scientific-minded physician, it is not surprising that he consulted "authorities" on this question. He says that the reason dicing is mentioned specifically is that in this particular form of gambling, it is easiest to cheat and rob one's fellow gambler by concealing another die between the fingers.

The Talmud, in discussing the law of the ineligibility of dice throwers (*Sanhedrin* 24b), says that the reason is that they do not participate in the maintenance of society (*yishuvo shel olom*). In other words, their life and their occupation have no constructive value to society. In fact, they are considered robbers; that is to say, their winnings are not earned by constructive work. Then Rabbi Judah is quoted, that this ineligibility applies only when they have *no other* occupation but gambling; but if they do have another occupation, i.e., if their gambling is only occasional and is not their main effort at livelihood, then they are quite eligible to be witnesses in the court.

The discussion then continues on to the next page, a *boraita* is quoted to the contrary effect, namely, that a gambler is ineligible to be a witness even if he is only an *occasional* gambler. But the law is not according to this *boraita;* it is according to Rabbi Judah. This is evident from the fact that the bulk of the later authorities do not declare the occasional gambler ineligible (see the *Mordecai* to this Talmudic passage, #690). So finally it is recorded in the *Shulchan Aruch* (see the laws of witnesses 34:16, in the middle of the paragraph). Thus it is clear that occasional gambling is not considered enough of a sin to make a man ineligible as a witness in the courts, as would be the case with an inveterate gambler.

Now as to the second question: What would be the attitude of the Jewish law to the legalized lotteries and off-track gambling instituted by various states of the Union? This question is hard to answer because, in general, Jewish law refrained from expressing itself as to the policies of Gentile governments, except, of course, if the policies were directed against Judaism and Jewry. This was the case of the oppressive Roman Empire, which was always referred to as "the wicked government." Of course Judaism took an attitude to specific government laws, but only insofar as they affected Judaism and Jewry. Thus there is full discussion in Jewish law of *dina d'malchuso,* government laws, as to when it is incumbent upon Jews to obey them and when not. If the government law did not interfere with our religion, if it was a law dealing purely with civil matters, taxes, etc., if the law was issued by a legitimate government, if the law applied with equal justice to all citizens and subjects, then that law of the government must, according to Jewish law, be obeyed. Other than with such government laws, Jewish law does not concern itself with the decisions of non-Jewish governments.

In the case of the new laws establishing state lotteries, these are not laws which compel action on the part of any citizen. No one is compelled to buy a lottery ticket or to bet on the races because of the government auspices. Therefore the Halacha need take no stand on these lotteries, etc., since the average Jew can completely ignore them and violates no law by so ignoring them.

Of course it may be argued that the government, by

legalizing gambling, while not compelling anyone to participate, nevertheless tempts people to participate and thereby encourages gambling. Thus the government might be deemed, according to the spirit of Jewish law, to be committing the sin of "placing a stumbling block," etc. But this would be true only if even occasional gambling were deemed to be a sin; but occasional gambling is not a sin, as has been mentioned above. Hence it would be safe to say that the Halacha takes no attitude to the lotteries established by governments. If a man ignores them, he has violated no government law. If he does play them occasionally, he has committed no sin.

50

ANNULLING RABBI'S ORDINATION

QUESTION:

Is it possible to have a rabbi's *semicha* taken away from him for reasons of moral turpitude? Have there been such cases in Jewish history? (Asked in a class of Rabbi J. B. Goldburg, Des Moines, Iowa.)

ANSWER:

THE QUESTION OF whether a rabbi can be "defrocked" is a complicated one because the meaning of ordination and the status of the rabbi have drastically changed in Jewish history. As for ordination, originally it was a mystical or spiritual transfer of sanctity by the laying on of hands. It was a process presumed to have begun by Moses, and carried on uninterrupted from ordainer to ordainee. This process ceased in the third century (although Maimonides hoped to restore it). It was, however, taken up by the Christian Church and greatly treasured as an evidence of the special sanctity of the sacraments by an ordained priest. Hence the dispute in the Church about "unbroken apostolic succession." As for us, in place of the mystical ordination, we have *hataras ho'roah*. This is popularly, but erroneously, called *semicha,* although no laying on of hands (*semicha*) is involved. Our modern *hataras ho'roah* is merely a teacher's certificate, a statement by one or a number of scholars that this person has studied and now has permission to serve as teacher, or rabbi.

It is clear that the two types of ordination differ as to their permanence inherent in the person ordained. It is hard to see how a sacred status, once bestowed, can ever be removed; but a teacher's certificate may certainly be retracted if subsequent events, for example, prove that it was given by mistake. Maimonides, in his responsum cited by David ibn Zimri (his successor in the rabbinate of Cairo), says that no one may be removed from the historic Sanhedrin once he has been appointed there. The reason for this inviolability of status in the Sanhedrin was due to the fact that no one could serve as a member of the Sanhedrin unless he had the true ordination. On the other hand, in his Code (*Sanhedrin* 17:9) he says that the head of a Yeshiva who has sinned is removed and is not restored to his position. David ibn Zimri explains it by saying that the members of the high Sanhedrin in Jerusalem could not be removed, but a teacher of the Torah may be removed.

However, there was great hesitation about the removal of a teacher or, as we would say, a rabbi. The Talmud states in two places (*Moed Katan* 17a and *Menachos* 99b) that if a teacher has sinned or has to be put under the ban, this must not be done publicly, but secretly. Resh Lakish bases this caution on the verse in Hosea 4:5, which says: "Therefore shalt thou stumble in the day, and the prophet shall also stumble with thee in the night." In other words, the disgrace that comes to the prophet is also a disgrace which comes to the people; both of them stumble together. Then Resh Lakish emphasizes the phrase "in the night" and says: "Keep the disgrace as dark as the night."

Thus, whenever it was necessary to rebuke or to punish a leader of the community, it was important to keep it quiet and so avoid public shame. Aside from the question of public shame involved, we must note that while the rabbinate is a profession, and a rabbinical position is based upon the choice of the congregation, the rabbi is considered to have a special status which gives him almost automatic tenure in his position. Note the following in the responsum on tenure in *Contemporary Reform Responsa*:

> To sum up: The general principle that "we do not degrade in holiness" (*En Moriddin Bakodesh*) stands against removal of any appointee of a congregation for sacred work. Such removal was possible, however, in

the early days when the rabbinate was not a profession. After it became a profession it is unheard of that a rabbi be removed after the formal term of three or five years mentioned in the rabbinical contract has passed.

Of course that does not mean that they were insensitive to an unworthy person functioning as a leader in public service. The Talmud (*Berachos* 32b) says that a priest who has killed somebody should not lift up his hand to bless the people, and the proof verse that is cited is from Isaiah 1:15: "When you lift up your hands, I will hide my face from you. Your hands are filled with blood." The *Shulchan Aruch* (*Orah Hayyim* 128:35), giving this as a law, says that even if the priest killed a man by accident, and even if he has made full repentance, he shall not publicly stand up to bless the people. (However, Isserles is more lenient to the repentant priest.) Thus we see that the law is, indeed, sensitive to ethical purity on the part of leadership, but it is hesitant in taking drastic steps because of the public shame involved.

The specific question asked here is whether any such cases have actually arisen. We may say theoretically that such cases must indeed have arisen, considering the complaints that are found in the literature about men who have received their rabbinate through the influence of the secular authorities. In other words, there is an awareness in the literature of unworthy men occupying the position. As to actual incidents, there are some discussions in the responsa literature. The great Hungarian authority Moses Sofer, in his responsa

(*Choshen Mishpot* 162), discusses the case of a rabbi against whom pious members of the community made a series of complaints. The first complaint was that the rabbi was not observant about hand-washing, grace after meals, etc.; the second, that he was too lenient in his decisions about *Kosher* and *Trefe*; and the third was that he gave divorce documents (*gittin*) in a city where no divorce documents should be issued. (There is an objection in Jewish legal practice to giving a *get* in a city where no legal *get* had been given before because the various spellings of the names and the status of the city on rivers were never settled, and the wording of a *get* must be precise. In the case discussed here, a well-known rabbi forbade any *get* to be written in the city where the accused rabbi lived.) As for the first two objections, Moses Sofer is doubtful whether the rabbi should be removed; but as for the third, with regard to the *get,* he states clearly that this cannot be forgiven. He says, therefore, that they should take away from him the *hataras ho'roah* because it was given to him by rabbis before they could have known the evil that he has committed (in other words, his ordination was an *ex post facto* mistake), and he says specifically: "They shall take from him completely the crown of the name of Rabbi."

On the other hand, a later responsum by the great Galician authority Sholom Mordecai Schwadron (II, #56) comes to a different conclusion (because the case was different). But it has its special interest: A rabbi of Rumanian origin was established as a rabbi in Manchester, England. He then moved to London. The

Chief Rabbi, Adler, wanted to have him removed from the rabbinate, but the Sephardic Rabbi Gaster (who was also a Rumanian) came to his defense. Schwadron discusses all the material cited above and comes to the defense of the rabbi.

In summary we may say that the rabbinate today is a profession and does not have the mystical holiness of the old ordination. Nevertheless, the rabbi's status is involved in the honor of the whole community, and therefore public disgrace is to be avoided. However, it is clear that cases came up in which scholars recommended that a rabbi be deposed. But even so, many scholars (cited by Moses Sofer, ibid.) said that the members of his community are not always to be trusted as witnesses against him because they may be motivated by hostility that has grown up between the rabbi and them. In brief, a rabbi can be deposed, as Moses Sofer says, and the title "rabbi" should not be used by such a man. Yet the cases are rare, and for the sake of the public good, they are handled with caution.

51

UNMARRIED COUPLES AND TEMPLE MEMBERSHIP

QUESTION:

There are in this community a number of couples who are living together as man and wife though not formally married. They do not consider themselves married. They are just living together. Some of them say that they expect to be married someday, and some have no such intentions. Some of them have children from this or from some previous relationship (legal or non-legal). A number of these couples have asked to join the temple, and their children (in the case of some of them) to join the religious school. The temple rules at present have provisions only for a family membership, not individual membership. Should we accept these couples as family members? (Asked by Rabbi Sheldon J. Harr, West Palm Beach, Florida.)

ANSWER:

THIS QUESTION WILL, unfortunately, come up many times and in many places. In the present state of relaxed morality, many couples are living together as if husband and wife, without any form of marriage. This is especially true in the resort areas of our country, where many people live detached from their older family ties. Besides young people who live together without marriage, there are many older, retired people who are living together and who, in order to retain their full Social Security, are not married legally. What is the status of such couples in Jewish law and also in civil law, and what should be the relation of the synagogue to them? What membership rights do they have?

It must be stated at the outset that the status of such people in the law of the various states must have a bearing upon our decision, first because we are citizens of our respective states and must respect its laws, and secondly because the laws of the state (*dina d'malchuso*) have a certain standing in Jewish law. Of course, in general, Jewish law accepts only the civil and not the ritual law or religious law of governments; for example, when some European governments forbade Jewish ritual slaughtering, Jews resisted the law. Marriage as an institution is both civil and religious. It is not a sacramental matter only, but involves many civil relationships, property, inheritance, all of which obligates the Jewish legal system to be concerned with the civil law of marriage.

I consulted a legal authority who informed me that from the point of view of the civil law, such couples are violating the laws against fornication and so are liable to punishment if any official bothered to pursue the matter. But whether punished or not, they *are* violating the law of the land. Some states have provision for common-law marriage. For a couple not formally married to have the status of common-law marriage, the parties must refer to each other and introduce each other, respectively, as "my husband," "my wife." This is not true of these couples. They do not declare or proclaim themselves husband and wife. They are just living together and so are violating the laws against fornication. And now, as in the case mentioned here, they are asking that this illegal status of theirs be acknowledged formally and publicly by a Jewish congregation by admitting them as a family couple to temple membership.

The status of such couples in Jewish law is somewhat more difficult to explain than their status in state law. As to the Jewish law involved, we must make a distinction between the ancient Jewish law and the law applicable in more recent centuries. According to the ancient law as stated in the Mishnah (*Kiddushin* 1:1), sexual intercourse in itself was one of the three ways of instituting formal marriage. If a man and a woman had sexual relations, and the man declared (with the woman's consent) that he meant this sexual act to be an act of marriage, the couple was thus formally and legally married. Thus in ancient times, if couples such as these wanted it to be so, their very living together could constitute a legal marriage. But for many centuries now this primitive form of marriage has been abolished (see *Shulchan Aruch, Even Hoezer* 26:1 and especially 26:4). Therefore these couples cannot be considered in Jewish law as married couples, but their relationship may have a certain status in the law. If a man lives with a woman without marriage, and if this is a relatively permanent relationship, and if the woman lives with him alone and not with others, she has a definite status in Jewish law. She is called a *pilegesh* (concubine).

Now having a concubine cannot be entirely forbidden in Jewish law. In Bible times the Patriarchs Abraham and Jacob and the Kings David and Solomon and many other honored Biblical characters had concubines. Of course their children were not deemed full members of the family as far as inheritance was concerned. Abraham gave gifts to the children of his concubines and sent them away, but only Isaac, his child by his legitimate wife, Sarah, was his legal heir (Genesis 25:6). Thus all through the Biblical period the concubine had a legal, if not an honored, status.

But the Biblical status of concubine has long been virtually abolished in Jewish life (see the famous responsum of the Ramban, Moses ben Nachman, in the "Responsa Ascribed" #284, in which he warns against permitting this concubinage). The Talmud (*Sanhedrin* 21a) describes a concubine as one without a marriage document (*ketuba*) and without having had a marriage ceremony (*Kiddushin*). Ramban amplifies this description as follows: She resides in the man's house, she is kept for him alone, and her children are called by his name. It is clear from this description that what he and the Jewish law call a "concubine" is what we would today call a "common-law wife." It is this sort of half-marriage which technically is permitted in Jewish tradition, even though Maimonides said that only the kings of Israel were permitted concubines (*Yad, Hil. Melachim*). All in all, it would be difficult for the later law to prohibit the common-law wife (or concubine) since, as the authorities say, all the great men in Scripture had concubines.

Yet though Scripture offers so much precedent for the common-law wife, the Ramban, while acknowledging that one is permitted to have one, nevertheless urges the rabbi who questioned him on the matter to prohibit such practice entirely lest it lead to adultery (z'nuss) and general looseness of morals (p'ritzus).

It is to be observed, however, that the couples referred to in the question have a much lower legal standing than that of concubine (common-law wife). First of all, the state from which the question comes has no legal provision for the status of common-law wife, and second, these couples say that they may be married sometime in the future but they do not claim to be married now. They are just living together. Therefore they are simply living in adultery. As Maimonides says (Ishus 1:4): "Whoever has relations with a woman without marriage incurs punishment by Torah law." So, too, Joseph Caro, in his commentary *Magid Mishna* (ad loc.), says: "Whoever has relations with a woman without intending marriage violates a positive commandment of the Torah." Clearly, then, both the civil law and the law of the Torah consider these couples to be living in violation of the law. This fact must determine the relationship of a congregation to such couples.

Let us assume that within the congregation itself there are rumors that certain members of the congregation are living together in this manner. It is not our duty to investigate every such rumor and to think of expelling such people from the congregation. They are indeed sinners, but it is a long-established principle that sinners have the right to remain in a congregation. In fact, as the Talmud says (*Kerissus* 6b), no fast day service is genuine unless sinners are included in the congregation. (See the response on homosexuality in *Contemporary Reform Responsa,* p. 25.)

Those within the congregation who are said to be sinful in this way (if such there be) are not to be deprived of the membership privilege they already have. But it is quite another matter to admit into membership nonmember couples who live openly and confessedly in violation of Jewish and civil law. Since this congregation has only family memberships, then to admit them as a family is tantamount to a public declaration by the Jewish community that those living such a life truly constitute a Jewish family and we formally acknowledge it as such. This we must never do.

It would seem to be wiser for the congregation to change its membership rules and to have, besides family membership, individual membership. A Jewish individual may join the congregation, and if he is sinful in one way or another, he *needs* the congregation. If he is notorious, the congregation may not honor him (or her) by some special status, but mere membership is the right of every child of Israel. We will do nothing to give official religious approval of the *couples* and confer on them the revered name of "Jewish family," but we will admit all Jewish individuals to membership.

As for the children, they have the full right to enter the religious school. Children of Jewish mothers, whether the mothers are married or not, are Jewish children. They may be illegitimate Jewish children if the couple is so closely related in blood as to make the union incestuous, or if the female partner of the couple is already a married woman. Only then is the child illegitimate in Jewish law. But even an illegitimate child has every right in Jewish law, including, of course, the right to a Jewish education, and our duty to educate him. The only right he lacks is to marry into a regular Jewish family. But the children of these unions, in which the union is neither incestuous nor the woman already married, are legitimate Jewish children, and without any question, it is our duty to educate them.

If the congregation will not change its rules, permitting individual membership, as I think it should, and if therefore these people cannot join the temple since we will not accept them as a family, then let them be required to pay a tuition fee for the education of their children. Whatever be their mode of life, it still is their duty, and it is also our duty, that the children receive a religious education.

52

TORAHS SOLD TO SUPPORT RABBI

QUESTION:

A congregation is losing its membership and is going to disband. The remnant will soon merge with another congregation. For some time this fading congregation had not paid its rabbi's salary, and the rabbi is now in dire need. This fading congregation has five *sefer Torahs* which the other congregation does not need, having a number of its own. May these five *sefer Torahs* be sold for the support of the rabbi (or be given to him to sell) and thus enable the fading congregation to fulfill its contract with him and to help in his need? (Asked by Rabbi Fred Pomerantz, Closter, New Jersey.)

ANSWER:

THE FIRST QUESTION involved here is whether the *Sefer Torahs,* which will now no longer be used in this synagogue, may be sold at all. Of course, *Sefer Torahs* are being sold all the time, either directly by the scribes who make their living writing them or by merchants who deal with them. However this question arises: If a *Sefer Torah* has once been used in the synagogue for the readings on the Sabbath and holidays, may such a *Sefer Torah* be sold like any other article of commerce?

Two famous authorities, Joseph Colon of Italy (15th cent. responsum #161, first ed.) and Solomon Luria of Poland (16th cent. responsum #15), both agree that once a *Sefer Torah* "has had the mantle put upon it," that is to say, once it has been used for a sacred purpose, it has now a special status (cf. the discussion in *Contemporary Reform Responsa,* pp. 106 ff.). The special status to which these authorities refer is as to the ownership of the Torah. If, for example, someone gives the *Sefer Torah* to the synagogue but says: This Torah is to remain my (or my family's) *Sefer Torah* and may be reclaimed by me, these authorities say he may *not* reclaim it once it has been used in the service. However, they do say that if he, at the time of his donation, formally declares in the presence of witnesses that this Torah will remain his property, then even if used in the service, he may still reclaim it. Therefore in the case mentioned in the inquiry it must first be clearly determined whether these five *Sefer Torahs,* or any of them, are still to be considered the *private* possessions of a certain family, or whether they actually belong to the congregation to dispose of as it wishes.

Whether they or some of them are still to be deemed private property depends upon whether this right was asserted at the time of the donation or loan or, more basically, upon the local custom as to such gifts to the synagogue. In these matters local custom, *minhag,* is the final determinant as to whether such gifts remain private or not.

Let us, then, suppose that some of these five Torahs are (by clear declaration at the time of the donation or by local custom) still deemed to be the property of certain families. In that case, may the family of the donor have the right to say: We are now willing that the Torah be sold for the benefit of the rabbi? The answer to that question is certainly clear (or at least clearly implied) in the statement of Isserles in his note to *Yore Deah* 259:2. He says: "If the local custom is such that it permits the donor to take the Torah back, then if the donor is in financial need, he may take it back to meet these needs." Clearly, then, if the donor may sell the *Sefer Torah* to meet his own needs, he may certainly sell it to satisfy the needs of the rabbi, for thereby he will also be fulfilling the additional great *mitzvah* of *zedaka*.

Let us now take the other alternative. Suppose by local custom, or by actual past purchase, these five Torahs do not belong to certain private individuals but are without question the property of the congregation. Does, then, the congregation have the same right as an individual has, namely, to sell the Torahs to meet the needs described? The *Tur* and the *Shulchan Aruch* in *Yore Deah* 259 discuss the whole question of changing the purposes or the financial currency of articles given to the synagogue. There is, of course, concern as to the varying degrees of sanctity of the various synagogue articles. But, in general, a study of this section of the law will indicate that there are two main purposes for which sacred articles may be exchanged. One is the support of the poor, and the second, the support of the study of the Torah. Both these aims are now embodied in the person of the rabbi. Supporting him is based on the assumption that the study of the Torah is being supported, and the fact that he is in dire poverty gives the congregation further right to make use of sacred objects for his support. Also, it must be stated that the contract which the congregation has with the rabbi is a solemn obligation which is incumbent upon the members of the congregation to fulfill.

Perhaps the simplest procedure would be to give the five Torahs to the rabbi if he wishes to attend to the sale. He can be relied upon to sell them to another congregation, if that is possible, rather than to a merchant. It is an established fact that each congregation is deemed to be of equal status with any other congregation. Therefore, for a Torah to move from one congregation to another can involve no diminution of its status (cf. Israel Rappaport, *Mahari Ha-Kohen, Yore Deah* #474; *Contemporary Reform Responsa,* p. 106). If, however, it is difficult for the rabbi to find another congregation which will buy them, he may, of course, sell them to a Jewish Torah merchant. If he does not wish to deal with the whole matter himself, the obligation still remains incumbent upon the members to provide for him and, if need be, by the sale of the *Sefer Torahs.*

To sum up: *Sefer Torahs,* even when they are no longer an article of commerce in stores, etc., may still be sold. A man who can maintain his claim that he still owns the Torah used in the synagogue may, according to Isserles, sell it in order to ease his poverty. If, however, the Torah is owned without question by the synagogue itself, then clearly the rights of the poor, fostering the study of the Torah, and meeting a solemn obligation of the community fully justify the sale of these five Torahs.

53

GENTILE PRESIDENT FOR SISTERHOOD

QUESTION:

Ours is a Reform Jewish congregation. A Gentile woman has been vice-president of our sisterhood. She has reared two children as Jewish and kept a Jewish home and worked with great devotion for the temple. May she become president of our sisterhood? (Asked by Rabbi R.J.B.)

ANSWER:

FIRST OF ALL, it must be stated that the congregation and the sisterhood should be grateful to this lady for her years of devoted work for the temple. This needs to be stated because some might imagine that a non-Jew cannot (and may not) properly serve a Jewish congregation. This is not so. The Bible in Isaiah 56:7 speaks of the offerings of non-Jews, which are received "favorably upon Mine altar." The thought of this Biblical verse is carried on in the Halacha. Provision was constantly made while the Temple was in existence for sacrificial gifts from Gentiles to be accepted and offered.

However, beyond her services, which are to be received gratefully, the question now comes as to whether she may be placed in a position of such leadership as will enable her to help determine the policies of the congregation. This is especially true in congregations in which the presidents of the sisterhoods are *ex officio* members of the temple boards. But even if this *ex officio* membership is not the rule in your congregation, the president of the sisterhood as such has authoritative standing and helps to determine congregational policy. Is such a situation bearable from the point of view of Jewish tradition?

It may seem at first that Jewish tradition can have no bearing on this problem because sisterhoods, as separate organizations with officers, were unknown in the Jewish past. But actually there is a relevant attitude revealed in the Jewish legal tradition. This is because the legal tradition worked by analogy, and there is a definite analogy which is applied in the law to congregational officers. This analogy is derived from the Biblical law in Deuteronomy 17:15 as to the appointment of a king: "One from among thy brethren thou shalt set king over thee. Thou mayest not put a foreigner [i.e., a non-Jew] over thee who is not thy brother." The Talmud, in *Yevamos* 45b, applies this to the appointment of *any* congregational officer, and the law then is stated that a man was properly appointed as officer because at least his mother was Jewish. Then the Talmud states it as a general principle that *all* communal appointments of authority must be "from amongst our brothers." The proof verse is the verse which I have cited

from Deuteronomy. This is embodied in the law in
Maimonides, *Hilchos Melachim* 1:4.

I do not know *why* this lady has refused to be converted after all these years of devoted work to a Jewish
congregation. She may very well have good reasons for
her refusal, but nevertheless her refusal has a practical
effect nowadays. We are living through a time in which
mixed marriages have increased. We would all prefer
it if the Gentile partner would become Jewish so that
we can have a family of unified faith. This is what we
would like to achieve with all intermarriages. But if
the president of the sisterhood herself has consistently
refused to become Jewish (whatever her good reasons
may be), her very presence as president would be an
obstacle to one of the important goals of the congregation.

Thus it is clear that the Jewish legal tradition against
appointing a non-Jew to a position of congregational
authority and influence has, also, practical importance
today.

54

TESTIFYING AGAINST A FELLOW JEW IN CIVIL COURTS

QUESTION:

Two rabbis representing a yeshiva were called upon to testify before a grand jury investigating corruption in the state's nursing home industry. The alleged scheme to defraud the state involved certain donations to the yeshiva by a supplier for the nursing home. The rabbis refused to reveal the names of the donors on the ground that the Jewish religion forbids handing over a Jew to a non-Jewish court (*mesira*). Is this refusal to reveal the names of the contributors to their yeshiva justified in Jewish law and tradition? (Asked by Rabbi H., New York.)

ANSWER:

LET US FIRST CONSIDER whether the yeshiva should have accepted such donations from people suspected of cheating the government. The question is not irrelevant because if the yeshiva was *wrong* in accepting these donations, then they should not hesitate and should say so and reveal the donors. Men who cheat the government out of monies that are justly due to the government are described in the law as *gazlanim,* malefactors (see *Choshen Mishpot* 369:6, also *Tur*), and in 369:3 it is stated that we are forbidden to enjoy any benefit from a *gazlan*, a malefactor. Of course it may be argued that these men have not yet been convicted (though some of them have been convicted). Nevertheless, Isserles adds there that it is forbidden to benefit from him even if he is just presumed to be, or probably is, one who has cheated the government (*she-huchzak m'mono shebo m'gezelo*). In other words, considering the whole complex of events, there is enough ground, at least for *suspicion,* that the yeshiva should have refused to benefit from such schemes. Since, therefore, the acceptance of the money is frowned upon by the spirit of Jewish law, the representatives of the yeshiva cannot claim complete innocence and clear conscience. They should be willing now to admit error and make full revelation.

Behind the fact that those who gave those donations as part of the defrauding scheme are to be deemed malefactors for having cheated the government, is the larger question of *dina d'malchuso.* Whenever *dina d'malchuso* properly applies, then it becomes a mandate of Jewish law that the laws of the government be obeyed. Of course *dina d'malchuso* does not apply in ritual matters. If a government forbade us to follow the laws of kosher slaughtering (as some governments often did), such *dina d'malchuso* must be resisted, but if it is a matter of government taxes and other civil matters, then Jewish law bids us obey. There is one moral restriction. Even in cases of civil law, it is not necessarily always incumbent upon us to obey. Only if the civil law applies equally to all citizens in matters of coinage value, taxes, etc., only then is *dina d'mal-chuso* operative and we are obligated by Jewish law to obey the government (see also *Tur, Choshen Mishpot* 369, end of sec.).

It certainly is incontrovertible that the laws of Medicare, of income tax, and of Social Security are the decisions of a just government applying equally to all citizens. Therefore it is our *religious* duty to obey those laws. Those who violate these laws violate a mandate of Jewish law thereby and are not to be protected.

The judge made the statement (as given in the *Law Journal*) "that to allow a prospective grand jury witness to excuse his failure to appear or testify because of his religious belief would be to make the professed doctrine of religious belief superior to the law of the land, and in effect to permit every citizen to become a law unto himself." The judge should be answered as follows: In all matters of civil law where the laws are just and apply equally to all citizens, our Jewish law puts upon us the duty to obey it.

In this particular case, another important element is involved. These witnesses are not merely *invited* to testify. They are *ordered* to testify under penalty. If they refuse to testify they are liable to fine or imprisonment. Therefore they are now under the special category of *moser b'ohnes*. One is permitted to testify to a non-Jewish court to save oneself from danger (see *Tur, Choshen Mishpot* 388 near the beginning and the *Bes Josef;* also *Yad, Hilchos Chovel* 8:2). In other words, if these witnesses, by revealing the names asked for, can save themselves from danger, they are permitted by Jewish law to reveal the names. For further references on this question of *moser b'ohnes,* see *Pachad Yitzchok* under that heading.

There is one further matter involved, and that is stated by Isserles to *Choshen Mishpot* 388:11. He says that if a man is engaged in forgeries, etc., thus endangering the community, it is permitted to hand him over to the Gentile courts (see also the *Tur* 388 near the end): "Whoever causes trouble for the community, it is permitted to turn him over to the government, to smite him and to fine him and to imprison him."

To sum up: The laws of *dina d'malchuso* apply fully to American laws since these laws do not interfere with Jewish observance but are in the realm of civil law and apply with equal justice to all citizens. Therefore, first of all, we may not accept benefit from what violators of American law may gain. Furthermore, since refusing to testify will bring the witnesses into danger of imprisonment, they are permitted by Jewish law to testify and save themselves. Finally, those who endanger the Jewish community should be turned over to the government to receive the punishment they deserve.

Of course it may be argued that these particular men have not yet been convicted and it is wrong of us to declare them guilty. Nevertheless, the whole complex of events has so developed and ramified that the good name of the Jewish community has been besmirched, and the people involved here are certainly to be considered under suspicion or under the presumption of wrongdoing and so should not be shielded.

55

ABORTION AND LIVE FETUS STUDY

QUESTION:

Since the Supreme Court recently made a decision with
regard to abortion, and since, also, there is legislation
pending on the question, the Central Conference is considering issuing a statement on this question, as other
religious bodies have already done. Specifically, two
questions need to be answered: Is there any relation
between Jewish tradition on this question and the Supreme Court decision, which makes a distinction between the first three months of pregnancy, the second
trimester and the third? Second, what is the attitude of
Jewish tradition as to the rights of the fetus if it has
been extracted from the womb in a living state? (Asked
by Rabbi Paul Gorin, Canton, Ohio.)

ANSWER:

THE QUESTION OF ABORTION has been discussed twice
before the Conference, once by Dr. Jacob Z. Lauterbach, and the second time by myself. Dr. Lauterbach's
responsum is, I think, in the *Yearbook*. My responsum
is in *Recent Reform Responsa,* #41. However, although the matter has already been discussed twice for
the Conference, new social conditions have developed,
and new governmental decisions have and will be

256

issued. Therefore, there is some need for a rediscussion
of the question.

As for the permissibility of abortion, the question
revolves around the status of the unborn fetus. Is it a
person, as, for example, the Catholic Church would
insist, or is it just a part of the mother's body? The
almost complete consensus of the classic Jewish tradition is that the unborn fetus is not a person (*nefesh*).
This conclusion is based mainly upon two situations in
the law. First, the law of Scripture (Exodus 21:22)
that if a man strikes a pregnant woman and thus destroys the child, he must pay damges to the husband.
But has he not killed the fetus? Is this not murder?
How, then, can the law let him off merely with paying
a fine? Clearly, then, the unborn child is not deemed to
be a person (*nefesh*). This law is codified in *Shulchan
Aruch, Choshen Mishpot* 423; and in the classic commentary to *Choshen Mishpot* 425, Joshua Falk, in his
M'iras Enoyim (end of his sec. 8), says simply: "While
the fetus is within the body of the mother, it may be
destroyed, even though it is alive, for every fetus that
does not come out into the light of the world is not to
be described as a *nefesh.*"

The second basis for this principle in the law is based
on the Mishnah, *Oholos* 7:6, and codified in the *Shulchan Aruch, Choshen Mishpot* 425:2, namely, that if
the birth is difficult and the mother seems likely to die,
one may destroy the child in order to save the mother.
Of course, if the child puts out from the mother's body
as much as its forehead, it is already a *nefesh,* and the

law is that one may not set aside (*dochin*) one *nefesh* in favor of another.

Since, therefore, the child is not a *nefesh,* abortion becomes basically permissible. Of course one may not destroy the unborn child without adequate reason, such as the health of the mother. But just as the mother, to save her life, may, if need be, sacrifice a finger or an arm or a leg, so she may sacrifice the unborn fetus if her health requires it, since the fetus is called "the leg or the thigh of the mother" (*uber yerech imo; Chullin* 58a).

The situation was summed up best by the late Sephardic Chief Rabbi of Israel, Ben Zion Uziel, in his *Mishp'tey Uziel,* III, 46 and 47. I quote his statement from *Recent Reform Responsa,* p. 193. Uziel concluded as follows: "An unborn fetus is actually not a *nefesh* at all and has no independent life. It is part of its mother, and just as a person may sacrifice a limb to be cured of a worse sickness, so may this fetus be destroyed for the mother's benefit."

Of course Uziel reckons with the statement of the *Tosfos* to *Chullin* 33a that a Jew is not permitted (*lo shari*) to destroy a fetus, although such an act is not to be considered murder. He says that one may not destroy it. One may not destroy anything without a reason. But if there is a worthwhile purpose, it may be done. The specific case before him concerned a woman who was threatened with permanent deafness if she went through with the pregnancy. Uziel decided that since the fetus is not an independent *nefesh,* but is only a part of the mother, there is no sin in destroying it for her sake.

It must be stated that there are some authorities who are reluctant to permit abortion unless it is extremely necessary. This reluctance is due, often, to the fear that the operation itself might be harmful to the mother.

So far we have discussed the general question of abortion much as it has been discussed in the two previous responsa mentioned. Now, specifically, as to the relationship of Jewish tradition to the trimester rule set down by the Supreme Court of the United States, namely, that abortion should be most readily permitted in the first three months, less readily in the second three months, etc.:

Jewish tradition makes no time division within the period of the nine months of pregnancy, except for the following: The first forty days of pregnancy are deemed the least important. The fetus is considered hardly to have developed, to have any form at all. This is based upon the Mishnah in *Nidda,* 3:7, namely, that a woman who has a miscarriage within the forty days of her pregnancy does not need the period of purification that is needed after the birth of a child. For the whole remainder of the period of pregnancy the child is still not a *nefesh,* even up to the time of giving birth. This can be seen from the fact that until the child actually puts out its forehead, it may still be destroyed to save the life of the mother.

The second question is with regard to whether scientific experiments may be made upon a fetus that is delivered from its mother's body alive. The status of the fetus (*nefel*) is discussed considerably in the law, but the discussion deals almost exclusively with the question of burial and mourning. Does this fetus need all the burial and mourning rites? The answer is no, as far as mourning is concerned, though burial is, of course, required when it dies. But while it is alive it certainly may not be put to death, as can be seen from the law that if it so much as puts its forehead out, then even if it endangers its mother's life at birth, we may not put it to death. How much the more must it be spared if it has not endangered its mother's life at its birth. Of course there are ways of studying the fetus today, even while it is in the mother's womb. These studies, chemical and x ray, that do not hurt child or mother and can be of great benefit to both are permitted, but anything that would destroy the life of the fetus after it is born and is no longer a danger to the mother would, of course, be prohibited.

56

ELECTRONIC EAVESDROPPING AND JEWISH LAW

QUESTION:

May a tap obtained through electronic eavesdropping be used as evidence in Jewish law? (Asked by Rabbi Richard F. Steinbrink, Saint Louis, Missouri.)

ANSWER:

JEWISH LAW IS basically religious (canon) law, and therefore it is not surprising that many of its rules are widely different from those governing secular legal systems. Thus the Jewish laws governing the eligibility of witnesses and the admissibility of evidence are much more severely limited than those of secular legal systems. For example, a Gentile is not eligible as a witness in a Jewish court (except in the special case of freeing a woman for remarriage when her husband has disappeared, *aguna*). Also, a child may not be a witness, nor a woman, nor a gambler, nor may any man testify in behalf of a near relative.

Since the laws of evidence in Jewish courts are so different from those governing secular courts, it would seem meaningless to draw any analogies between the two on any matter involving the rules governing witnesses or admissible evidence. Yet such a question *can* be meaningful if we go beyond the actual rules (or certain rules) of evidence and try to reach the ethical basis upon which they rest. In this deeper sense, the older (Jewish) system may give some moral guidance in some of the newer legal problems. This is surely the meaning of the question here. What really is asked is: According to the *ethical* standards underlying Jewish legal procedure, would it be deemed morally right to use a tape obtained by electronic eavesdropping as evidence in a secular court case?

Of course it is obvious that classic Jewish law could not possibly know of the modern devices whereby voices recorded on a tape can be repeated in the hearing of the court, and used thus as testimony of guilt or of financial obligation. Furthermore, as has been stated, Jewish law as to testimony is extremely strict in defense of the innocent, or the possibly innocent, and thus reveals an especially high ethical standard. Then let us assume that the sound of the voice from the tape may be considered the same as the voice of a witness testifying. Would such a witness be accepted as competent in Jewish law even though the tape is not a living witness?

First as to criminal law, even if it were accepted as a witness (assuming that for the moment), it would not be *sufficient* testimony because in Jewish criminal law there must be two witnesses together in the court at the same time, both testifying as having observed the same crime at the same time. So, along with the tape, there would have to be a living witness as the second witness, and he would have to testify that he has personal knowledge through his own senses of the same crime to which the tape attests. The tape alone could not be admissible because we would not have here two independent witnesses. If it were possible for a living witness to attest the alleged fact, it is not likely that there would also be need of surreptitious eavesdropping. But at all events, the tape, even if it *were* acceptable as a witness, is invalid in criminal law unless there is another witness who can testify of his own knowledge to the same facts at the same time.

With regard to civil law, disputes as to debts, etc., the two witnesses do not need to have observed the facts in dispute simultaneously. However, there are certain definite restrictions to testimony other than those mentioned above which are relevant to our question. The crucial fact in Jewish legal testimony is that the witnesses must hear the words of the judges and the judges' warnings against false testimony, and they must submit to cross-examination by the judges (this is *always* the rule in criminal cases, and in case of doubt also in civil cases). It is for this reason that the preponderant weight of Jewish law is against testimony in writing (i.e., by affidavit); see Rashi to *Gittin* 71a). The *Tur* (in *Choshen Mishpot* 28) cites Rashi's opinion, but adds that Rabbenu Tam permitted written testimony. However the *Shulchan Aruch* (ibid.) upholds the general rule that only *oral* testimony is acceptable. It is because the witnesses must hear the warning of the judges and accept cross-examination that deaf-mutes are considered incompetent to serve as witnesses in a Jewish court (see *Choshen Mishpot* 35:11 and also the *Tur;* see also Maimonides in *Yad, Hil. Edus,* IX. 9). Such restrictions are all based upon the Talmud in *Gittin* 71a, where certain rights are assured to deaf-mutes with regard to marriage and divorce, but they may not testify against someone else, since Scripture in Deuteronomy 17:6 says that only "from the *mouth* of the witnesses" can a man be condemned. There are, by the way, certain alleviations to this rule; for example, a woman who is an *agunah* may be freed from her unhappy state through the testimony of a deaf-mute. But this is testimony to help her and is, of course, a special case. In general, the law in all the Codes based on this Talmudic passage is that a deaf-mute is not a competent witness because he cannot hear the warnings of the judges or be subjected effectively to cross-examination.

The moral basis of this restriction is clear enough. No

man can be justly condemned unless the witnesses and their testimony can be carefully scrutinized and weighed. For similar reasons (that the witness must hear the judge and may be cross-examined) only oral testimony (but not written testimony), according to most authorities, is admissible. This certainly applies to the admissibility of an electronic tape. At best it is written rather than oral testimony. At worst it is equivalent to a deaf-mute because it cannot be questioned and it cannot be warned. If a living witness cunningly concocts a false testimony, he can be questioned and perhaps trapped in his deceit. But if a tape is cleverly faked, the tape itself is like a deaf-mute and cannot be spoken to.

Therefore one may say that by the moral high standards of Jewish court testimony, a tape cannot be accepted as a witness or as testimony.

Addendum

I consulted Eugene B. Strassburger, a prominent lawyer, and asked him whether any of the objections to electronic eavesdropping in American law are based upon reasonings analogous to those in the Jewish legal tradition. He answered that he has not seen a case where objection was made on the grounds (mentioned in the responsum) that the tape could not be cross-examined. He mentions, however, the right of the people to be secure in their houses (i.e., privacy). Then he continues as follows: "The Fifth Amendment to the Constitution provides: 'No person . . . shall be compelled in any criminal case to be a witness against himself.' Electronic devices by which a defendant in a criminal case is heard to make a statement against himself violate this amendment."

There are, indeed, similar regulations in Jewish law defending the privacy of private premises. One may not make a window overlooking a neighbor's court. The neighbor can object on the basis of *hezek r'iah* ("the damage of looking"), i.e., invasion of privacy (*Choshen Mishpot* 154:6 ff., Maimonides, *Yad, Hilchos Shechenim* VII).

But more significant in Jewish law is the prohibition against a man being compelled to incriminate himself. The Talmud, in *Yevamos* 25b, speaks of a man's relatives being ineligible as witnesses, and then says: "A man is considered to be his own relative and therefore may not declare himself to be evil, or criminal." See Rashi to the passage in which he says: "A man may confess to a debt, but he may not make any confession against himself in criminal law." So, too, Maimonides in *Yad, Edus* XII, 2. In fact, Jewish law seems to be even stricter than general law in this matter. Not only may he not be compelled to incriminate himself, but he may not incriminate himself even of his own free will. He is simply ineligible as a witness (even if voluntarily) against himself. Certainly by the electronic tape he is, as Mr. Strassburger says, made to incriminate himself. This is against Jewish law, as it is against American law.

INQUIRIES

1

INQUIRY

POSSIBLE PIDYEN OF SECOND SON

QUESTION:

In the law of redeeming the first-born son, Scripture speaks specifically of "opening the womb." Therefore the following question arises: Suppose the first-born child was born by Caesarean operation and is, therefore, not eligible for *pidyen,* not being "the opener of the womb"; then a year later a son is born in the normal way; does the second son, being "the opener of the womb" require a *pidyen?* (Asked by Rabbi Kenneth Segel.)

ANSWER:

THE LAW IS STATED in Scripture in Numbers 18:15 as follows: "Everything that openeth the womb . . . both of man and beast . . . the first-born," etc. The law thus mentions *both* requirements for redemption, namely, "the opener of the womb" and "first-born." This dual requirement in the law becomes relevant in the later discussions of the question raised here. The *two* qualities are mentioned, for example, by Rashi to *Bechoros*

19a, in which he speaks of the first-born of "Vlados," i.e., the order of birth, and the first-born of "Rachamim," "the opener of the womb."

Since Scripture mentions in the same verse both the redemption of a human child and also the redemption of the first-born of cattle, the law involved in the question asked is discussed both for cattle and for humans. The Mishnah (*Bechoros* 2:9), speaking of cattle, discusses the situation in which one calf is taken out of its mother's body by Caesarean and the other is born naturally from the womb. In that situation, Rabbi Tarfon thinks that there exists some doubt as to which is truly the first-born, and therefore, because of this doubt, neither may be used by the owner. Both calves must be allowed to graze until they become overaged. However, Rabbi Akiba says that neither is "first-born" (in the sense of requiring redemption). The law is according to Rabbi Akiba—namely, as the commentators explain, for the calf to require redemption it needs to have *both* qualities, "first-born" and "womb-opening."

Now this question is raised in the same tractate (8:2) in the case of humans. If the first child is born by Caesarean and the second is born from the womb, Rabbi Simon has the same doubts which Rabbi Tarfon voiced with regard to calves, and thinks that each child has some qualities of "first-born." But the anonymous Mishnah states that *neither* requires redemption; and that is the law. Thus, too, the law is given by Maimonides (*Yad, Hilchos Bekurim* 11:16), who says simply that if one child is taken from the side (i.e., by Caesarean) and the other is born normally, both of them are free from redemption; the first because he did not go forth from the womb, and the second because another child had preceded him. And so the law is given in the *Tur* and the *Shulchan Aruch, Yore Deah* 305 (*Y.D.* 24).

Thus the law seems clear enough that the second son does not require redemption. However, there is some doubt involved in this question due to what might be called medical reasons. Both the commentator Bertinoro and Lifschitz (*Tiferes Yisroel*) say that this situation can only apply to twins, first of all because the analogous law with regard to the birth of the calves clearly deals with twin calves, and second for the following medical reason: Bertinoro says that the Rambam (who was, of course, a famous physician) said that in the case of a human mother, it is impossible for her to undergo a Caesarean operation and heal up sufficiently so that at a later date she can have a normal birth from the womb. Therefore, these commentators say, this law applies only in the emergency case of human twins, which evidently means that the mother will be dying of the Caesarean but before she expires the second child is born normally.

However, it is to be noted that Maimonides himself, in giving the law, does not restrict it to the birth of twins, nor does the *Shulchan Aruch* or any of the Codes so restrict it.

As for the statement ascribed to Maimonides by Bertinoro, Maimonides may have stated it so elsewhere, though not in his Code, as far as I can see. It is true also that the opinion ascribed to Maimonides by

Bertinoro was held up to modern times by physicians. The rule was often cited as follows: once a Caesarean, always a Caesarean. But I inquired of a well-known gynecologist, who told me that medical and surgical practice has improved in recent years and that if, for example, the first Caesarean was made, not because of a narrowness of the passage but because of some infection, then it is quite possible, and, indeed, it happens, that the mother recovers from the Caesarean operation and at a later time can give birth in the normal way.

It is not an infrequent situation in the law that the law takes cognizance of changes in medical practice, and so it is clear in this case that the law is as stated. The second child, born a year or so after the Caesarean, requires no *pidyen,* since the two qualities mentioned in the original Scripture text, "womb" and "first-born," do not apply to him.

ADDENDUM

It is worthwhile noting that Bertinoro (16th cent.) actually overstated the medical opinion of Maimonides (12th cent.). According to Bertinoro's commentary (*Bechoros* XIII, 2), Maimonides said that it is *impossible* for a woman to recover from a Caesarean operation and be able to bear a child normally in the future.

The statement which Bertinoro refers to was made by Maimonides in his commentary to that Mishnah. What Maimonides actually said there (although it amounts to nearly the same thing) is the following: As to what people tell about (i.e., that a woman can recover from a Caesarean and later bear a child in a normal way), I cannot explain it; for that would be a very astonishing occurrence (*davar nifla m'ode*).

The modern edition of the Mishnah commentary of Maimonides was made by Joseph David Kapach (Jerusalem, 1967), and he comments on Maimonides' strong doubts. He says: "What was astounding in the days of our teaching [Maimonides'] is now, with the progress of medical science, an everyday occurrence." In this way the legal literature takes note of medical progress.

At all events, while Maimonides would consider a normal child-birth after a Caesarean (except for twins) as "an astounding phenomenon," that opinion of his would not lead him to state that if such an astounding phenomenon *did* occur, the second child would need redemption. Therefore in his Codes, as in all the Codes, the law is simply stated that neither child needs to be redeemed.

2

INQUIRY

CANNIBALISM

QUESTION:

The newspaper reports that the survivors of a plane wreck in the Andes Mountains were not found for a number of weeks after the accident. Those who survived admitted that they survived by cannibalism. Is there anything in Jewish legal literature which would be relevant to this situation? (Asked by Rabbi Daniel Syme, New York, New York.)

ANSWER:

THIS TRAGIC circumstance has indeed occurred a number of times in the past. One, at least, occurred in American history. The survivors of an immigrant train toward the Pacific Coast survived by cannibalism in the sadly famous Donner Pass.

Of course, if certain weak members of the expedition or the group of survivors were put to death in order to provide sustenance for the stronger and more violent members, this would be an unforgivable sin. There is a famous anecdote in the Talmud, the concluding line of which applies here. A man came to

Rava saying that the governor of the province had told him that if he did not kill X, the governor would take his (the inquirer's) life. The man came to the rabbi with the question, therefore: May he save his own life at the expense of another man's life? To which the rabbi responded: "No! Why do you think your blood is redder than his?" In other words, we have absolutely no right to save our own life at the expense of another man's life, except, of course, in a clear case of self-defense (*Pesachim* 25b).

Now assuming that certain members died (of starvation or exposure), and it was the flesh of these bodies which sustained the rest, did they do right in sustaining their own lives this way? Of course the body of a human being in no sense constitutes permitted meat, although it must be stated here that human blood is not absolutely prohibited, as is animal blood. Thus, for example, if human blood were completely prohibited, and a person had a bleeding gum and swallowed some of his own blood, he would be committing a sin, which in fact he is not committing (*b. Ketubos* 60a). However, human flesh is certainly forbidden for food (cf. *Yore Deah* 66:10).

Nevertheless, it must be remembered that this was a case of *pikuach nefesh,* absolute danger to life, and the law is clear, especially as stated by Maimonides, that in a case of *pikuach nefesh,* if, for example, a doctor orders you to eat something which is absolutely *trefe,* you must obey the doctor and sustain life (*Yore Deah* 155:2, 3; *Yesode Torah* V:6). Of course what Maimonides had in mind was nonkosher animals, but the same thing must apply to cannibalism.

As a matter of fact, the following related question came up during wartime: If soldiers were in a position where it was absolutely impossible to get kosher food, and they simply had to eat *trefe* food to sustain life, were they required to make a *b'rocha* over the *trefe* food? The answer is clear: they certainly must, since they benefit from the food, and the blessings of food are called the blessings of benefit (*ha-nehenin*). The law is clearly stated in *Orah Hayyim* 204:9 as follows: One who because of danger has eaten food or drink which is forbidden must pronounce a blessing before and after (see, also, *Kitzur Shulchan Aruch* 50:8).

To sum up: In those tragic circumstances in the Andes, if nobody was put to death in order to sustain the others, then forbidden flesh of the dead was permitted because of the supreme duty of sustaining life (*pekuach nefesh*), and a blessing must be recited over that horrible food.

3

INQUIRY

JOINT MIKVEH AND BAPTISTRY

QUESTION:

The military is working on new plans for the building of chapels for the joint use of the different religions. Consideration is being given to the inclusion of a pool which can be used both as a baptistry by Baptists and a *mikveh* by Jews.

The purpose of this inqury is to learn whether, if the pool is built as a kosher *mikveh,* would those who follow the traditional Jewish law be able to share their kosher *mikveh* with those who use it for baptizing Christians.

Of course the oceans and streams were the original sources of *mayim hayim*—used by both Jews and Christians to meet their respective needs. (Asked by Rabbi Aryeh Lev, Director of the Commission on Jewish Chaplaincy.)

ANSWER:

BASIC TO THE INQUIRY is the larger question, whether a chapel used by Catholics and Protestants may also be used by traditional Jews for regular worship, provided, of course, that the ritual objects specific to one religion are removed before the chapel is used by another re-

ligion. It is true that this question was settled prag-
matically during the war, but that was under war
conditions. Now that we are not at war, the question
of the propriety of using such a joint chapel may well
arise again. Besides, the question of the usability of a
joint chapel has direct bearing on the specific question
asked here, namely, the joint use of an immersion pool
by Baptists and traditional Jews.

All the laws stemming from the Bible against close
association with non-Jews refer specifically to idolaters,
which all the non-Jews in earlier days were. However,
it must be clearly stated that in the eyes of Jewish law,
Christians are *not* idolaters and, in fact, Rabbenu Tam
and other prime authorities state that when Christians
speak of the Trinity, etc., they really mean God (see
the references given in Isserles to *Orah Hayyim* 156).

Nevertheless, although Christians are not deemed
to be idolaters, many of their ritual objects, such as
crucifixes, etc., are deemed to be idolatrous objects
(indeed, many Protestants also consider them to be
such). Therefore the question arises in the law as to
Jewish worship in a place where there have been or
there are such objects as crucifixes, etc. Specifically
the question is asked: Suppose crucifixes were brought
into a Jewish house of worship and then removed;
could the house be used for Jewish worship thereafter?
Elijah Mizrachi (in his *Kenesses Hagdolah, Orah Hayyim* 151) says that a synagogue is *not* invalidated if
the idols are removed from it, and the *Mogen Avraham*
to *Orah Hayyim* 154 (end of par. 17) says that the
reason this is so is that the building *itself* was not dedi-

cated to idolatry, and therefore it does not lose its
sacredness after the objects are removed.

Now, if a synagogue is not invalidated if Christian
symbols are removed from it, then this applies all the
more to a *mikveh* for the following reasons: A *mikveh*
is not a sacred object, as a synagogue building is. A
synagogue building has sacredness inherent in it even
when it is in ruins. But no one would argue that a
ruined and abandoned *mikveh* has any inherent re-
sidual sanctity and therefore must be respected. A
mikveh is only a convenient appurtenance to the *mitzvah* of the ritual bathing, which in fact can take place
anywhere. The bathing can be legally fulfilled in a
river, provided that most of the water in the river is
not rain water, but comes from the river source. So,
too, a ritually legal bath can be made in an overflow-
ing wave from the sea. Surely no one could argue that
since John the Baptist baptized people in the Jordan,
the Jordan thereafter could not be used for Jewish
ritual bathing; or that a seacoast would be forbidden
if Christians were baptized a little farther up the coast.

But actually we do not need to rely upon this *a
fortiori* argument (i.e., if a synagogue once used by
Gentiles is usable, then surely a *mikveh,* which is less
sacred, is usable). The actual fact is that they frequently used *mikvehs* that belonged to Gentiles and
were on Gentile premises. Asher ben Jehiel takes that
fact for granted in the question that was asked him
about such a *mikveh* (see his responsa, sec. 18, #8).
All he is concerned about is whether or not a Gentile
might be suspected of filling the *mikveh* with rain

water from the roof when it needs replenishment; to which he replies that if the diminished *mikveh* still has twenty-one *seahs* of proper water (i.e., more than half of the forty *seahs* required), the addition of the rain water will not invalidate it. This is cited by Asher's son, the *Tur,* in *Yore Deah* 201, and a full discussion is given by Isserles in *Yore Deah* 201:4, and he indicates that if we know that the *mikveh* was filled by a Jew according to law, it is certainly a legal *mikveh.*

To sum up: A synagogue is not invalidated by the fact that idolatrous objects were once in it. All the more is it true that a *mikveh,* which is a mere appurtenance to the *mitzvah* of ritual bathing, is not invalidated if it were used by non-Jews. Furthermore, the law specifically mentions *mikvehs* actually belonging to Gentiles, which are kosher if properly filled, just as a river, which is generally kosher for Jewish ritual bathing, is not made useless by the fact that Gentiles baptize in it, even in the vicinity of Jewish bathing. We might add that Baptists certainly avoid crucifixes, etc.

The military authorities may well be informed that if the *mikveh* is made according to Orthodox rules, its use is not inhibited if Baptists use it also.

4

INQUIRY

TWO BROTHERS CALLED TO THE TORAH

QUESTION:

What is the basis of the custom not to call two brothers in succession to the Torah? (Asked by Rabbi Fredric Pomerantz, Closter, New Jersey.)

ANSWER:

THE SHULCHAN ARUCH (*Orah Hayyim* 141:6) says plainly: "We *may* call two brothers in succession," etc. If the *Shulchan Aruch* finds it necessary to insist that we *may* call them in succession, then evidently it is trying to contravene a widespread opposite opinion that we may *not* call two brothers, etc. Sure enough, the various commentators to the *Shulchan Aruch* say it *is* a widespread custom not to call them in succession because of the "evil eye." So, also, the *Kitzur Shulchan Aruch* (23:13) says plainly that we do not call two brothers to the Torah in succession because of the evil eye.

But this is folk custom, not law. Otherwise the *Shulchan Aruch* would not have presumed to gainsay it. By the way, the custom may also be based upon an

older folk fear against doing anything by pairs, such
as drinking two cups in succession, eating two things
in quick succession; all this is mentioned in the Talmud
in *Pesachim* 109b. There is also a relevant Midrash.
When Jacob sent his sons to Egypt to buy corn, he
warned them not to enter by the same door because
people would give them the evil eye.

5

INQUIRY

THE "KERIAH" RIBBON

THE LAWS GOVERNING the tearing of the garments at
the death of a relative (*keriah*) are detailed, extensive,
and very strict. In the *Shulchan Aruch*, they occupy
an entire large section of thirty-nine subdivisions (*Yore
Deah* 340). There the law is given that whoever is
present at the death of a worthy Israelite must tear his
garments. Even if not present at the death, relatives
must tear their garments for the seven relatives for
whom they are in duty bound to observe mourning.
For a parent the laws are stricter than for other relatives. While for other relatives it is sufficient if one
garment is torn, for a parent all the garments must be
torn until the heart is exposed.

With all these strict detailed laws, it seems strange
that it has become customary among modern Orthodox

in America not to tear the garments at all, even for the death of a parent. It is now a widespread custom in many (modern) Orthodox funerals for the undertaker to pin a small bit of black ribbon (about four inches long) onto the garment of the mourners and to cut that ribbon in lieu of *keriah*. Greenwald, in his compendium of mourning laws, is shocked at this new custom. He calls it "a mockery and a joke," and he blames it on the undertakers, who, he says, violate the old laws and make laws for themselves.

Yet, although this black *keriah* ribbon is a mere evasion of the required tearing of the garments, nevertheless questions of observance and proper usage have already begun to cluster around it. People ask for guidance as to how long the ribbon should be worn. Should it be transferred from one garment to another during the week of *shiva,* or during the thirty days of mourning, *shloshim?*

Of course there can be no definite answer to these questions because they are based upon a new American usage which all Orthodox authorities would scorn (as Greenwald did) as an avoidance of the basic religious obligation. Nevertheless, evidently rabbis are groping about for answers to the questions that are now being asked of them in this regard.

If an answer can be given at all, it must be based upon the distinction which the laws of *keriah* make between the *keriah* observance for parents and the observance for other deceased relatives. For parents, if during *shiva* the mourner changes from one garment to another, he must tear this second garment, but for the other relatives one need not do so. So one might answer, then, that if it is a mourning for parents, the ribbon should be transferred from one garment to another during the mourning period.

And people also ask how long the ribbon should be worn. That, too, may be answered by analogy. For all other relatives the tear may be basted up after seven days (and permanently sewn after thirty days). But for one's parents, one may not even baste it until after thirty days. Thus one might extend this to apply to the ribbon and say that the ribbon, when mourning for a parent, should be worn for thirty days and for other bereaved for seven days.

But it must be understood that all the above suggestions are merely theorizing on the basis of analogy. The whole use of the ribbon, instead of actual tearing of the garments, is brushed aside as meaningless by Orthodox authorities.

6

INQUIRY

SONS AT FATHER'S BURIAL

QUESTION:

Asked by Dr. Abraham Bernstein of San Francisco after a visit to Jerusalem, where he was informed by a resident of that city that a son is not permitted to accompany his deceased father's body to the cemetery. What is the source and the meaning of this unusual custom?

ANSWER:

THIS CUSTOM IS OBSERVED by some in Jerusalem and referred to in two sources which specialize in dealing with the customs in Jerusalem. One is *The Bridge of Life* (*Gesher ha-Chayim*) by Tekuchinski. The work was begun by the father (Jehiel) and completed by the son (Nissim). The custom reported is found in this work in Vol. I, pp. 109 and 112. The author here says that the custom began with Joseph ben Abraham Molcho (about a hundred years ago), who, before his death, forbade his sons to accompany his body to the grave.

The reason for this strange custom is given most clearly in another work which deals with Palestinian customs (mostly Cabbalistic), *Ha-Kuntres Ha-Jechieli*

(Vol. II, p. 18b), where the custom is clearly explained.

This Cabbalistic custom is based upon the law which declares it is a sin to waste seed (the male seminal fluid; see *Shulchan Aruch, Even Hoezer* #23). The Talmud (*Nidda* 13b) says that a person who consciously wastes his seed is like a murderer, the theory back of that statement being that *each* drop of seed might have produced a living being.

Now the Cabbalistic elaboration of the idea (that each wasted drop of seed might have become a living being) is that each wasted drop actually *does* become a living being, a ghostly being, a dangerous spirit (*ruach*). This superstitious idea is elaborated still further as follows: These *ruchos* (spirits), created by whatever seed a man may have wasted in his lifetime (voluntarily or not), all claim to be his sons. When the man dies, these ghostly spirits demand the right to accompany "their father" to the cemetery. In order to prevent this, a solemn ban (*cherem*) is proclaimed, calling upon *all* his sons not to accompany the father to the grave. This strange Cabbalistic ban, which is primarily meant to exclude these supposed ghostly sons, therefore necessarily also excludes his normal, human sons. This is the origin of this curious Cabbalistic Jerusalem custom.

7

INQUIRY

PERMISSIBILITY OF GRAFTED FRUIT

QUESTION:

> Whereas mixtures of different cloths are prohibited (and also planting together and grafting different species are prohibited), the laws of *kashruth* do not follow through on the principle enunciated against mixtures. Thus we eat a variety of fruits that are hybrid in nature, such as nectarines (which are a combination of plum and peach). Please clarify this apparent discrepancy. (Asked by Rabbi Daniel Syme, New York.)

ANSWER:

FIRST OF ALL, it must be made clear that those who eat hybrid fruits are not doing so in disregard of the law. The fact is, the eating of hybrid fruits is not only not prohibited but is specifically permitted. Thus the Mishnah (*Kelaim* 8:1) states definitely that while mixed plants are forbidden to be made or to be kept, the fruit is permitted to be eaten. So, too, Maimonides (*Yad, Kelaim* 1:7) says: "One who grafts trees of different species is to be punished [for the act of grafting], but the resulting fruit is permitted to be eaten." This does seem to be a contradiction. How can it be forbidden to graft trees of different species and yet be permitted to eat of the fruit?

In order to answer this apparent discrepancy, the law should be traced from its beginning. The prohibition against such mixtures is given in two places in the Torah, Leviticus 19:19 and Deuteronomy 22:9–11. In his commentary to the passage in Leviticus, Rashi says that these laws have no known reason but are simply the decree of the King, which we must obey. A similar statement that there is no human logic to be found in the laws of mixture is made by Bachya in his *Chovos Ha-L'Vovos* (cited in *Ozar Yisroel*, article *"Kelaim"*). So it is difficult at the outset to explain these laws logically. One could leave the answer at that and say, following these two great scholars, that we should not be surprised at any lack of human logic with regard to these particular laws.

Nevertheless, if we follow the development of the law in sequence, we will see some reason for this permissibility. In the first place, the prohibition against mixing species of fruit trees is nowhere specifically mentioned in Scripture. This prohibition is assumed to be implied in the general prohibition of not sowing mixtures in the field, even though the term "sowing" usually means planting grain (cf. *Yore Deah* 295:1). Then, secondly, the Mishnah enumerates (*Kelaim*, chap. 1) various plants which are mutually dissimilar plants but which may be mixed since they are really of the same species. A second permission is to allow the planting together of the *seeds* of different species. What is prohibited with regard to trees is the grafting of a twig from a tree of one species to another. Any other planting together, as of seeds, would be permitted. The only prohibited act with regard to mixing tree species is the act of grafting. Moses Sofer, in a responsum (*Yore Deah* 288), has an interesting discussion which came as an answer to Jewish agriculturalists in Hungary. They would buy orchards of already mixed trees from Gentiles who planted and grafted them. Moses Sofer says that these Jewish agriculturalists may keep and use the fields and the fruit, but as a precaution he would suggest that the fruits be plucked by Gentile workmen. Then the fruits would be permitted.

To sum up, then, the following may be the reason why the Mishnah and Maimonides, etc., permit the eating of the fruits of grafted trees. First, the species brought together, though apparently dissimilar, are not dissimilar at all, and therefore may not be technically *kelaim*. Second, it may be that the mixture was brought about without actual grafting (as, I believe, we do with hybrid corn). Third, if the tree *is* to be grafted, a Jew is prohibited from doing the grafting, but if a Gentile did it of his own accord, the fruit is certainly permitted. All these considerations are, I believe, sufficient to explain the apparent discrepancy as to why the fruit of a prohibited action is permitted.

8

INQUIRY

COSMETIC SURGERY

QUESTION:

A young, unmarried Orthodox girl wants a nose plastic operation and her face lifted. She realizes that according to Halacha she must not inflict unnecessary injury to herself. Should she have these operations? (Asked by Dr. Abraham Bernstein, San Francisco, California.)

ANSWER:

IN TRADITIONAL LAW there is ground for debate whether *any* operation which cuts the human body can be freely consented to. Of course if it is a question of saving an endangered person's life, then *no* prohibition among the commandments is allowed to stand in the way of the necessary operation. All commandments are waived in cases of *pikuach nefesh* (danger to life). But suppose the operation is not one for saving a person from real danger but is for a relatively minor purpose, such as improving the shape of the nose, are such operations permitted by Jewish law?

In order to answer that question, we must first look into the question of a person giving consent to an operation. The law is fairly clear that just as a person may not wound another (*chovel*, "to wound, to injure") so he may not wound himself (or arrange for someone else to wound him—in this case, the surgeon). This law is stated clearly by Maimonides in his Code in *Hilchos Chovel* V, 1. However, where the law is stated in the *Shulchan Aruch* in *Choshen Mishpot* 420:31, it is not stated as positively as Maimonides does. The *Shulchan Aruch* says: "He who injures himself is free [from punishment] although it is not permitted to do so." The reason for this ambiguous statement of the law in the *Shulchan Aruch,* which seems to say you may and you may not injure yourself, is that Rabbi Akiba, who is the chief authority for this law, himself seems to have two diverse opinions. In the Mishnah (*Baba Kama* 8:6), he states the law just as the *Shulchan Aruch* quotes it, namely: "You should not injure yourself, but if you do so, you are free from punishment." But in a *boraita* quoted in the Talmud (*Baba Kama* 91a at the bottom), Akiba says flatly that a man is free to injure himself. Clearly this vagueness in the law of self-injury leaves room for discussion of the question asked here and of many analogous questions.

An interesting recent discussion was made by Moshe Feinstein, the prime contemporary Orthodox authority (in his *Igros Moshe, Choshen Mishpot* #103). The specific question with which he was dealing was the following: May a man give his blood to a blood bank for pay? On the face of it, this should be prohibited because the man is arranging for his self-injury. After a minute analysis of the two semi-contradictory statements of Rabbi Akiba, Moses Feinstein comes to the conclusion that it *is* permitted, first because they used to do bloodletting in Talmudic times; second, because the injury is slight and painless; and third, because the man may, of course, need the money.

On the basis of the law, the line of our inquiry must be as follows: First, how dangerous is the cosmetic surgery as a procedure? What risks does the patient incur? Second, how important a benefit is the beautification of the woman? Is it important enough to justify whatever danger there is in the surgery?

It may be assumed that cosmetic surgery deals mostly with the outer parts of the body and does not generally involve disturbing the vital organs. As for the benefit derived by whatever risk this surgery entails, this question has a remarkable place in Jewish traditional literature. The Bible and the Talmud pay a surprising amount of attention to cosmetic matters. First of all, the various spices and lotions used in women's beautification are mentioned many times in Scripture. In the Song of Songs 3:6 and 4:10, and in Esther 2:12, various spices are mentioned. Also in the Talmud (*Baba Kama* 82a) we are told that when Ezra brought the people back from Babylonian captivity, among his special ordinances was one permitting peddlers of cosmetics to travel freely throughout the country so that these ointments, etc., would be readily available.

The law permits a woman to go through extensive beauty treatment on the half-holidays (see *Orah Hayyim* 346:5). The husband must provide means of his

wife's beauty material (see *b. Ketubos* 64b). One of
the most touching narratives in the Mishnah (*Nedarim*
9:10) concerns Rabbi Ishmael. A man had made a
vow that he would not marry a certain woman on the
ground that she was homely. Rabbi Ishmael then took
the girl into his house and beautified her. Then he presented her to the young man who had made the vow
and said to him: "Is this the girl you vowed you would
not marry because you said she was homely?" The
young man looked at the beautiful girl and said: "No,
I would gladly marry her." Then follows the saying:
"The daughters of Israel are beautiful. It is their poverty which makes them homely." Then we are told that
when Rabbi Ishmael died, all the daughters of Israel
sang a dirge for him.

It is clear from Jewish tradition that the right of a
woman to beautify herself is one that is honored in
Scripture and in Talmud. It is not at all to be considered as a trivial matter. It is clearly the spirit of the
tradition that a woman has the right to strive for
beauty.

Since, therefore, the cosmetic purpose is an honored
one and an important one, and since the operation is
not likely to be a dangerous one, then the ambiguous
law of *chovel* against self-injury does not apply here,
and this woman is not prohibited by Jewish law from
undergoing cosmetic surgery.

9

POST-BURIAL INQUIRY

PEBBLE ON TOMBSTONE

QUESTION:

What is the basis and meaning of the frequently observed Orthodox custom of visitors to a grave leaving a pebble on the tombstone or the grave? (Asked by Rabbi Fredric Pomerantz, Closter, New Jersey.)

ANSWER:

THERE IS SOMETHING rather surprising about the custom, which can be seen in many cemeteries in America. One would think that a custom so widely observed would be referred to in almost all the books on *minhagim*. But of all the fairly modern books on *minhagim,* I was able to find it in only one, and that is a book called *Ta-amay Ha-Minhagim* by Abraham Sperling-Danzig (first ed., Lemberg, 1896). The book concentrates chiefly on customs instituted by the various Chassidic groups. Therefore it is certainly presumed that it is practiced primarily by the Chassidim. The author explains the custom as follows: "We put grass and pebbles on the grave. It is to show one's respect to the dead and to show that he [the visitor] was at the grave." In other words, it is a sort of a visiting card to tell the dead that you have paid him a call.

However, although this is one of the few, if not the only, recent works which refer to the custom, it was certainly known a century or two ago. Actually, the custom and the explanation are quoted word for word from the *Be'er Hetev* to *Orah Hayyim* 224:8. And he in turn cites *Derashos Maharash* as his source.

As to the purpose behind the custom: It is certainly deeper than merely giving notice that one has been at the grave. This can be seen from the earlier form of the custom. Nowadays the people who observe the custom leave a pebble at the grave or on the tombstone, but the *Be'er Hetev* (end of 17th cent.), quoting his source, says that people left pebbles and/or grass. This fact proves that the custom has a close relationship to the more established custom which is followed at the end of a funeral. The *Shulchan Aruch* gives this custom in *Yore Deah* 376:4. Picking up the grass and the earth is in reference to Psalm 72:16: "They shall spring up like the grass of the field" (see *Be'er Hetev* to *Orah Hayyim* 547:7: "The grass that is plucked up after the burial of the dead is a symbol of resurrection"). The custom of plucking and throwing the grass and dust as a symbol of resurrection is referred to by Israel Bruna (15th cent., Germany) in his responsa (#181). Therefore it seems evident that the custom of picking up pebbles (or dust and grass) after a later visit to the grave is a repetition of the reverent and devout feeling at the time of the funeral itself, which the visitor to the grave now recalls and experiences anew.

Also, it is quite possible that some Chassidic scholar recommended the practice on the basis of the Midrash which says that when Jacob buried Rachel by the road-side, each of Jacob's sons took a stone and put it on the grave (see Ginzberg, *Legends of the Jews,* Vol. V, p. 319, n. 310; the Midrash is found in *Lekach Tov* 35,20).

10

POST-BURIAL INQUIRY

WASHING THE HANDS AFTER A FUNERAL

(Asked by Rabbi Stephen S. Pearce, Forest Hills, New York.)

ANSWER:

THE SPECIFIC QUESTION asked was about washing the hands before entering the house after returning from the funeral. This custom has no foundation at all in the law. It is brushed aside by as important an authority as the Gaon Paltai. His opinion is cited by Isaac Ibn Gayyat in his *Shaare Simcha* in the laws of mourning (ed. Fuerth, 1861, p. 42). The Gaon was asked about the custom of washing the hands before entering the house after a funeral. He answered: "They do not need to do so, but if they have developed a custom to do so, it does not matter much." This opinion is echoed by Israel Kremsier (14–15th cent.) in his Notes to Asher ben Jehiel (at the end of *Mo'ed Katan,* sec. 86). He says that it is not necessary to wash the hands on returning from the cemetery, but if the people have become accustomed to do so, there is no harm in it.

There is, however, another washing of the hands which all authorities accept and approve. It is part of a three-part (or four-part) ceremony at the cemetery. After the burial the departing mourners pluck grass and earth, throw it over their shoulders, and then wash their hands. This throwing of grass or earth back over the shoulders suggests immediately the folkloristic basis of the custom—the attempt to repel or evade the various spirits (*ruchos*) that hover in the cemetery. Joseph Caro mentions this custom in *Yore Deah* 376:4. The *Be'er Hetev* (Judah Ashkenazi of Tiktin, first half of 18th cent.) cites the Ramban to the effect that all this is for the purpose of cleansing oneself of the *tuma* of the cemetery. He says that this *tuma* is so intense that it needs the three methods of cleansing, namely, water, dust (symbol of the ashes of the Red Heifer), and hyssop (symbolized by the grass). There is also a folkloristic reason for an additional custom on leaving the cemetery. In some countries the people sit down seven times (in other countries, three times) on going away from the grave, so that the spirits (*ruchos*) will give up following them.

An ethical meaning was given for the hand washing at the cemetery by Joseph Schwartz in his *Hadras Kodesh* (in the section "Likkute Dinim," p. 44, #103). He connects it with the hand washing which the Biblical law (Deuteronomy 21:8) requires of the elders of a city when a corpse is found on the road near their city. The elders perform this ceremony of hand washing to proclaim their innocence of this death. So do we (says Schwartz) wash our hands after the burial to proclaim our innocence of any neglect of the deceased during his illness. This explanation, that the washing of the hands at the cemetery is a declaration of our innocence, is found as early as the thirteenth century. It is given in *Shibbole Ha-Leket* (Zedekiah the Physician, 13th cent.) in the laws of mourning.

So the hand washing at the cemetery is properly (and traditionally) a part of the multiple observance after the burial, namely, dust, grass, sitting down three or seven times, and washing the hands. Evidently, then, this washing of the hands at the cemetery was transferred by some, perhaps for mere convenience, from the cemetery to the door of the house, where water would always be available. This later custom, though not forbidden, is deprecated by legal authorities. It is definitely not a requirement of the law. It is only an extension of the *cemetery* custom of washing, which itself is based upon folk apprehensions.

11

INQUIRY

SHA'ATNEZ WITH REGARD TO TZITZIS

QUESTION:

What is the reason that *tzitzis* are free from the laws of *sha'atnez,* thus, why one is permitted to have woolen fringes on a garment of linen? (Asked by Rabbi Mark Staitman, Pittsburgh.)

ANSWER:

FIRST OF ALL, it must be stated that it is not always possible to find a logical explanation for all the laws involved in the prohibition of mixed breeds, namely, the mixing of seeds in the vineyard, of cross-breeding animals, of grafting trees of different species. Rashi to the text in Leviticus 19:19, where the prohibition of mixing seeds is given, says that these laws must be obeyed simply as a decree of the King since we have no logical reason for them. Thus, while we might wonder at the permissibility of mixed textiles in the *talit* (or the *talit koton*), we notice that this is not the only commandment with regard to *sha'atnez* that seems to need explanation. Thus, for example, the shrouds made for the dead are free also from the prohibition of

sha'atnez. So, too, and strangely enough, the garments
which the priests wore in the Temple at the Temple
Service were a mixture of linen and wool (see *m.
Kelaim* 9:1).

Of these three exceptions, perhaps the one easiest to
explain is the permissibility of the shrouds to be of
sha'atnez. The verse in Psalms 88:6, "Free among the
dead," is explained in the Talmud (*Shabbas* 30a) to
mean that the dead are free from the mandate to obey
the commandments. Therefore, the commandment
against *sha'atnez* (in their shrouds) does not apply to
them any more than do the other commandments. See
the statement of the Rambam to his commentary to
Kelaim 9:4, in which he says that the freedom of the
dead with regard to *sha'atnez* in their shrouds applies
also to freedom from *tefillin, mezuzos,* etc.

As for the reason that the priests in the Temple wore
sha'atnez, this permissibility is analogous to that which
we will see is the reason given for the permissibility of
sha'atnez in the *tzitzis,* namely, that the makeup of the
priestly garments is specifically described in Scripture
and so constitutes a definite commandment independent of the commandment of *sha'atnez.* Furthermore, it
is to be observed that the Rambam specifically forbids
priests to wear these garments *outside* the Temple
service, since the specific permission of Scripture describing the precise makeup of the priestly garments
applies only to the specific purpose of the Temple
service (*Yad, Hilchos Kelaim* 10:32). In other words,
outside the Temple the priest wearing the sacred garments would be wearing them for his own benefit, for

example, for warmth; and actually the specific prohibition of *sha'atnez* applies to the *wearing* of the garments for warmth, etc. It is not forbidden, for example, to manufacture such garments for sale to non-Jews. It is only forbidden to a Jew to wear them for warmth, etc. Even for the use by Jews, *sha'atnez* cloths that are *not* worn on the body, as, for example, a tent cover or even a bed cover, are not forbidden by Torah law, although some scholars forbid it by rabbinical restriction.

Now specifically as to the question asked, namely, the permission to have the *tzitzis* of *sha'atnez,* Rashi states (to Deuteronomy 22:12) that the permission to have the *tzitzis* of *sha'atnez* is due to the fact that the verse prohibiting *sha'atnez* and the verse commanding *tzitzis* follow directly upon each other in Scripture (i.e., Deuteronomy 22:11 and 22:12). Rashi's brief remark as it stands is somewhat cryptic; but it becomes quite clear when we look at the source from which Rashi cites his comment. Rashi's statement as to the juxtaposition of the two verses comes from the words of Rabba in the Talmud, *Menachos* 39a. There the discussion involves the permissibility of "the woolen fringe in a linen garment" (*s'din b'tzitzes*). Rabba explains that Scripture mentions the prohibition of *sha'atnez* and then immediately follows it with the commandment to make the *tzitzis,* which indicates that the commandment to make the *tzitzis* is a separate law, i.e., is independent of the prohibition of *sha'atnez.* See especially Rashi's fuller comment to this Talmudic passage.

To sum up: As Rashi indicates, the laws against mixed breeds, etc., cannot be explained by human logic, but must be obeyed as God's decree. Therefore, we should not be too surprised that there are exceptions to the law of *sha'atnez*, as in the case of shrouds, priestly garments, *tzitzis*, etc. The shrouds may be *sha'atnez* because the dead are free from all commandments. The priestly garments and the *tzitzis* are given specifically in Scripture as independent commands and so are not subject to the laws of *sha'atnez*. This is clear from the fact that the law of *tzitzis* is mentioned as a specific duty immediately after the law of *sha'atnez*. This explanation is quoted by Rashi from the Talmud in *Menachos* 39a, where his comment is fuller and clearer than his brief comment to Deuteronomy 22:12.

12

INQUIRY

THE U'N'SANA TOKEF

QUESTION:

The community of Mainz and other Ashkenazic communities have the *U'n'sana Tokef* prayer only on Rosh Hashonah. Others have it both on Rosh Hashonah and Yom Kippur. Which of these observances is more justified in the liturgical tradition? (Asked by Rabbi Josef Zeitin, Odessa, Texas.)

ANSWER:

THIS FAMOUS PRAYER is ascribed, as is well known, to Amnon of Mainz in the time of the Crusades. Even if Amnon of Mainz is only a legendary figure, as some scholars say, nevertheless, since he is associated with the community of Mainz, it may well be presumed that the community of Mainz would be more likely to have kept the prayer in the appropriate service than other communities. Therefore, theoretically, we could assume that Rosh Hashonah is the appropriate occasion for the prayer. Furthermore, the theme of the prayer is that God passes judgment on who shall live and who shall die, etc., and it is Rosh Hashonah which is more properly and completely *Yom Ha'din,* the day of judgment, than Yom Kippur. Yom Kippur, of course, *seals* the judgment, but the judgment itself is made on Rosh Hashonah.

But we do not need these theoretical considerations in this matter. The literary evidence, even though meager at best, points to the fact that Rosh Hashonah is the proper day for this prayer. Incidentally, the most available and complete source for the various references to this prayer in the literature is in Landshuth's *Amude Ho-Avoda,* (I, p. 45). The first reference to the prayer is by Israel of Krems, who wrote the notes to Asher ben Jehiel, the Rosh (*Ha-gohos Asheri*). His reference to this prayer is on the very first pages of the Rosh to tractate *Rosh Hashonah.* He has no such note, as far as I know, to tractate *Yoma.* As for the Maharil, he also comments on the wording of the prayer but *only* in his *minhagim* to Rosh Hashonah and not to Yom Kippur. Incidentally, a beautifully complete version of the story of Amnon of Mainz is given in the early edition of Heidenheim's *Machzor* to Rosh Hashonah. If you lack this book, I am enclosing a copy of the relevant page.

So, clearly, its original place is Rosh Hashonah. But how does it happen that so many *machzorim* have the prayer not only in the *Mussaf Kedusha* of Rosh Hashonah but also in the *Mussaf Kedusha* of Yom Kippur?

This is not a surprising phenomenon. The same thing occurred with *Yizkor.* Its original place and origin in the Rhineland were only on Yom Kippur. Then it spread to the last day of the three festivals (see my article on *Yizkor* in the *HUC Annual*). The same thing, therefore, must have occurred with the *U'n'sana Tokef*. It spread from its original place to an additional place in the liturgy (namely, Yom Kippur).

The motivation for the various rituals repeating this prayer on Yom Kippur seems clear and logical. The prayer describes the various tragic ways in which God may decree that our life might end, "in famine, or war, or fire," etc. This prayer, therefore, belongs logically on the Day of Judgment, namely, the New Year, as has been said. However, God's judgment is, after all, not yet decided. There still follow the Ten Days of Penitence; and so it may be that if we repent, the tragic judgment will, after all, not be "sealed" against us. Hence, we repeat the prayer on Yom Kippur, confident that its last line will apply to us, "repentance, etc., avert the evil decree."

Nevertheless it is noteworthy that even this understandable extension of the prayer from Rosh Hashonah to Yom Kippur did not occur too early. The prime source of the *minhagim* of East European Jewry is *Mateh Moshe* by Moses Mat of Przemysl (1550–1606), the pupil of Solomon Luria (Maharil). In his *Mateh Moshe* (par. 818) he speaks of the prayer *only* on Rosh Hashonah.

To sum up, then: For the reasons mentioned above, the prayer belongs primarily to the *Yom Ha'din*, Rosh Hashonah. From there, in some *minhagim*, it was later extended to Yom Kippur. In our *Union Prayer Book*, we have the prayer only on Yom Kippur, for a practical reason, namely, that the Yom Kippur service, lasting all day, needed to be enlarged by additional prayers.

13

INQUIRY

ESTHER AND THE SECOND SEDER

QUESTION:

Is there actually a *minhag* to dedicate the second Seder to Esther and to the woman of the house because it was on that night that Esther prepared the fatal banquet for the king and Haman? (Asked by Rabbi M. Arthur Oles, San Francisco, California.)

ANSWER:

NONE OF THE classic books of *minhagim* available to me even mentions such a *minhag*. For example, the *Ta'amey Ha-minhagim,* the *Ozar Kol Minhagey Yeshurun,* and the classic *Mateh Moshe* have no mention of such a *minhag.* Of course there well may be such a custom *somewhere,* especially nowadays, when the Seder is being extended in various ways as a means of honoring different groups in our recent history, as, for example, an extra *matzo* to recall the heroism of the Warsaw ghetto and the third Seder for some similar purpose. So if some modern writer thought up this *minhag* that you mentioned, it would not be surprising.

Yet as a matter of actual tradition, if there *is* such

a *minhag* somewhere (of which I have been unable to find any specific notice), or if someone started it, there does exist a large amount of material in the traditional literature that might amply justify it.

In the first place, it seems clear that many of the important events involving the rescue of the Jews on Purim began to occur on Passover of the preceding year. The record of the official decree to slaughter the Jews of Persia is mentioned in Esther 3:12 as follows: "And the scribes of the king read on the first month, on the thirteenth day of the month [i.e., *Erev* Pesach]." This dating of the murderous decree left its mark in the *minhagim* observed in the preparation for Passover. The *Sefer Hamatamim* (p. 26b, item #15) states that when we make the formal search for leaven before the Passover (*b'dikas chometz*), we place around the house *ten* pieces of leaven to be found in the search. Why ten? Because the scribes mentioned in the verse were actually the ten sons of Haman; and as a symbol of their ultimate removal, we have ten pieces of leaven which we remove in preparation for the Passover.

More directly, when Esther called for a fast of three days (Esther 4:17), it is understood that these three days were the thirteenth, fourteenth, and fifteenth of Nisan. See Rashi to the reference in *Megilla* 15a, who also explains the next verse in the Book of Esther, "And Mordecai passed" (*va-ya-avor Mordecai*), as meaning "And Mordecai *transgressed*," i.e., he transgressed the Halacha by having a fast day on the first day of Pesach. This is amplified in the Midrash to Esther, verse 4:16, in which Mordecai complains to

Esther that the three-day fast she is proclaiming for the Jews to observe will include the first day of Pesach. To which complaint by Mordecai she rejoined: "If there will be no Jews left, what becomes of Pesach?" Furthermore, Esther is praised in many ways as being especially meticulous in observing the law, and among these various praises of her as an observant Jewess, it is said that she actually observed the ritual of cleaning out the *chometz* from the house (*biyur chometz*). See *Koheles Rabba* to the verse in Ecclesiastes 8:5: "He who observes a commandment will not know any evil thing." To which the Midrash there says: "This verse refers to Esther, who engaged in the *mitzvah* of removing the *chometz.*"

Perhaps the closest justification for the possible custom that you mention is the statement in the *Pirke Rabbi Eliezer* (chap. 50) that the banquet which Esther arranged for the king and Haman actually occurred on the sixteenth of Nisan, the day before the second Seder. This is the source of the statement to which you have referred.

Therefore, while I cannot find in any source among the *minhagim* that the second Seder is (or should be) *dedicated* to Esther, nevertheless, if such a custom does exist somewhere, i.e., if it is not merely a modern concoction, it has plenty of classical justification, as mentioned above.

14

INQUIRY

HIGH-RISE CHURCH AND RESIDENCES

QUESTION:

The Sixth Presbyterian Church is planning to raze its present church building and to build on the site a high-rise building which will house a Presbyterian church, commercial office space, and housing for the aged. Since the church is in a neighborhood (Squirrel Hill) where there is a large Jewish population, the question has arisen as to whether Orthodox Jews or Jewesses might object to living in a building which contains a Christian church. Is there any objection in the Jewish legal literature to residing in such a building? (Asked by Eugene B. Strassburger, Jr., Pittsburgh, Pennsylvania.)

ANSWER:

THIS QUESTION could never have been asked in the past, since the building of tall buildings, and the awarding of government aid to churches to provide residences for the aged, is a new and an American phenomenon. Of course, considering the wealth of the churches in Europe, it must certainly have happened that Jews resided in buildings owned by a church; but such a situation has, as far as I know, left no record in the legal literature. Besides, even if there were such a record in the Middle Ages of Jews living in properties owned by a church, it still would not be closely relevant to our question. The building in question is not only owned (or controlled) by the church, but the church itself is in the building, and Jewish old folk would be living in the *same building* which contains a church; and that is our question.

First it must be established that the large body of Jewish law in relation to non-Jewish religious institutions, etc., were originally developed in the time of idolatry, and the objections to the various religions were objections to idolatrous religions. It must be clear at the outset that Judaism does not consider Christianity or Mohammedanism idolatrous. (Please see the responsum on "Church Use of the Synagogue Building" in *Contemporary Reform Responsa,* pp. 44 ff.) However, although Judaism does not believe Christianity to be an idolatrous religion, nevertheless such objects as crucifixes, etc., are still deemed to be idolatrous objects (as, indeed, many Protestant sects consider them to be). Hence there are many questions in the law as to the usability by Jews of church objects. Such questions as these are asked: If the stubs of the wax candles used in the churches are remelted, may they be used as candles in the synagogue? May a Jewish tailor and embroiderer make the cloak used by the priest with a cross embroidered on its back? May a Jewish jeweler or pawnbroker buy and sell crucifixes, etc.?

Among these questions are some that are relevant to

our inquiry. For example, it is asked: If such objects
as crucifixes, etc., were brought into a room and used
for Christian worship, and then they were removed,
could that room be used for Jewish worship? The
answer is yes, because the *objects* were worshiped, but
the room itself was not worshiped. So, for example,
if a house is built for general use and then changed
(by the painting of images on it, etc.) for non-Jewish
worship, if these paintings are removed, the house may
be used for Jewish worship. So it all depends on
whether the house itself is worshiped as sacred. If,
therefore, the religious articles are not present, the
house may be used for general purposes (see *Yore
Deah* 145:3 and *Mogen Abraham* in *Orah Hayyim*
154, end of par. 17). In this special case, the building
itself is not dedicated for worship. In fact the main
part of the building is definitely set aside for secular
purposes. Besides, even in the church itself, Presby-
terians make very little use of crucifixes, etc.

Therefore, since the building itself is not intended
for non-Jewish worship, and the part that is for worship is well separated from the rest, there is no ground
in Jewish law for a Jew to object to living in parts of
the building; or even, for that matter, to having a little
synagogue in one of the rooms. Of course, some old
Jewish people may object to living in the building, but
their objections would be based upon personal feelings,
unjustified by the law.

Combined Index for "Reform Responsa" (I), "Recent Reform Responsa" (II), "Current Reform Responsa" (III), "Modern Reform Responsa" (IV), "Contemporary Reform Responsa" (V), "Reform Responsa for our Time" (VI).

synagogue near, II, 41
vandalized, V, 224
visiting, before thirty days, VI, 109, 110
visiting on Sabbath and holidays, VI, 188
visiting the, V, 232
see also Burial, Tombstone
Cemetery memorial service:
on second day Rosh Hashonah, VI, 57
Chanukah: I, 29
lights, I, 25; IV, 90
non-linear arrangement of lights, IV, 87
Shamash ("servant") IV, 90
Chaplain's insignia:
Hebrew letters on, V, 120
Charity:
status of recipients, VI, 65
Chaverus, promise of: II, 123
Ethical Culturists, III, 183
Jews raised as Christians, III, 217
Chevra Kadisha: I, 128
Child named:
after Gentile grandparents, IV, 134
after deceased person, IV, 136
Children:
Christian service, attendance at, I, 115
Christian Sunday School, II, 59
Christmas celebration at school, I, 112
custody of, I, 33, 200, 209; III, 193
Children ("Sons") of Noah:
I, 89, 110, 114, 116; IV, 71
Christian cemetery:
body of Jew to, III, 163; VI, 179
convert buried in, V, 151
memorial services in, I, 143
officiating for Christians, III, 175
worshiping in, I, 144

Christians:
not idolators, IV, 71
officiating at funerals of, III, 175
relatives memorialized, IV, 226
Sefer Torah, called to, II, 49
"Sons of Noah," IV, 71
substituting for on Christmas, V, 131
taught Torah, V, 47
temple organ used for Christian hymns, II, 47
Christmas:
celebration of in school, I, 112
Church:
use of synagogue building, V, 44
Church membership and conversion:
I, 82
Circumcision:
anesthetic for, III, 103
before eighth day, I, 90
CCAR debate, VI, 71
child of unmarried mother, III, 100
children of mixed marriage, IV, 165
Christian surgeon, I, 93, 111
dead child, I, 96
Gentile doctor, VI, 93
irreligious Jewish doctor, VI, 92
Jewish adult, I, 100
naming of orphan, II, 91
naming when circumcision is delayed, II, 94
of proselytes, VI, 71
on eighth day, I, 38
son of Gentile wife, II, 99
who may circumcise, I, 105
woman doctor, VI, 90
Coffins: I, 155
lights at head of, V, 177
two in one grave, VI, 100
wife's ashes in husband's coffin, IV, 237
wooden nails for, II, 153

Kaddish for unmarried child, I,
167
last hours, IV, 195
postponement of, IV, 188
presumption of, II, 107
time of despair, II, 105
Deconsecration:
of old synagogue, V, 9
of synagogue in large city, V, 10
Dedication:
of a synagogue, V, 9
Disinterment:
due to labor strike, V, 160
from Christian cemetery, VI, 175
of Jew from Jewish cemetery for
reburial in Christian cemetery,
VI, 179
services at reburial, VI, 177
Divorce:
father, natural, and Bar Mitzvah,
I, 33
father, obligation, I, 33
for doubtful marriage, V, 82
daughter, custody of, III, 193
Dog:
burial of, III, 165
seeing-eye dog at services, III, 74
Drugs, psychedelic: III, 247
Duchan: I, 41
Dues:
synagogue, nonpayment of, IV,
179
Dying patient:
Caesarean operation for dying
woman, I, 212
in agony, asks for death, VI, 85
infant, naming of, IV, 223
informed of condition, I, 122
kept alive, I, 117; terminal, IV,
197
last hours *chaye sha'a,* VI, 88
organ transplants, III, 118
relieving pain of, VI, 84
requests no funeral, II, 110

Electronic eavesdropping:
and Jewish law, VI, 260
privacy of private premises, VI,
265
prohibition against self-incrimina-
tion, VI, 265
English name for congregation: I,
78
Esther and second Seder: VI, 303
Eternal flame:
in cemetery, IV, 249
on grave, VI, 106
"Ethiopian Hebrews": III, 112
Etrog:
frozen, III, 26
last year's, III, 48
Eulogy: I, 27
for a Christian, I, 145; III, 175
for a suicide, II, 119
Eunuch (*saris*): I, 27
Euthanasia: I, 118
Excommunication, laws of: IV, 180

Falashas as Jews: V, 297
Falasha woman: II, 85
Fallen Israeli soldiers:
temporary burial of, V, 205
Fast:
proclaiming a new, VI, 47
Fasting:
if Torah dropped, V, 117
Father's name forgotten: V, 32
Feebleminded:
sterilizing the, V, 74
Fertility pill: VI, 205
Fertilized ovum implant: VI, 215
Festival:
burial on, I, 49
Flowers, belated: VI, 108
Foetal material:
study of, V, 155
Food:
diminishing world supply, VI, 63
Foundling:
"son of Abraham," V, 34

made from metal Torah rollers, III, 37
non-linear Chanukah menorah, IV, 86
Mezuzah:
affixed diagonally, VI, 82
to Gentiles, VI, 27
Midwifery: I, 188
Mirrors, covering of: I, 179
Miscegenation: II, 83
Mixed couple:
temple membership, II, 63
Mixed marriage:
CCAR attitude to, IV, 112
circumcision of children of, IV, 165
Kohen and child of, II, 158
on temple premises, IV, 108
Mohel:
woman doctor, VI, 90
Money matters on Sabbath: I, 47
Mother's name:
in Yizkor, VI, 120
on son's tombstone, VI, 116
when praying for sick, VI, 120
Mourning:
dates of, in different time zones, IV, 243
delayed burial, I, 151
dishes returned, I, 178
for stillborn and infants, I, 166
greeting mourners, III, 156
when body lost, I, 147, 150
Muggers:
on Sabbath, VI, 28
Museum case, Torah in: V, 110
Music in synagogue:
organ and Christian, II, 47
secular music, III, 33

Naming child of unmarried mother: V, 91
Negroes:
see Races

New Testament:
rabbi reading, IV, 73

Oath of office: V, 279
Ordination, annulling rabbi's, VI, 232

Pants suit, lady's: V, 123
Pardon asked of the dead: V, 293
Passover:
spices prohibited, V, 287
Patient:
terminal, allowed to die, IV, 197
which to save, IV, 203
Physician:
atheistic, I, 109
Christian, I, 93
divine emissary, I, 119
Jewish, I, 106
Pidyen ha-Ben: V, 28
possible pidyen of second son, VI, 266
one child by Caesarean, VI, 267
Plants or flowers on grave: V, 284
Pornography: III, 240
Posul Torah in Ark: V, 114
Prayerbooks, burning of: I, 71
Priest (Kohen):
apostate, I, 196
community composed of, I, 40, 41
marrying daughter of mixed marriage, II, 158
Prohibitions, Biblical and Reform: IV, 102
Proselyte:
accepted into family, IV, 162
born anew, I, 84
indelible allegiance of, IV, 162
pregnant, IV, 143
reverting, IV, 159
Proselytism:
questions from Israel on, V, 269
Prostration, on Yom Kippur: III, 49
Protest, halting religious services as a: IV, 82

Rabbi:
    participating in Christian funeral,
        III, 175
    reading or responding to passages
        in New Testament, IV, 73
Rabbinate:
    fees and salary, III, 199
    questions from Social Security,
        III, 209
Rabbinical Tenure: V, 263
Race:
    adopting Mulatto children, III,
        196
    "Ethiopian" congregations, III,
        112
    mixture of, I, 200; II, 85
Raped woman, marital rights: VI,
    216
Reconversion, of ex-nun: V, 141
Red Cross, identification card of:
    IV, 175
Redemption (Pidyen ha-Ben): V,
    29
    father's right absolute, V, 30
Reform attitude to conversion: IV,
    157
Reform Judaism:
    change, VI, 4
    marriage formula, VI, 191
Responsa:
    computerizing, VI, 2
    first Reform literature, VI, 5
    statistical survey, VI, 3
Rosh Hashonah:
    mood of, VI, 58
    two days in Israel, IV, 286

Sabbath:
    caterer working in synagogue on,
        III, 225
    communal business planned on,
        V, 58
    congregational meetings on, I, 46
    eighth day Passover, III, 42
    Gentile funerals on, VI, 142

Gift Corner open, I, 51
    healing sick, VI, 30
    hiring musicians, II, 35
    lights, I, 24; on table, IV, 91
    loaves, pre-sliced, IV, 95
    memorial mood, VI, 59
    memorial service, I, 26
    muggers and money, VI, 28
    money matters on Sabbath, I, 47
    muktsa, VI, 29
    New Year Shofar, II, 36
    reading memorial list on, IV, 24
    school dance on, II, 32
    sports in community center, VI,
        11
    wedding on, II, 167
Sabbath candles:
    composition and size of, V, 49
    prekindled in synagogue, VI, 9
Sabbath candlesticks:
    weekday use of, V, 53
Samaritans: I, 64
Seder:
    congregational, I, 55
    Esther and second Seder, VI, 303
    wine, types of, III, 43
Sefer Torah: See Torah
Services:
    dog, seeing eye at, III, 74
    interfaith, IV, 69
    halting, as a protest, IV, 82
    lengthened on Yom Kippur, V, 59
Sha'atnez with regard to tzitzis: VI,
    296
Shiva
    and quarreling family, VI, 136
    in house where deceased died, VI,
        138
Shofar:
    New Year Sabbath, II, 36
Shroud, extra, for Kohen: V, 276
Sinai, stones from, for decalogue
    tablets: IV, 40
Social hall of synagogue: I, 75